PAST IMPERFECT

Ilka Chase

PAST IMPERFECT

Doubleday, Doran & Company, Inc.

GARDEN CITY   1942   NEW YORK

PRINTED AT THE *Country Life Press*, GARDEN CITY, N. Y., U. S. A.

To MOTHER
who thought it would be a good idea to try
and to BILL, who prodded me until I finished it
this book is dedicated.
It is their chicken, and it has
come home to roost.

CONTENTS

Contents

PAST IMPERFECT

CHAPTER ONE

Life with Grandma

I AM ALWAYS IMPRESSED, WHEN I READ AN
autobiography, by the amazingly accurate memory of
the writer and the detailed background of his life, which
he can evoke with the twist of a brain cell. My own
memory is distressingly spasmodic, and I have destroyed
or mislaid most of the old letters which others always
seem to have prudently garnered and stored in the
upper left-hand drawer. To be frank, I never had much
of a collection. Either my friends don't go away, or if
they do they are wretched correspondents; and since the
flowering of American Tel and Tel, there is a dearth of
epistolary material. I dare say the Messrs. Plutarch, Bos-
well, and their ilk wouldn't have been so glib with their
reminiscences if all they had had to go on were a few
remembered phone calls and here and there a telegram
relaying the latest ribald story, cunningly cleaned up for
the chaste eyes of Western Union.

But if I am impressed by the correspondence-savers,

I am even more awed by the diary-keepers. They seem to me creatures of iron determination. Who would voluntarily lash himself daily to his desk and write for the simple pleasure of it, with no thought of fame or gain? I am not at heart a diary-keeper, always having believed that once a day is past, it's past, and the hell with it. There is also my feeling about blackmailers. Belonging, as I do, to the candid school of self-expression, it is better not to lay oneself open in black and white. This same idea must have occurred to me in my extreme youth, as I remember getting a letter from an early beau which began: "Dear Ilka, I have just received your note, written with one eye on the jury box." Would that my youthful caution had prevailed throughout my maturity! Many's the pretty pickle I would be saving myself.

Also I have been much influenced by the movies where the heroine goes to the cad's apartment to recover the slim diary or the bundle of letters he has rifled from her secretary (the inanimate variety). In her bag is a small pearl-handled revolver which she whips out and applies when his attentions become too pressing; and she is certainly lucky to be married to Herbert Marshall, whose brilliant plea to the jury clears her fair name. Mr. Marshall not being as active in these matters as he once was, a girl should indeed look lively and watch her step when committing herself to paper.

However, if this is to be an autobiographical treatise, I suppose it would be more orderly if I got myself born. As they say in novels, no inkling of the dark future disturbed that early spring morning when I first saw the light of day. Taking a leaf from my betters, who all seem to have firsthand data about these things, I recall, after some consultation with my mother, that I was born at 2 A.M. on April 8, on East Fifty-ninth Street in New York City, by which it will be seen I am no average New Yorker, as most of them are born in Scranton, Buffalo, or Des Moines. The world-shaking event of my birth took place in a small hospital, in the shadow of the Queensborough Bridge.

I was a tall baby. Indeed, I remember the doctor observing that I came by the yard; and on his first look my father promptly christened me "Stubbs," owing to the button formation of my nose. This has plagued me through life, my husband even now referring to it as negligible. There seems to have been some division of opinion as to my early appearance, with my mother further confusing the issue according to her mood—one day saying I looked like a little Chinese doll, with straight black hair and eyes like violets, and the next remarking irritably that I was so dark, so low of brow, that I looked alarmingly like a monkey. Certain it is, however, and to my eternal regret, that the violet eyes turned humdrum brown. "It was awful, darling," says Mother. "I looked at you one day, and your eyes were full of coffee grounds, nasty little black specks, and a couple of days later they were quite dark." Ochi cherniia!

Although never much of a hand at family-tree tracing, I gather that I am the product of a long line of Quakers on my mother's side and of New Englanders, many of them seafaring, on my father's. To judge from daguerreotypes, I look remarkably like my maternal great-grandmother. This has always secretly delighted me, as I consider her something of a glamour girl. During the Civil War she ran away from her children, Grandma among them, and her first husband, who was

a stanch Abolitionist, to marry a Southern doctor. She
lived with him for many years in Florida, raised another
family, and, when he died, returned to my great-grandfather, whose second wife had by that time died too, and
remarried him. This seems to me nice going at any time,
but in that day and age a truly remarkable feat. Somewhat harried and, I should imagine, dazed by such goings on, Great-grandfather eventually passed to eternal
rest, but Great-grandmother hung on till the age of
ninety-two, when she died from injuries received in an
automobile accident while out joyriding with a beau.

From occasional outspoken remarks I gather Grandma
never approved of her mother. That she left her husband, Grandma could understand; she left two herself, and she frequently said that sex was the devil's
invention. When you consider the trouble it gets you
into, she may have had something there. But she could
never forgive her mother for having deserted her when
she was an infant. Even at the age of eighty Grandma
was not past referring to herself as poor little motherless
Laura. She was a peppery old party with a will of solid
granite and a hot, flaring temper. Had she possessed
self-discipline with her fabulous vitality, she could have
succeeded at anything she'd had a mind to. At the age of
seventy-eight she took up painting, and although it was
not art, her grapes and flowers and birds were entirely
recognizable as such, and the family was delighted that
she had found an occupation. She sang rarely, but she
had a singularly sweet and true voice, and she and I
both thought she should have gone on the stage. Certainly her gift for self-dramatization was second to none.
We always used the Quaker "thee" when talking to
Grandma, although occasionally the Friends' locution

must have sounded a little odd, such as the time a friend of mine, arriving unexpectedly, crumpled up with laughter because, Grandma having driven me into a frenzy, I was shouting at her, "Thee is a horrible old woman."

The sense of the theater was strong in Grandma, and she fancied herself in the role of a dear little old lady in cap and lavender taffeta, until an opinion was uttered which challenged her own. Then she would let fly. She never used bad language, but she had a shattering fierceness of attack and lung power totally unexpected in so frail a being. She became tiny in her old age, like a little gray leaf, but her periodic rages, instead of destroying her, seemed to infuse her with new vitality. Many subjects could rouse her ire, and she was inaccurate, but violently opinionated on politics. When she died, the New York *Times* lost its most faithful subscriber. Any argument she settled once and for all by the flat statement that such and such was obviously true, as she had read it in the *Times*. I do not know whether it is because of her convictions, but I find myself humbled and convinced by the *Times*, whereas even the *Herald Tribune* will leave me cocky and self-opinionated. As for Mr. Hearst's press, I frequently enjoy it, but aside from the sporting and theatrical pages, I think they make the whole thing up. I feel I might grow to like the *News* if I could ever get myself disentangled from the Ludwig Baumann ads.

I once suggested the *News* to Grandma, as she took a lively interest in murders, and I thought the pictures might prove stimulating. "If I may venture a criticism," I said, "the *Times* is a bit conservative with its murders." Grandma looked at me coldly and said, "Thee obviously doesn't appreciate the New York *Times* newspaper. Besides, I know my way around it. At my age I haven't the time to go gadding about in the tabloids." Grandma's gadding *was* pretty limited, being chiefly confined to the movies around Fifty-seventh Street, where she lived. When I was in Hollywood, she went faithfully to see every picture I was in. Indeed, she would follow them around the neighborhood playhouses and see them five or six times, and she would announce that my performance on Thursday was, she was happy to see, a good deal better than the one I had given Monday. I tried once or twice to explain that in a picture the performance doesn't change, but she would glare angrily and say, "Thee doesn't have to explain that to me. I'm not a fool, dearie. I tell thee Thursday was better than Monday."

According to Grandma, whenever she went to the movies, the lady sitting next to her would always be the one to open the conversation. Carried away by enthusiasm, she would remark, "My, my, who is that attractive girl?" "Well, dearie, I had no intention of mentioning thee," Grandma would say, "but when she asked, what could I do? It was only polite to tell her thee was my granddaughter; then she got so interested I told her that my daughter was the editor of *Vogue.*"

As Grandma was, to say the least, somewhat *dégagée* about her appearance, feeling that comfort was more desirable than chic, Mother and I would receive this revelation with mixed emotions. I was torn between annoyance and laughter; Mother would say with considerable irritation, "Really, Mother, it isn't necessary to tell thy business to everybody," and Grandma would grin maliciously. There was nothing she relished so much as others' discomfiture.

One time when she was ill, Mother, in an effort to bring some order into her apartment, had removed about half of her works of art, because Grandma created them in such profusion that they completely covered the walls and stood on the floor four and five deep. Grandma had barely emerged from the Valley of the Shadow, however, when hell began to pop. She demanded to know where her pictures were. Mother, playing for time, said they were in the country in the Oyster Bay house, but Grandma, scenting mice, was not to be put off. She called the police and had them send a detective to search every cupboard in my apartment. When the poor man, somewhat upset by this want of family tact, asked her why she suspected her own granddaughter would filch her paintings, Grandma replied with sirupy satisfaction, "I'm sure she's hidden them in her closets. Ever since she's moved into that new apartment she's been boasting of the wonderful closet space. I'm sick and tired of hearing about it. Thee go and have a good look. Likely there are skeletons to boot."

When I realize the great good the Quakers do in the world, I am proud I can claim kinship with them, but I fear our particular branch has not always been entirely in line with the teachings of the founder, all our family having been quicker on the uptake than on turning the other cheek. I like to think that it is because injustice is still the vice that goads us to swiftest action. Grandma once took her umbrella to a man who was beating a horse, and when she was through with him, he was glad to be turned over to the police.

As far as I can learn, none of the Woolmans was a

very mild character. There is certainly nothing namby-pamby in John Woolman. He was Grandma's great-great-uncle, and the wintry beauty of his famous *Journal* still stands as testimony to the man's spirit. Many of the old Quaker relations were preachers, but I think they would have got on well with the New England Chases and Coffins of my father's family, as they seem to have been straightforward men of action. Daddy has sometimes said to me, "Well, dear, what you don't know about some of those seafaring ancestors won't hurt you. I'm damned sure a couple of them hanged. They were good men, though; great sailors."

My father himself loved the sea and sailed it for many years before he married Mother. As a young man he was sent to the University of Heidelberg. I don't know how much he learned there, but I am pleased that he avoided the saber cut from dueling—an affectation considered *de rigueur* by the bloods of the time and place. It has always seemed to me a phony Germanic concept of heroism, smelling of ham, and all too reminiscent of Erich Von Stroheim made up for a De Mille epic. Daddy's father made and lost two or three fortunes, and when my father was a youngster, his family had a big house in Boston and one in Nantucket, where he was always fiddling with boats. When I was a baby, Daddy would walk the floor with me, singing ribald sailor chanteys instead of conventional lullabies, and I loved them. Mother was a little shocked by this, feeling it would have a bad effect on my subconscious, but Daddy figured that the chances of my understanding them were dim. I don't know, though; I still prefer "Blow the Man Down" to "Rockaby Baby."

During one of the flood tides in Grandfather's affairs

he got grandiose ideas about horses and started to build a stable with marble stalls. Then he went broke, and the estate got no farther than the marble slabs sticking up like teeth. They stood for many years and were known as "Chase's Folly." I think as a child I was once taken to see them, but nobody is quite sure.

Many of my childhood summers were spent in Brookhaven, a small village stretching for about a mile inland on the south shore of Long Island. When I was a little girl, it was a flourishing colony of artists and writers. Everybody ate at Mrs. DeArcas' boardinghouse, and on Sunday afternoons used to gather for tea at Mother's. I enjoyed those tea parties—I sensed that the guests were entertaining, but my most immediate concern was the sumptuous chocolate cake made by the woman who lived across the road from us, and which it was my job to fetch on Sunday mornings. My companion on this agreeable errand was a bright yellow duck named Kiki, who followed me everywhere, and who was as passionately devoted as I to the neighboring cuisine. If ever I saw a duck who couldn't be trusted with chocolate cake, that Kiki was the one. This reprobate fowl was a handsome character with feathery deep golden plumage, orange bill and feet, and shoebutton eyes. We loved each other dearly, and when he was a tiny duck he slept in a basket in a grass nest under my bed and chirped to me softly through the night and smelled rather high. He met a swift and brutal end while doing battle with a weasel. We had bought a wife for Kiki; her name was Miss 'Arriet, but she was a banal white duck, and I never cared for her much.

An earlier object of my consuming affection had been a small teddy bear. One day when I was at school, while cleaning out my closet, Mother had given him away to "some little poor children." I reproached her bitterly. "But, darling," she said, "how was I to know you treasured that particular bear? You have so many toys."

"You should have known," I cried passionately. "You should have known!" And I burst into a storm of sobbing. It was my first experience of loss, and to this day, whenever bears crop up in the conversation, Mother regards me uneasily, with the expression of one who fears that an old wound has never quite healed.

I was sent to boarding school when I was very little— about five, because my mother and father were both working, and away from home all day, and they couldn't afford anything so starchy as an English nurse or a French governess. Mother did not relish the idea of delegating my upbringing entirely to the slap-dash, if devoted, care of an Irish or colored maid, so she hit on the idea of sending me to a convent. We are not Catholics, but there were two reasons for this choice. One was that most boarding schools did not take such young children, and the other was that Mother felt that the nuns, whose lives were dedicated to devotion and service, would be affectionate as well as disciplinary. In this she was not wrong, the only trouble being that, as I was the baby of the school, I ran the risk of being spoiled beyond redemption.

After a brief miserable brush with the Ursuline Sisters, I was sent to the Convent of the Holy Child Jesus, on Riverside Drive, where, except for occasional violent attacks of homesickness, I was, on the whole, very happy.

Homesickness seems to me one of the most terrible maladies, and one which you do not necessarily outgrow

with age. It lies in wait like a recurrent illness, and sometimes, quite unexpectedly, the old familiar pain will
surge over you. The desperate longing for home and the
people you know will so engulf you that nothing on
earth matters but the urgency of your need.

As I was at boarding school so much as a child, my
bouts of homesickness assumed something of the quality
of an occupational disease, from which I would recover,
however, with resiliency, and then be for long stretches
quite spoiled and happy. I was much impressed by the
nuns, especially one Mother Mary Dismus. That was a
long time ago, and her face is very dim, but she has
always seemed to me one of the sweetest souls I ever
knew. We called all the nuns Sister except the Mother
Superior, who was called Reverend Mother, and who
was an awesome character. Even for my mother, though,
the convent proved something of a mixed blessing. The
difficulty was that convent authority lingered over those
week ends when I returned to my pagan home, and my
dear parents suffered considerably from my reiterated
tales of convent standards, invariably prefaced by "Sister
says——"

"Never mind what Sister says," they would remark
tartly. "You think up something on your own, or else
just depend on us." Sister once said it was impolite to
blow your nose in public, which elicited from Mother
the retort practical: "What are you supposed to do?
Let it run?"

A cause of keen aesthetic discomfiture to Mother
was the unfortunate rule which stated that at all recitals
or social functions in the convent we should wear black
silk gloves. She thought this bad taste and said so. She
also thought that the idea of children from six to ten

piously singing, "Weary of life and laden with my sin, I look at Heaven and long to enter in," while piquant, was too idiotic to be borne with equanimity.

Opposed to that, however, was the credit column. The nuns were teaching me nice manners. I fear, alas, that the wear and tear of life has rubbed off most of them, with the exception of my reaction to door-banging. The precept that no lady slams a door was so firmly imbedded in our minds that to this day if I bang a door accidentally, I quickly open it again, even if the room is empty, and I have caught myself murmuring politely: "I beg your pardon."

They were teaching me manners; I was moseying along among the three R's; scholastic standards were not high; and I was learning a very smooth game of pool. This last may seem an odd accomplishment to have absorbed from the dear Sisters, but it came about quite naturally.

After I had spent two years on Riverside Drive, Mother decided I needed country air, and so she sent me to the house in Suffern which had been given to the Order of the Holy Child by Thomas Fortune Ryan. The upper rooms had been remodeled into dormitories, but the downstairs was left pretty much as it had been during the tycoon's incumbency. There was a pool room, and in the room, a pool table; and the dear Sisters had seen no reason for removing it. We all played continually, and it was a pretty sight to see Mother Mary Agnes, who shot a mean ball, leaning backward over the table, her veil slightly askew, while with her cue tucked under her arm she aimed swift and true for the corner pocket.

Among my fellow students of this game of skill and chance were three whom I still know and sometimes see: Elizabeth Keyes, who married Earnshaw Cook, and who now lives in Tuxedo Park and is a great hand with sailboats; Ellin Mackay, the little girl who grew up to marry Irving Berlin; and Natica Nast, Condé Nast's daughter, whom I have known since our infancy. Natica is now Mrs. Gerald F. Warburg, and she has two children and lives in a charming house on Long Island, but in those days she was a rather sallow child with dark eyes and braces on her teeth. I was torn between envy and annoyance, because she was always having extras added to the convent diet. The extras generally took the form of cereals and thick cream. I was annoyed because I hated thick cream, and Natica used to eat it very, very slowly, and as we sat at the same table, I had to watch her. But I was envious, because, as the doctor had ordered it, it made her seem delicate, a state of grace I longed to attain. I was a skinny, wiry child, but never delicate, and although I ran through measles, mumps, chicken pox, whooping cough, and scarlet fever with abandon and dispatch, they only made me stronger.

Ellin Mackay had extra things too, but everybody knew it was only because her father was so rich and they had nothing to do with her own complex organism, and so I never envied her. Her father was always giving statues to the chapel, and everybody else had cells in the dormitory, but Ellin had a whole big alcove with bay windows all to herself. Apparently it never made her feel superior though, because I remember that once when she was sick in her pitcher, she put her bath sponge on top of it, as she was afraid to tell Sister.

Aside from other activities, my time was occupied by my studies of military tactics. I had organized an army of about ten moppets and elected myself general. Natica

Nast was the captain, and there were no other ranks. One of the privates, Rita McAleenan by name, had a generously inclined father, who sent us two fine army tents. I stuffed the ten soldiers into one of them and kept the other to myself, where I presided in solitary grandeur. I remember this giving rise to a small mutiny—Natica, as captain, claiming she had a right to share it with me.

This same Rita McAleenan was unwittingly the cause of one of the tragedies of my childhood. Her mother gave a birthday party for her and invited a group of her school friends. My mother had called Mrs. McAleenan to ask if the children were to be arrayed in party finery, and Mrs. McAleenan said, no, it was a very simple affair, to send me along in anything. Mother did, but the affair was not so simple. I was faultlessly attired in an imported blue serge from Hollander's, an extravagance Mother had found irresistible, but all the other children flowered in net and organdie over pink and blue slips. My humiliation was intense, and further deepened when, in playing games, I was made to be the teacher because I had on a dark, prissy dress.

Although I don't think I was a mean child, and I never bore grudges for very long, I still remember one injustice perpetrated on me which I bitterly resented. It was when I was ill in the convent—chicken pox, I think—anyway, it was a light case, and two or three of us were quarantined together and couldn't go to classes, and we had a high old time. It was around Easter, and on Easter Sunday afternoon one of the nuns came in to see us and said, "Ilka, dear, your mother sent you the most beautiful plant."

"Where is it, Sister?" said I, buggy-eyed, because I

loved plants and I loved my Mother and that seemed to me a fine combination.

"Well, dear," said Sister, "as it's Easter, I was sure you would want our Lord to have it, and as you're quarantined, if I'd brought it in here for you to look at, we couldn't have put it in the chapel, so I took it there directly." She was quite wrong: the idea of giving my plant to our Lord would never have occurred to me and filled me with cold rage, but there I was, trapped and impotent on a sick bed and feeling very sorry for myself.

On the whole I got on fairly well with the religious aspect of my training. I thought Catholic ways curious and interesting, but I was never tempted to adopt them. I was much impressed by the solemnity of the Mass and used to hold dawn services for my dolls when at home on Sundays, pinning two bath towels over my shoulders in the manner of a sandwich man. I would mumble unintelligibly, just like the priest, coming out strong on the "amens." This would sometimes madden my father and mother, who, having been up late of a Saturday night, did not take it in the proper spirit. Also I loved retreats. You were supposed to retreat into silence for several hours over a course of days, and during those periods, so that our minds might be exalted, the nuns gave us holy pictures to paste into scrap books. Those who had the artistic urge were encouraged to paint wreaths around their pictures. I had it, and can still see my St. Theresa, thick-embowered in forget-me-nots, which were what I painted best—four little blue dots close together, then a yellow one for the center, then lots of curly green leaves.

It seems to me that children accept unquestioningly the religious concepts of their elders without having the vaguest idea as to what they mean. Sometimes the ideas roll off them like water from a duck's back, which was true in my case, and sometimes they absorb them; but I think they rarely understand them. Curious misconceptions can exist in a child's mind of which adults are completely unaware. My own idea of God was of a being dressed in white, with a chef's cap, emerging from an enormous cloud bank; and for a long time I thought the phrase, "fruit of thy womb, Jesus," in the Hail Mary was one word: "Hail Mary, full of grace, Blessed art thou amongst women, and Blessed is the fruitofthywombjesus." What it meant I neither knew, asked, nor cared.

Throughout her life Mother has had recurrent attacks of interest in Christian Science, and during one of these, when I was a very small child, she sent me to a Christian Science Sunday school. I do not remember it, but she says that when I came home and she asked me if the little children had given testimonies, I replied, "No, Mummy, just nickels and dimes."

Actually, my earliest memory is a religious one—I had a devout Catholic nurse who thought I was headed for limbo or worse, as I had no saint's name, and so one day, while Mother was at the office, she took me to a church and had me christened Catherine. I must have been tiny at the time, but I remember a huge, dark place, a woman who was Queenie, my nurse, beside me, and a man who flicked an icy drop of water on my head.

One day I told this memory to Lawrence Langner, a director of the Theatre Guild, who has studied psychology, and Lawrence said it meant I love comfort and am cynical and not easily impressed by pomp and outward form. There is a good deal of truth in this

analysis, but I think he was able to hit on it more because he knows me well than because the memory was
significant.

It is probably due to so much orthodoxy in my youth
that my religion today is, so to speak, freehand, but I
think an honest, functioning faith is the solution to the
problems besetting us, and spiritual integrity is in a very
literal sense our soul's salvation.

However, these long thoughts did not occur to me in
the convent, and I was content to swallow the catechism
whole and gobble up all the prizes for learning by heart.
I was a whiz at learning by heart, and while the dear
Sisters may have hoped it was the content of the catechism that inspired me, they probably secretly realized
it was only because I had a photographic memory and
could imprint an entire page on my brain, complete
with punctuation. This trick will not help you to probe
and analyze your subject, or to so completely absorb it
that it becomes as your own, but it is invaluable when
all you have to do is to repeat what it says in the book.
"Who made you?" "God made me." "Why did God
make you?" Today the reply all too frequently seems to
be, "Why, indeed?" But then it was easy: "To know,
love, and serve Him in this world, and to be happy with
Him forever in the next."

CHAPTER TWO

"An Actor's Life for Me"

TO JUDGE FROM THEATRICAL BIOGRAPHIES, convents have long been cold frames for sprouting actors. Ours was no exception. Lots of people around there loved the theater, and we were always putting on plays. When I was eight I acted the title role in *Puss in Boots,* and though the cast was limited, I was not. In Act One I did not appear as Puss, but I wore a sign around my neck which said, "I am the Miller, the First Son, and the Second Son." In Act Two I burst forth in glory in a kind of gray flannel union suit with feet in it, a long tail, and a cat mask with whiskers. There was one slight anachronism: as a monsignor was to be present at the performance, the nuns, apparently deciding that eight-year-old spindle shanks were somehow indecent, made me wear a brief flaring blue-serge skirt and a bolero. The effect was that of a Gold Dust Twin with a tail. I do not remember much about my performance—it makes me happy to imagine it as triumphant—but I remember distinctly the anticlimactic epilogue. As the leading character I was supposed to present the monsignor with a bouquet of red roses—a reversal of the usual procedure, by the way—but the cat mask slipped around on my head and I couldn't see, so that I walked straight into Reverend Mother's lap. I can still hear her social laugh and slight hiss in my ear as she gave me a shove toward his Right Reverence.

The following season I starred in *Little Lord Fauntleroy.* I had the curls, painfully acquired by sleeping on hard rag knobs, the lace collar, and the black velvet suit, only mine had a skirt instead of pants. My uncle, the earl, was an athletic girl of eighteen with densely powdered hair and a flannel dressing gown, leaning goutily on my shoulder. When I saw Freddie Bartholomew and C. Aubrey Smith play these parts years later in the movies, I thought they were effete—they had polish, but we had gusto.

After *Little Lord Fauntleroy* came *Sara Crewe, or The Little Princess,* still one of my favorite stories. The scene where little Sara, cold, tired, and hungry, climbs to her bleak attic room to find it transformed into a snug haven with a fire crackling in the chimney, the table set with a delicious hot supper, and the little monkey who had escaped from the Indian servant sitting watching her with bright beady eyes, is my idea of heavenly escapism.

Another of my childhood literary passions was *Racketty-Packetty House,* a wondrous tale about some poor but merry wooden dolls who lived in a dilapidated old doll's house in one corner of the nursery and who were obliged to watch the cavortings of the rich and snobbish dolls who lived in a palace in the opposite corner. The Racketty-Packetties were debonair, with wit and spirit, and they had jolly times in spite of their hardships. I suspect that actually it was a subversive bit of literature, as the rich dolls were undoubtedly entrenched Tories bent on grinding down their weak neighbors. The only count which might save them from this indictment was the fact that the neighbors could not be said to represent Labor, for they toiled not, neither did they spin, but spent their days laughing and making long noses at the Palace crowd; and though they had nothing to eat but turnips, they dined on ten courses of them, calling each one by a fancy French name. It is a fine book, as can be seen, full of conflict and comedy, and the merry hearts triumph in the end. I wish I could have appeared in a dramatization of it.

After *Sara Crewe* there seems to have been a long hiatus in my theatrical activities, a phenomenon which reoccurs with distressing frequency in my adult career.

I will not go into a dissertation on what is wrong with the theater, as that is discussed regularly in learned articles in the Sunday papers and *Theatre Arts Monthly,* but I will say that what is wrong with it as far as I am concerned is that I don't get enough jobs. When you long to be active in your work, enforced idleness is a bitter thing; a painter, even if he doesn't sell his pictures, can still paint. A writer can sweat over a book because he can't help himself—the book will out, and their very efforts will give them satisfaction. But you cannot act alone—it's no good. Acting is like an electric-light bulb; if you can't establish contact, it won't light. The contact with the audience is the current which illuminates a performance.

I remember how clearly that was once brought home to me at a time when I had forgotten the sensation. I had been playing in pictures in Hollywood for about two years, then I came back to New York and got a part in Philip Barry's *The Animal Kingdom,* with Leslie Howard. We went through the usual rehearsal period, and it was interesting, but uneventful, until the opening night out of town. When the curtain went up, and we felt the audience, the play seemed suddenly to rise out of the printed page, instinct with life, and three-dimensional. It was a thrilling moment. I think all actors feel this need of public reaction, and if you are an actor, you are, of course, an extrovert—an exhibitionist in one form or another. Actually I am using the term *actor* collectively. The same feeling is experienced by all those who work in the theater and who are continually frustrated by inactivity. It is as though an athlete, used to running and leaping, were imprisoned in a little room. His suffering would be intense. So it is with anyone eager and able to do a job when he finds no job to do. It happens to me time and time again, and it is not to my consolation but rather to my rage that the same thing happens to hundreds of others, many bigger and better than I.

The theater is a baffling business, and a shockingly wasteful one when you consider that people who have proven their worth, who have appeared in or been responsible for successful plays, who have given outstanding performances, can still, in the full tide of their energy, be forced, through lack of opportunity, to sit idle season after season, their enthusiasm, their morale, their very talent dwindling to slow gray death. Of their finances we will not even speak; it is too sad a tale. However, in my youth I knew nothing of these future disappointments, and it never occurred to me to be anything but an actress.

After five years I left the convent. Although there were no signs of it, Mother thought I might be converted to Catholicism, and as it was not the family faith, she felt it would be wiser for me to wait until I was old enough to make up my own mind. After some backing and filling I went to Mrs. Dow's School in Briarcliff Manor. There were some two or three in between the convent and Mrs. Dow's, but as I went to nine schools, I am confused as to the chronological order.

One might think I would be educated as all get out, but such, alas, is not the case. I never learned to spell properly. When I engaged a secretary, my first question was whether she could spell. My Miss Koehler assures me she can, and I only hope she speaks the truth, as I have no means of checking up. I still remember my childhood humiliation when I was put out of a spelling bee for flunking on the word *raisin*. I forgot the first *i*. Mother, in despair, used to return my letters to me with angry red circles drawn around every misspelled word. It sometimes looked like an interlocking design. To further complicate matters, when I was sixteen and it began to seem as if in the light of mature reason I might penetrate the mysteries of the written word, I went off to school in France, and the whole thing blew up, because where the words were similar—*apartment* and *appartement*, for instance—I unintentionally but perversely adopted the French form and never have got myself straightened out.

It was at Mrs. Dow's, however, that I was first introduced to the classics. We did a condensed version of *Twelfth Night*, and I appeared as Malvolio, in bright yellow hose and duly cross-gartered. Mother came to see me and brought some friends, and they all said wasn't I wonderful to remember all those lines. I received this compliment frostily. It seemed to me scarcely professional criticism, although, at that, remarks of about the same caliber are frequently heard in dressing rooms after an opening performance on Broadway, especially when the offering is doomed to quick oblivion. One's hapless friends, having just witnessed the debacle, nevertheless feel constrained to offer some kind word, so they say brightly, "Well, dear, you *looked* lovely"; or, "It's not a good play, but there are lots of laughs"; or most ominous of all, with a note of defiance in their voice, "Well, *I* liked it." That "I liked it" is a death knell almost invariably confirmed by the morning papers.

The first professional production I ever saw as a child was at the old Hippodrome. I went with Daddy, so that we were in our seats before the cleaning women had left. He was a tartar for punctuality. It seems I sat in rapt silence for a long time, then suddenly started to bellow. My father, embarrassed and alarmed, demanded to know what was the matter. The matter was that I had been promised diving horses and disappearing mermaids, and they hadn't materialized. For a limited period I had been enthralled by the spectacle of the huge circular curtain, surging with allegorical figures and beasts—I thought that was the show—but when it palled, I considered I had been gypped and I demanded action.

I had a good many brushes with the theater before we began to calm down and understand each other. At a far too tender age I was taken by my mother, who since that time has never been remarkable for her love of music, to hear *Die Walküre*. We sat in a box at the Metropolitan, and when the flames began to mount around Herr Wagner's goddess, I began to scream. I was

hastily yanked from this scene of grandiose doom and
dragged through the corridor, shrieking my head off.
The tympani were hard put to it to top me.

I must have been hard to please, theatrically, because
when I was sent to the recitals of Miss Kitty Cheatham,
a very genteel lady who dressed as a shepherdess and
sang little songs for children reflecting the spirit of love,
I made rude noises and cried for redder meat.

The first time the theater and I really got on a co-
operative footing was when I was taken to *Hop o' My
Thumb*. The script I have forgotten, but there was a
sensational scenic effect when Hop o' My Thumb
climbed high in a tree. The walls fell away, and the
surrounding country lay before my astonished eyes. In
my childhood, when there were trees on the stage, the
foliage was caught in a kind of coarse fish net, and I
loved it. It was so unreal. To this day I am a pushover
for plays that deal with the weather. I love thunder in
the theater, and *Boris Godounoff* is my favorite opera because of the snow scene. There is a lovely one, too, in
the *Affairs of Anatol*, and I remember when I was at
school in France and went to see *Cyrano de Bergerac*,
I wept copiously, less at the death of hapless Cyrano
than because the autumn leaves came drifting down the
air and settled on the stage with soft little slaps.

Hop o' My Thumb also impressed me for another
reason, other than sheer worth. It was the first play I
ever saw at night, and I was baffled, on emerging from
the theater, to discover it was no darker at eleven than
it had been at eight. I had imagined the night grew
progressively blacker. The performance was memorable
for me all around, because it was then that I officially
decided, like J. Worthington Foulfellow in the Disney

masterpiece of some years later, that it was to be "Hi diddle dee dee, an actor's life for me."

It is interesting, I think, the way plays assume an importance in our lives which has nothing to do with the intrinsic value of the script.

Broadway was one of the biggest hits ever produced, but I always associate it with heartache, because I saw it on one of the unhappiest nights of my life. On the other hand I once appeared in an indifferent little flop which everybody t'ched t'ched over and said, "How unfortunate!" But I thought it a most graceful affair and cherished its memory because I met at the time a charming beau.

I suspect myself of light-mindedness in such matters, and it is all too obvious that that is no way to Get Any Place. The smart ones are those who build their careers deliberately, block by block, and I would be more than willing to do so, but often there are no blocks at hand.

It is a problem most actors have to face at some time in their careers—whether to appear in bad plays and at least be seen, however briefly, so that people may know they are still alive, or to hold out until a good play comes along and run the risk of not acting season after season.

My own career frequently strikes me as being one long lull, and in my childhood my professional appearances were far too infrequent for my happiness—the difference being that then they were treats; my real work was boarding school, and so I was always in a job.

I held my job at Briarcliff for about three years, with varying degrees of popularity, depending on whether or not Mother, who had by then assumed the editorship, was crusading against fashions for the young in *Vogue*. Issue after issue would go by with young ladies of finishing-school age properly relegated to the back pages or, more generally, ignored altogether. Then would come the holidays. Mother would meet me at the station, and she would gaze with unbelieving and outraged eyes upon the wardrobes of the young misses of seventeen and eighteen. I myself was still one of the comparatively small fry, and for the most part we were safely enveloped in Bramley frocks and chinchilla reefers, but I had violent crushes on the dazzling creatures who were three or four years my senior, and Mother's verbal flaying of their sequinned frocks and mink coats, their lipstick and mattresslike coiffures, though merited, filled me with distress.

When I attained that age myself, I bought a negligee of gold lace, pink marabou, flowers, and pleated chiffon, of which Mother remarked, with the candor which has always distinguished her, that it was a tart's idea of Heaven.

After one of these pilgrimages to Grand Central, when the daughters of the new rich passed in review, Mother would publish a blast in *Vogue,* detailing what well-dressed young ladies of good family *should* wear. As *Vogue's* circulation has always been large in the glossier finishing schools, it was inevitable that these philippics should meet the eyes for which they were intended. The eyes stared stonily at the sound advice, and in a sad and roundabout way it all reflected on me. I was the daughter of the editor, wasn't I? Even if I was a child, I must have known something of my mother's intentions—probably put her up to it. I had an unfortunate way of aggravating matters by saying priggishly, "My mother is quite right. I'm not even allowed to powder my nose." It is small wonder that I was periodically and intensely disliked. After a few days the crisis would abate, and I would be restored to good odor until the next vacation.

When I was about sixteen, Mother offered me the choice of going to school in France or going to college. I had always longed to go to Europe, and college had no appeal for me. It was only four more years of the same, and I was sick of boarding school. I knew very few boys, and was terribly shy of them, so that I could never understand how the other girls could talk lightheartedly of proms. The very idea terrified me. As it turned out, I needn't have worried; I never went to one in my life. When I came back from Europe I was out of touch with my old school friends, and any boys I would have met through them who might have asked me to dances were lost to me. Soon after that I got my first job in the theater, and my interest in men developed suddenly into something a little too mature for college proms.

My first trip to Europe was the most glamorous experience of my life. Mother and I crossed on the old *Adriatic,* and the second night out there was a frightful storm. The furniture slid all over the ship, and two passengers had their arms broken. My stepfather radioed to find out if we were all right, and we certainly were. We had split a bottle of champagne between us and slept like clams through the raging night.

We landed in Cherbourg, and everything about France entranced me; the shouting, angry porters in their blue blouses, the ingenious use of straps for carrying luggage, the lovely cultivated countryside, and the wonderful food on the train to Paris. I remember the blue plates, and the chicory coffee, and that it was the first time I had ever seen green almonds. They were served in little baskets lined with leaves.

We came into Paris early on a June morning and went to a hotel in the Rue de Rivoli, overlooking the Tuileries, and my first French breakfast was hot chocolate and *croissants,* with strawberry jam and round, flat butter pats with a cow embossed on them. I was sixteen; I was in Paris; and it was the most wonderful thing that had ever happened to me.

We stayed there a few weeks, and then Mother and I went with Nancy McClelland, the decorator, to Italy. We called Nancy "Mamma," because Italy was an old story to her—she spoke the language perfectly and was the one who ordered the meals and looked after the luggage and generally bossed us around. We went on the Simplon Express to Venice. Arriving in Venice was not like arriving in any other city, for other stations are loud, with the thunder of busses and the squawk of taxis, but Venice was quiet, so quiet it came as a shock, with the canal lapping against the steps, and gondolas instead of cabs jockeying for position. Also, in Venice nobody ever went to bed. People strolled in the Piazza di San Marco, feeding the pigeons and sipping *apéritifs* and ices at Florian's, and they dined at ten, and drifted for hours in gondolas, and the gondoliers actually sang "Santa Lucia." Our rooms opened on a balcony overlooking the Grand Canal; and the whole atmosphere was like a perpetual comic opera. I was young and impressionable; there was an intoxicating magic about it, but it is better to go there with a lover, because otherwise frustrations may set in.

I went to the island of Murano, where for centuries they have made the exquisite Venetian glass. We saw the huge flaming ovens and watched the men blowing and shaping the hot liquid glass; while I watched, they made a beautiful rose for me, and two days later I went back to fetch it, because it had to have time to cool. I carried it everywhere with me, and then, alas, it slipped from my hand and crashed on the stone floor of one of the innumerable churches. We did them all in true sight-seeing style, and when I couldn't read any of the Latin inscriptions Mother was good and mad to think she had spent all that money on my lack of education.

Our hotel room in Venice was vast—the corners vanishing into the shadowy distances, and in a great alcove were twin beds of black tin, inlaid with mother of pearl. There was much red plush and many gilt mirrors, and it was by far the most theatrically sumptuous apartment I have ever slept in.

We left the magic, odoriferous city at four o'clock one morning and betook ourselves to Florence. Some day I should like to have a heart-to-heart talk with the pixies who arrange European train schedules. In Florence we met a most helpful man, whom I will call Coletti. He was an Italian business friend of Nancy McClelland's who knew Italy like his pocket, and he took us every place. In Florence our hotel windows overlooked the Arno, and a muddy, noisy, turbulent flood it is. There was a sign outside the bedroom door which said, "Please lock your door and hang the key on this hook." We decided that "when in Rome" probably applied to when in Florence as well, and so we obeyed instructions, and I must say nothing was ever stolen.

The Florentines were very flattering and used to follow me around the streets, murmuring, "Oh, *que bella signorina,*" as they did to all Americans, who, they had been assured, apparently by unreliable sources, were only too eager to accept their advances. Having a formidable idea of what these advances might be, I would hop into a carriage and try to escape, but then it was even worse, because the driver would go very slowly, and the gentlemen would walk beside the carriage, exchanging pleasantries with him which were obviously directed at me. Then the driver would turn around on his perch and peer down at me and deliver himself of his opinion—all this in Italian, which I couldn't understand, and it made me extremely uncomfortable. It also scared me to death. Americans are less aggressive in their attentions; it all seems more in the spirit of good, clean fun. I expect it's fun to the Italians too, but lacking the antiseptic element. Unfortunately I have outgrown my maidenly reserve and, I fear, got myself a bad name, because now if anybody tosses me a quip in passing, such as "Hi ya, Toots," or "Hello, Babe," I burst out laughing. I don't mean to, and I think it shows a shocking lack of control, but such things strike me as comic.

From Florence we toured the hill towns: Siena, Assisi, Perugia—those crumbling symbols of the past, picturesque and beautiful and smelling to high heaven. We approached Perugia late one rainy night, and as we drove up to the gates of the city two soldiers with guns leaped on the running boards and told Coletti— we were in his car—to drive to the city hall. Mother and "Mamma" and I went into a little restaurant across the square to wait for him and ordered dinner. It was late, and they would only make us an omelette. The room was dimly lighted, and the tablecloth was dirty, and we were the only people there. From time to time we would go to the door and peer across the square at the car standing in the rain, and at the rain slanting in the beams of the headlights. A long time later Coletti came into the café. He looked white but said it was all right; we could go on now. He had talked them out of confiscating his car. It seems there was some trouble in the country; he had thought his papers were in order, but the law had been changed while we were on the way from Siena to Perugia, and the armed guards—incidentally they had not laid down their guns during the interview—claimed that the car and luggage rightfully belonged to them. Coletti, by what persuasion I don't know—probably a conspicuous pile of lire—had talked them out of it, and we were allowed to proceed. That was a sample of Fascism in diapers—Mussolini yet to come. I haven't been back to Italy since, but they do say that the trains now run on time and that the smell of the canals and of the ancient cities has been elminated. It has been replaced by a stench even more offensive to those who crave the fresh air of freedom, but perhaps a people to whom the building of roads and arranging of timetables seemed an insuperable problem feel they are getting a run for their money.

Although I had been wide-eyed over Italy, I loved returning to Paris. If going to Paris is grand, going back is grander. The beautiful city—surely the world's loveliest. It is still standing, but at a price which must seem bitter indeed to those French who hold the honor of France more dear than her greatest city. Those who reason that the French could not have won the war by defending Paris, thus laying her open to destruction, perhaps reason soundly enough. The tragedy is that such a city should have become only a beautiful shell, enclosing a corrupt and cynical body politic. Through her lovely streets walk the men who betrayed her.

In the fall Mother returned to New York, leaving me in school at Groslay. Groslay is a small village north of Paris, not far from Enghein, and if you drive there by motor, you pass through Saint-Denis, where lie buried the kings and queens of France.

The school was an old château, which had once belonged to Josephine de Beauharnais before she met up with Mr. Bonaparte of Corsica. It was a pleasant country house which in no way resembled a castle, but the French have a blithe habit of referring to any country residence which is not an out-and-out bungalow as a château. The bungalows they refer to as villas. This is at times misleading, but on the whole it lends an agreeable air of grandeur and does no harm.

There was a lovely garden at Groslay, part of it enclosed by a high wall, against which were espaliered apricot and peach trees. When the fruit was ripe, I would sneak into the garden and filch it.

The school was run by a couple whom we called Petite Mère and Petit Père. Petite Mère was a small, plumpish, and rather luscious creature, the type the French call *popotte*. She had a little mouth and sherry-colored eyes, and she wore a beautiful auburn transformation which none of us ever saw her without. Petit Père looked like nine million other Frenchmen—medium height, dark, slender, with a mobile face and a mustache. It gave me great pleasure when I once discovered, on his bedside table, a strange masklike contraption, which he wore at night to keep it in place. They were extremely kind to us, and not much on discipline, except for Petite Mère's occasional furious outbursts, which would send us scampering before her, like leaves in a gale.

The food was good, but the commissary department was presided over by a huge, smelly, incredibly slovenly creature, who padded around in felt slippers. She wore a red wig, reminiscent of the mistress's, but of poor design and coarse hair. I always thought she was some distant cousin of Petite Mère's, as I couldn't imagine keeping her otherwise. She lived in a little hole off the kitchen, called *l'office,* and although she never ate anything, she was enormously fat. She used to say it was her glands, and I guess it was. One of the mistresses had lived for twenty-five years in Russia. She referred to the inhabitants as *"les barbares"* and had picked up the habit of chewing sunflower seeds. There was another little elderly, bright-eyed teacher who said she bet I wore pink underwear, and when I asked her why, she said because I was *"le type gai."*

The school was not large, perhaps twenty-five or thirty pupils in all, but we had as many varieties as Mr. Heinz. English and Americans predominated, but there were also Belgians, Rumanians, and Egyptians.

I would suggest to Mr. Hitler that he give up now— he will never conquer the British, because even their young girls have stamina undreamed of by other nations. On raw, bitter November evenings, muffled to the eyebrows, my feet in fur-lined sabots, I have gone into their rooms to find them dressing for dinner, running around in the briefest and sheerest of combinations, the windows wide open, the wind and the rain beating in. "My God, aren't you freezing?" I would blurt out between chattering teeth. They would look at me blankly. "Why, no," I have heard them say, with my own ears, "we find it rather close."

I have absolutely no memory of classes at Groslay,

though obviously we must have had them, but I did learn to speak fluent French. I loved the language, and I loved to read, and so I quickly absorbed it. On the whole we were fairly good about speaking French to one another, although I remember one of the English girls, when asked by Petite Mère why she wasn't as conscientious about it as the rest of us, replying that the spirit was willing but the French was weak.

We were allowed to go into the village alone; it was about a quarter of a mile from the school, and there was scant danger of our getting into mischief. The streets were winding and cobbled; the women clattered along them carrying water in buckets from the village pump. The houses were wired neither for sound nor plumbing, and the little town had a peculiar, personal, slightly sour smell, compounded of rotting straw, poor drainage, and freshly baked bread. There was a tiny shop where I used to buy licorice. I have never liked licorice before or since, but in Groslay it was delicious. It came in endless narrow strips coiled up like rolls of tape.

A couple of times a week we were taken into Paris to the Opéra, the Comédie Française, or the museums. The *Ceinture de Chastité* at the Musée Carnavalet was the most popular exhibit, and I remember the first time I went to the Louvre and saw the Venus de Milo, set against black velvet at the end of a long vista. I cried. It seemed so wonderful to be seeing the original, after all those copies and pencil trade-marks. But the theater was my real passion. My desire to act, which had lain more or less dormant since my convent days, flared up again in Paris.

CHAPTER THREE

Coming Out — And Getting Out

THE MATCH WHICH REKINDLED MY AM-
bition was a production of Rostand's *L'Aiglon,* at the
Théâtre Sarah Bernhardt. The unhappy prince was
played by Vera Sergine, a slender, husky-voiced creature with enormous dark eyes and a feverish, unhealthy
quality which had the peculiar fascination of the de-
cadent. I saw her in many parts, and always you felt she
was consumed by an inner fire. There was a kind of
sexual intensity in her acting which compelled attention
and packed the house. Other French actresses, notably
Piérat, shared something of that quality, but I have
never seen it in our native product. Our girls are sometimes intense. There is a whole sect who go around with
hunched shoulders—the raised shoulder, according to
Miss Frances Robinson-Duff, a well-known dramatic
coach, denoting emotion—but the effect is more one of
poor carriage than sexual prowess. The temptation to
shout "Relax!" as these damsels stalk the stage has to be
sternly resisted.

I was so carried away by Mlle. Sergine that I saw *L'Aiglon* five times. I would have seen it twenty-five, but my pocket money ran out, and so did the patience of the mistress who had to chaperon me into Paris. I then bought the text and learned all the parts by heart. Because L'Aiglon toyed with them on his deathbed, I purchased countless bunches of violets from the flower market at the Madeleine, and back at Groslay, after the matinee, I would stand in front of my mirror and intone with sonorous splendor the lengthy speeches of L'Aiglon, Flambeau, and Metternich. The tears poured down my face as I died, murmuring brokenly, *"On batise à Paris mieux qu'on n'enterre à Vienne."* I was splendid as Metternich too—dry, brittle, ruthless.

I had, of course, developed a violent crush on Vera Sergine and wrote so many letters begging to see her that finally, in self-defense, the unfortunate woman sent word I might come to her dressing room after a matinee. I was paralyzed by ecstasy and fear, and the school mistress who accompanied me was almost as bad. We made our way through the dark drafty backstage corridors of the Théâtre Sarah Bernhardt and debouched at last into a hot, brilliantly lighted, heavily scented dressing room. There stood my idol, but I think I must have fainted mentally (I am, alas, too tough for physical vapors), because I cannot remember a single word that passed. The only impression I retain is the atmosphere of the room, which was thick, and the great masses of Parma violets which must have been sent to her by every stage-struck youngster in Paris.

My meetings with the Great have never been very fruitful. My memory is sometimes clearer than on that particular occasion, but the Great's remarks, to me, are never epic. I notice that other writers and reporters are continually quoting pregnant comments, but I apparently do not inspire such confidence. It is like my visit to George Moore in Ebury Street the winter I lived in London. Horace Liveright, the publisher, took me to call on him. I never liked Horace much—he was rude to waiters—but he promised me Bernard Shaw and George Moore. Shaw never materialized, but he was as good as his word on Moore.

We went to Ebury Street one evening after dinner, and there were just the three of us. I felt that history was in the making, but the occasion somehow lacked stature. Moore was a spindly-legged, potbellied, bejowled little man, and he unexpectedly pinched my behind. I felt rather honored that my behind should have drawn the attention of the great master of English prose, but it was embarrassing too, as I didn't know whether to respond or whether it wouldn't be kinder to let the whole thing drop. I listened respectfully, however, while he and Horace discussed literature, and at last ventured to ask him what he thought of Conrad. There was a slight pause. "I don't know, my child," he said testily, "I can't read Polish."

Sometimes I think the Brains do not take me seriously. I have heard that Mr. Henry Luce once remarked he had never yet met a mind to equal his own. My acquaintance with him is of the sketchiest, but once or twice, after chatting with him for five minutes, I have received the distinct impression that the Luce Quest of the Golden Fleece has still to bear fruit. This makes me sad, and I read the best books when they are not too long, but it is obvious I do not have a steel trap in my skull. I have lots of fun, though, and I sometimes think it is better not to be burdened with too much mentality, which is just as well, as I am not.

While I was still going to school in France, Mother came over for the summer holidays, and we went to Antibes. Dwight and Steve Wiman were there, and Clifton Webb and Grace Moore, and Townsend Martin and Kenneth MacKenna and Marilyn Miller and Ben Finney and his beautiful police dog. Marilyn laughed all the time, which could be a little wearing, but she looked like a daffodil, and I can still see her on the rocks, between a swim and luncheon, in dazzling white silk Chinese pajamas, with a parasol over her golden head and the sun in her eyes.

Captain Edward Molyneux's villa was near by, and there used to be magnificent luncheon parties on his rocks. I was never a member of these de luxe affairs, but we used to have picnics just as grand on the rocks belonging to Charlotte and Jan Boissevain; and Lady Mendl lived near by and gave dinner parties to which came Mary Garden, still walking like a goddess, and the Grand Duke Dmitri and Audrey, his American wife, so that in the end the desirable chic was spread evenly, like butter, over the whole colony. I fell in love with a giant of a man, an explorer named Babe White. Like Desdemona, I hung upon his lips, listening to his tales of adventure, but Mother, with the cynicism of Iago, remarked they were doubtless fabrications to ensnare the young. I don't believe they were, though possibly a little embroidery was here and there appliquéd upon the solid fabric. In any event, my love was unrequited, but my idol, all unaware of my delicious excitement, taught me to aquaplane. It was the only athletic accomplishment I ever had, and I was very proud.

That summer we also went to Biarritz, where I saw a man drowned. The undertow there is treacherous, and he had gone swimming and couldn't get back to shore. They threw him a rope, and he had half managed to scramble back on the rocks when the rope, which was old and frayed, broke, and he was swept out to sea. It was a tragic and typical example of French inefficiency—the necessities never worked: a rope to save a man's life, the hot-water faucet; and inevitably the elevators were always out of order, forever decorated with little signs saying, "Ne Marche Pas." It never seemed to occur to them to fix things—they hung up the sign, you had been duly notified, and that was that. You could jolly well take a cold bath and walk the five flights. That is bad enough, but to pile Pelion upon Ossa, they have that hellish system of the electric light. You press the button at the bottom of the stairway to illuminate your passage, but before you are halfway there the bulb, which is maliciously timed, goes out, and you grope your way upward in unrelieved black. It is these petty economies which drive one mad. The French are a great race, but in the debit column must be noted the concierge, the lack of free matches, and the fact that if you want extra ice for a cocktail party, the only place which has enough is the undertaker's. As the full implication of this idea sinks in, you really need the drink. There is also the matter of *l'appareil*, ze telephone. I once arrived in Paris and tried to phone a friend at the Ritz. The service was so bad that I sent a *petit bleu*, which took a couple of hours to get there, but at that, he received it before we got a telephone connection.

While we were at Biarritz we one day motored into San Sebastian with Alexander Moore, who was at that time our ambassador to Spain. He was a kind of Al Smith American: no grammar, but supposedly a heart of gold; they said the Queen of Spain was delighted by him. She must certainly have been surprised. We crossed the border in the embassy car with an enormous United States great seal on the door. It was ostentatious, all right, but fun too. I have never been one to care about great wealth, but I adore special privileges— not having to wait in line, and getting good theater tickets.

In San Sebastian I saw my first bull fight, and though we know there are only two sure things in this world, I am willing to bet that it was also my last. To see the horses with their guts spilling onto the hot sand and their vocal cords cut so that they couldn't scream was unendurable. When the toreador finally killed the bull, the great beast sank to his knees, and a shout of triumph went up from the mob. He heard it in his dying brain, and his huge brown eyes looked up bewildered. I was screaming hysterically, "O God, kill the man—make him die in the most terrible agony!" The Spaniards were furious, and they rushed me out, and I was sick all over San Sebastian. Mr. Ernest Hemingway to the contrary, I do not think it is a beautiful and gallant sport.

All my holidays in Europe, however, were not so turbulent. There was the long, peaceful summer I spent with a French family near the forest of Fontainebleau. I didn't go through the château till twenty-four hours before I left, but I used to wander every day through the forest, and once there was a great thundering of hoofs, and a troop of cavalry galloped by, the sunlight splashing through the trees on the blue uniforms and shiny chestnut haunches of the horses.

The French family consisted of an old mother, her two daughters, and her writer son. She was a charming old woman, like a fairy godmother. She had soft white hair, and her head shook continuously from side to side, ever so slightly. The elder daughter was an aging spinster, and the brother had white hair, too, and used to come out on Sunday to spend the day with his family. He had written several well-known novels, and they were tremendously proud of him, but personally I found his product heavy going.

The other daughter came to the little house for two or three weeks at a time. I fell in love with her, but she was something of an enigma, with a mysterious husband she referred to vaguely and whom I wasn't to see till the summer was over. I think they were all fond of me, and I was making great plans for seeing her in Paris when school opened again, but since they felt, with a strong bourgeois sense of decorum, that I was a *jeune fille bien élevée*, the mystery husband had at last to be explained. It was a sad and commonplace little story. He was, of course, no husband at all, but she had lived with him for many years. He was a brilliantly educated orthodox Jew, who supported her in the greatest comfort, but who would never marry her in opposition to his father's wishes. Because she was a Christian, the old man was unalterably opposed to the match. At the time I knew her she must have been in her early forties and was beginning to get quite deaf. I suppose the truth was that her lover was bored by that time, and didn't want to marry her, and used the religious barrier as an excuse. I did meet him once. The three of us lunched one Sunday at Voisin's. He had a distinguished head and a subtle intelligence, with that fund of literary and historical information which is the heritage of the well-educated Frenchman who, even if he is not intelligent, is almost always knowledgeable. He had a shining mind, but I think his heart had gone dry.

His lady was not a pretty woman, but she had beautiful eyes and dressed with great chic. She also served in her house the best *moules marinières* I have ever eaten. I lunched with her occasionally, or she would take me to tea when I could get away from school in the afternoon, and I sensed that she led a lonely life. Her friend she apparently saw rarely; she had nothing of the *grande cocotte* in her make-up—I think, as a matter of fact, she didn't know any of those glittering ladies. She was a simple, charming, not overly intelligent little woman, who should have lived a quiet married life, but because she was not married, the bourgeois homes where she belonged were closed to her. She was not an artist, so there seemed to be no niche into which she could properly fit—she had fallen afoul of the social scheme.

She appealed to my youthful imagination as a lonely, romantic figure, and I continually championed her, to the violent alarm of the nuns when they found out about her. As Groslay had not turned out too successfully, and as the Order of the Holy Child had a house in Neuilly, Mother had packed me back to the Sisters, hoping they would prove as efficacious as they had in my childhood. Alas, it was too late. I had grown older and had seen something of the world; I felt confined, and the Sisters felt confused. When they wrote to

Mother, suggesting that she remove me, they put it very tactfully: said I was a dear girl, but a bird in a cage. However, sugar-coat it as they would, the fact remained that I was expelled. There were many contributing causes. I read everything I wanted to, preferably French novels on the Index, and I was constantly going into Paris for diction lessons, which necessitated a chaperon. I used to concoct a thousand errands for the unfortunate nun whose duty this was, so as to be left alone with my diction teacher, who gave me lessons in *"la déclamation"* and with whom I was in love. My fickle affections forgot the brown giant of Antibes, and I dreamed of the lined, mobile face of my actor-manager. I used to hope he would attack me with passion and tenderness, but he never did. His Siamese cat would sometimes spring at me when I was intoning the measured Alexandrines of Racine's *Phèdre,* but it was more in the spirit of criticism than desire.

My special courses disrupted the convent routine; my flaunting of the Index the nuns found shocking; also my reference to Popes as fallible humans—"Look at the Borgias," I would cry triumphantly—grew tiresome. All this they bore, however, accepting me, I suspect, as a kind of spiritual hair shirt, until they found out about my lost lady. Then their endurance snapped, and they dispatched a frightened squawk to Mother to the effect that I was associating with fallen women.

In France they take these things very seriously, and there is a sharp dividing line between virtue and vice. This was brought home to me on another occasion when, walking in the Champs Elysées, I waved to a couple I knew and was coldly ignored. The man was one of the heads of French *Vogue,* and his companion was an attractive woman, the *première vendeuse* at Jenny's, the famous dressmaker's. As they were both friends of mine when I saw them separately, I was baffled by their conduct when I met them together. Claire Avery, the artist, who worked on *Vogue* and was a close friend of Mother's, lived in Paris and kept an auntlike eye upon me. She explained that in France there were great social differences, and that it was not considered *comme il faut* for a gentleman, when walking with his mistress, to acknowledge the salutation of a *jeune fille*. This little convention seemed to me then, and still does, the rudest thing I ever heard of. Certainly the *jeune fille* has every right to be annoyed by the slight, and I should think the mistress would slap his face and leave him flat. If the affair is secret, such blatant betrayal is inexcusable, and if it is generally known and accepted, why should the conduct of those involved be such as to embarrass everybody else?

There is an interesting little treatise to be written on *Behavior toward the Loved One*—the chapter on "Common Courtesy" taking precedence.

Mother was very nice about the fallen woman part, not taking it too seriously, but at the distance of three thousand miles the idea of my being expelled was a jolt, and stringent punishment had to be meted out. I had been invited to Brussels to visit a school friend for the Christmas holidays, and she forbade me to go. This seemed to me brutal and unwise, and I felt like the butterfly on the wheel. I still regret it, as the nearest I have ever been to Brussels is the Belgian Pavilion at the World's Fair.

At that time I loved Europe and all things European, and even the aggravating bits, like the "Ne Marche Pas" signs, and the uncomfortable bits, like *strapontins* in the theater—those little seats that let down into the aisles, making the place a perfect firetrap—seemed quaint and rather charming. Most of the French people I met I found delightful. Mother was a great admirer of the French too, having infinite appreciation of their taste and intelligence, but as she had to deal with them in business, her affection was not so unstinted as mine. Their devious circumlocutions drove her crazy. In her simple Quaker way she was always more than a match for them, but the waste of time involved appalled her. Most of the trouble she laid at the door of "that damned charm." The leader of the French *Vogue* charm group was a Madame Fernandez. I have rarely met a more enchanting woman. She was in her fifties with short-sighted blue eyes, through which she squinted gaily, and a delicate mustache. From many years of bleaching, the mustache had stiffened slightly, and the hairs clung to her upper lip in the manner of a small and elegant walrus. She wasn't frightfully efficient, but her family was impeccable, and she could charm the birds off the trees. This ravishing creature had a swarthy son who used to beau me around, but I never cared for him much.

Madame Fernandez spoke English like a stage French-man—her vocabulary was full of "zeses" and "zoses." From being so much with foreigners, Mother picked up a kind of pidgin English. She would speak to them slowly and rather loudly in little broken phrases, always in the present tense, with much rolling of the *r*'s. I used to rock with laughter, but it was a great success with the French. It was easy for them to understand, and so they thought they were making progress in English; Mother felt vaguely that her French was improving, and everybody was pleased. Sometimes Mother was up against a Problem who spoke no English, and I occasionally acted as interpreter. The Problems were generally the artists—Pierre Brissaud, Georges Lepape, Benito, Martin: the school of brilliant French moderns who had turned their talent to the fashion world and who contributed to *Vogue*. They were Problems temperamentally and linguistically, but their wants were simple—more money. The French staff always demanded to be paid in dollars, which was understandable, as the rate of exchange was generally in their favor, but occasionally it was not, and their rage at this injustice, which they took as a personal insult, was glorious to behold. They considered it was doubtless instigated by Condé Nast, their publisher, and clannishly abetted by the United States Secretary of the Treasury.

I sometimes thought dear Mama took a malicious pleasure in these reversals of their fortunes, as she was heard to murmur sanctimoniously that it was a pity they couldn't get it coming and going.

The happy Paris life finally came to an end. It was time for me to return to America and make my debut. I had become vaguely engaged to a lissom half-Russian, more because our mothers liked each other, and there was no particular reason for not doing it, than because we were in love. On the boat coming home, however, it suddenly swept over me that I couldn't possibly marry him, and I sent a radiogram to that effect and felt greatly relieved. I don't doubt that he did too.

I don't know what it is about the ocean, but my emotions almost always suffer a sea change. Somewhere between Sandy Hook and Land's End the magnet ceases to function. Whether it is lack of stamina on my

part or a recrudescence of a submerged critical sense
I am not prepared to say, but the procedure is all too
familiar: the tearful farewell, the broadening sea, the
ties that bind stretching more and more tenuously, till
finally, with a soft little pop, they disappear into the
salt air; the carefully composed cable, half gallant, half
rueful, the deep breath, and the fresh start. It gets so
a girl is leery of the tub, lest she find on emerging that
the tender emotion has gone with the bath salts.

We returned to New York in the early fall, and
December found me, dressed by Worth, embowered
in flowers, standing beside my mother in the Cosmopolitan Club, being duly inducted into society. It was
awful. All the humiliating, tragicomic, heartbreaking
things happened to me in my girlhood, and nothing
makes me happier than to realize I cannot possibly re-
live my youth. When people regret the passing of their
young days, I don't know what they are talking about.
The embarrassment, heartache, and sense of insecurity
which most young people suffer are surely the badlands
of life, which, once traversed, are never to be revisited.

These, it seems to me, are the normal afflictions of
youth regardless of class or place, but in the social life
of a big city they are intensified. The three months
which were to launch me into society and, it was to be
hoped, matrimony, were as bleak a period as any I have
known. Since I had pretty clothes, a good home, and
friends, the charge of self-pity can easily be brought
against me, but for all that, I was lonely and unhappy.
During the years I had spent in Europe I had lost track
of people of my own age, and although the launching
of a girl into society is such an organized racket that,
whether one knows one's contemporaries intimately or

not, one is automatically included in most of the functions of the debutante season, I was still an outsider to the tight little cliques and groups which composed that year's younger set. I was invited to the parties, but I was not asked to dance, or if I was, there was the ever-present dread of being "stuck" with one man. How awful if the stag line didn't cut in on you, how desperate the pretense that you were enjoying yourself till your face ached from smiling brightly, and then the laughing little excuse that you really had to powder your nose, and the escape into the ladies' room. There would be an instant of blessed relief, but then you didn't know which was worse, the one or two other girls who were in the same fix, or the chattering darlings of fortune who had been so rushed all evening that they legitimately had to take time out for repairs before being whirled into the waiting arms of twenty beaux.

Oh, those ladies' rooms—brief, unhappy refuge for wallflowers, where more young things have closed the little doors, collapsed on the toilet seats, and cried their hearts out than are dreamed of by the society columnists or their doting parents. One of the most rueful stories I know is about a lady whose gallant adventures as she grew older made Ninon de Lenclos look like a spinster schoolmarm, but who swears there is one scar from her debutante year which she will carry to her grave. She is a lovely creature, Amazonian and beautiful, and many gentlemen have suffered acute heart attacks because of her; but when she was eighteen she was only thought of as big, and boys made fun of her. She had been invited to a gala debutante evening, most of which she was spending in tears in one of the cold comfort stations of the Ritz. In came two Dresden-china shepherdesses, laughing and poking fun at "that enormous red-haired creature, my dear, with those big feet." In her terror and shame, lest they see the telltale feet under the half-door, she drew them under her and crouched there, strangling her sobs until the two gentle hearts had withdrawn.

I don't know what comes over my sex in the town's tonier powder rooms. To this day I am chilled by the cold eyes, the curiously unfriendly ways of ladies repairing the evening's ravages. The swanker the night club, the worse they are: smart, hard, glittering, and unlovely. Significantly, it is the drunken ladies who are the most sympathetic. They have always been done dirt by their escorts, and it has cracked the veneer. I don't forget the trenchant comment of one frail blossom who, when her friend observed through maudlin tears, "You're awful mean to Jack," remarked grimly, "You bet. You've got to keep the upper hand."

In my debutante days it wasn't so much a question of keeping the upper hand as of getting a foothold. Owing to my mother, I apparently belonged socially to the upper stratum. The hitch was temperamental. I wanted to go on the stage; the other girls wanted to go to parties. I liked older men, because they liked me; my friends liked college boys, who frightened me, and whom I bored to death. I suppose the gents with whom the current debutantes associate must still present the same problem. The very young ones are incarcerated in the halls of higher learning and are only allowed out on the leash occasionally. If those who live in town are free to stay up all night, dancing their glazed boots through, it is because they can sleep all day, *ergo* are out of a job, *ergo* broke. The hard-working ones in good jobs—

i.e., the eligibles—are generally older or cannot take time out to go gallivanting about the grog shops with their lights of love, and a debutante who iş not seen at all the better taverns and balls is no debutante and might just as well be buried in the Maine woods or holding down a job herself. One can see that gentlemen are ladies' problems from the tenderest age.

Of course beaux and dances are the thorniest questions, but another prickly aspect of high life is female luncheons. Debutantes lunch in herds, and the routine meal in my day was filet of sole with grapes and breast of chicken under glass. Also, especially if the debutante's family came from the Middle West, there were likely to be bunches of sweet peas tied with silver ribbon beside each girl's plate.

I do not wish to give the impression that I do not like my sex—some of my best friends are women—but I think many will agree with me that in the coming-out season one is apt to acquire a bright yellow view of femininity which fades but slowly through the years.

During this stormy time Mother was sweet and perplexed. Because of the aura of glamour surrounding the gilded children of the Best People, she wanted me to be one too; but because of her infinite common sense and experience of life, she saw clearly what a manufactured setup the whole business was; and although she put up a gallant front and cheered me on, and said I was silly to be shy—"After all, darling, you are really sweet and look far more distinguished than many of these Totty Coughdrops"—in her heart she knew as well as I did that I was not cut out for the Social Life. Not, mind you, that the Prince of Wales wouldn't have been lucky to get me, but even so . . .

I think part of my difficulty was Mother's insistence on Distinction. When all the other girls were wearing their hair in great fluffy masses, I longed to dress mine in the same way and look pretty; but Mother wanted me to look smart, and so I wore it like a black lacquered cap. And I slithered in slim, reedy frocks, where others swished in robes *de style*. I looked distinguished all right, but I looked a good fifteen years older than I do today, and outside of a few *Vogue* artists who said, *"Quelle chic,"* and "What individuality," none of the boys knew what I was driving at. They would stare at my small head, long throat, and tubelike dress and turn quickly to a blonde snuggle-bug. Young people want to look like peas in a pod, and there is no use trying to make them different.

At last, after a three months' losing battle, Mother capitulated, and I withdrew with exquisite relief from the field of the cloth of gold. That was in March. In April I joined Stuart Walker's stock company and life began in earnest.

CHAPTER FOUR

I Played Maids

I IMAGINE ONE REASON STUART WALKER gave me a job was because he was something of a snob and thought it would be profitable to have the daughter of the editor of *Vogue* in the company. He may have had visions of de luxe publicity, but they never materialized.

Every summer he would take a few young people for training—they were called disciples. Stuart was a tough taskmaster, using sarcasm like a lash, working himself up into frightful rages, but within his limits he knew what he was about. As he was something of a bully, he was never too hard on me, thinking probably that I would sass him back or else run howling home to Mama, and there would be journalistic repercussions. This was highly improbable, but Stuart, like the rest of the theater world, stood in irritated awe of the press, and the eternal shadowboxing between the two antagonists was as brisk in Cincinnati as any bout on Broadway. In any event, he let me alone, not that I would have sassed him back—I am far more of a Milquetoast than anybody believes, and I only hope my enemies don't find out—but I can't stand seeing little people picked on, and so there were a couple of occasions when, though the most minor member of the company, I flew at him like an enraged mother tigress. Stuart subsided quite suddenly and started to laugh, and one time the frail young gentleman whom I had championed wept his gratitude on my chest and quite ruined an olive-green Vionnet, to my intense annoyance.

Our manager was always dying to act himself, and the company had to sit on him hard and frequently to deflect his ambition. It was a service to the community, actually, as he acted very badly. However, he could direct very ably, and it was he who first taught me to cope with inanimate objects. He once told me to cross upstage left, and I observed that the sofa was in my way. "Good God, child," he shouted. "Haven't you got more brains than a piece of furniture? Go above, go below it, but get the hell over to that door." This so impressed me that ever since I have been able to slither between coffee table, floor lamp, and chair with the ease of an adder. Of course, if they have any sense, the scenic designer and the director will not deliberately arrange a Hampton Court maze just to test the actor's ingenuity, but such ability stands one in good stead in a pinch.

Although the full summer stock season was played in Cincinnati, we opened with six weeks in Baltimore, which is where I first set foot on any stage; so far as I know, there is no plaque commemorating the event. It was in a play by Edward Sheldon and Dorothy Donnelly, called *The Proud Princess,* in which, I forget how or why, the Italian ambassador disguised himself as an organ grinder and went slumming with a monkey; but he ended up by marrying a rich girl who also pretended to be poor in order to be loved for herself alone. And in the last act, when the disguises were cast aside, were they surprised to find out the true state of affairs! Surprised and, I should think, damned well annoyed that they had taken all that trouble for nothing. I do not wish to give the impression that I was the Proud Princess. Far from it; I was an Italian immigrant in Mott Street, where the wedding scene took place, and we all danced around the happy couple, and I handed them a pink cotton rose and said, "I give you this rose that love may always blossom in your hearts." Mother came all the way to Baltimore from New York for the occasion and couldn't hear a syllable.

I remember that I have never been so tired in my life as at the end of my first rehearsal; not that I had anything to do, but I watched it so intensely that I was drained of all vitality for hours afterward. It was to me the most exciting, wonderful thing in the world, and still is. I feel terribly sorry for people in other businesses—their lives must be so drab. To my way of thinking, rehearsals are the most enjoyable part of acting, but of course there is the opening night too—half horror and half ecstasy—and then the first few weeks of playing, while it is still fresh and before the job becomes mechanical. But the working out of a character, watching a play come alive, has a curious excitement of its own, and if you have a director in whom you have confidence, and a real character to play, it's as stimulating as having a baby. The feeling between actor and director has inevitably a little something of the relationship between a woman and her obstetrician. He sees you through the tightest spots. Between you, you create a person. No matter how much theater people may dislike one another, and many of the antipathies are cordial, they are against their wills bound to one another by mutual understanding of common struggles.

Howard Dietz, who is in charge of publicity for Metro-Goldwyn-Mayer, and the lyricist responsible for such hits as the *Little Shows,* the *Bandwagon,* and others, once said that to be in the theater was to follow an orgasmic career, and he is right. It may start gently enough, but a production inevitably works to a crescendo, of which the opening night is the resolution. This is perhaps most emphasized in musical plays.

I have been in two musicals, *Revenge with Music* and *Keep off the Grass,* which were both flops, but even had they been good I wouldn't have liked them. You have no chance to really build a scene, because just as things get interesting, on come the girls, and the next time you appear you have to start over again from scratch. Most legitimate actors who have never tried them long to do musicals. They say, "It must be so gay when the music plays," but that depends on the music. The one real advantage is the salaries, which are lush.

If, however, you have a weakness for illusion, that old sobersides, the legit, is your dish, although I remember a curious experience in my Stuart Walker Baltimore days when, in learning something of backstage mechanics, I temporarily lost my illusions and could no longer enjoy a play. I knew that the rest of the house did not lie beyond the stage set; I knew that the walls—flats, they are called—were propped up by braces and whipped together by cords; the actors weren't characters, but people I knew. In short, like Psyche, by looking too closely at my love I had lost it. Fortunately, after a little time, I regained it. I was once again an ingenuous audience, and am to this day. I laugh and cry and turn cold with fear, and to me all the stage is a world, and one I much prefer to God's effort.

The theater can play curious tricks of fancy, though, even on those who are in it. I once did a play in New York, and I was mildly in love with the leading man. The scene was laid in the Middle West, and toward the end of the third act he would leave me, presumably to go to New York, where I was to meet him. I used to wonder what went on in his life as the character between the time I bade him good-by on the stage and the time I saw him again in the dressing room ten minutes later.

Once with Stuart we did a play called *Three Roses*. The first act was the lawn in front of an old Southern house before the Civil War. Peggy Wood came from New York to star in the play, and she and Ruth Hammond and I sat on the grass, our hoop skirts pooling around us in the soft light, and Miss Wood sang "The Last Rose of Summer." The scene evoked a nostalgic mood, and after the performance, when I had to cross the bare, darkened stage from my dressing room to get to the street, I had the oddest feeling that there had been a real garden there, where three girls sat in the twilight long ago.

That summer was an eventful one for me all around, because I fell in love, passionately and hopelessly. How hopelessly I didn't realize until later, as I couldn't and

wouldn't accept the truth—my idol, my darling, with
his quick, ringing laughter, his masculinity, and his
gentleness, not only didn't care for me; he didn't care
for women. I walked the floor at night, whispering his
name, and was swept by fear as by a fire, because when
I tried to read a love story I suffered so much I thought
literature must be forever closed to me. When I looked
at the sunset, the ache in my heart was unbearable. I
thought the rest of my days would be informed with
sadness because of unrequited love, and although the
pain was genuine and acute (it was also the first of
many), the sense of being a lost lady was not unpleasant. It was at about the same time that that tower
of tripe, *The Green Hat*, was published, and romantic
young women were much influenced by it and went
around being gallant, doomed, and as promiscuous as
their luck provided. They prudently stopped short of
crashing into oak trees. My own promiscuity was decidedly limited, as my offering was in vain. I have had
my heart shattered several times since, but, on the
whole, I never again suffered so much for so little.
Occasionally I have seen my love in the course of the
passing years, and so changed are we that the only
reaction is boredom. I am hard put to it to remember
the turmoil. When I do, I murmur incredulously to
myself, "Was this the man?" How many times, alas,
the fickle heart repeats the question. And yet, who
does not long to love truly and forever? How many
ladies have lain down in a new bed hoping to arise
enchanted for the rest of their lives, only to find that
they had installed themselves in a mirage.

In plays they arrange these things better; even when
there are mistakes and disappointments, there is a suc-

cessful clinch at the final curtain, and it is only the writers who are busy with the looking glass, mirroring our current problems, of whom one must beware. With them, if you are not very careful, you are apt to find yourself looking at a nasty little slice of life right on the stage. These are generally the better plays—and the ones to which Mr. Richard Watts, of the *Herald Tribune*, who is socially conscious, gives good notices, always provided that they are sound theater, for he plays fair in such matters and will give them a pat on the back but not a real boost if they are only propaganda—but they are also the plays which harry one. In a normal world this would be a healthy stimulus, but with the current headlines shrieking about one's ears, there is scarcely time for much complacency, and perhaps a couple of hours in Never-Never Land are permissible; a couple of hours where the honeymoon shines forever and where to be meek is to inherit the earth and not the dive bomber, the depth charge, and the ghetto.

In my Baltimore and Cincinnati days the theater was more foolish. Love held sway on stage, and off stage there were jealousy and affection, tears and laughter and parties—poisonous prohibition gin and a touch of high life in the person of Miss Julia Hoyt, who had social position. Julia was in the Stuart Walker company, and she was fun and always very nice to me. Later on we married and divorced the same man. I got there first, but she lasted longer, and although we rarely see each other now, I would say that our mutual sentiments are friendly if tenuous. A month or so after Julia married my ex-husband, I was playing in Chicago, and in going through a trunk which had been sent on to me from New York, I found a box of calling cards

engraved "Mrs. Louis Calhern." They were the best
cards—thin, flexible parchment, highly embossed—and
it seemed a pity to waste them, and so I mailed the
box to my successor. But aware of Lou's mercurial
marital habits, I wrote on the top one, "Dear Julia, I
hope these reach you in time." I received no acknowl-
edgment.

I was impressed by Julia, because she had been
presented at the Court of St. James's and once said
she got more of a thrill when a stagehand complimented
her on a performance than she did when she bowed to
George and Mary. I don't know how true this was,
but it showed a nice feeling for the worth-while things.

Along with the disciples there were, of course, some
real actors in our company, and they were very good.
The year before I joined them, Stuart had Elizabeth
Patterson, and in my summer we were blessed with
Beulah Bondi, who is now earning rich sums in Hollywood; but no matter how much they pay her, she is
a bargain, because she is one of the finest actresses you
will ever see.

At the end of the season I returned to New York,
steeped to the eyebrows in theatrical lore and superstition—don't put your shoes on the shelf, don't whistle in
the dressing room, green is bad luck—and as full of
theory as Stanislavsky. I still lacked some of his polish.

My first New York appearance caused a furore backstage. I got more flowers than I have ever received at
an opening night since, and Mother gave me a small
ruby heart on a silver chain. In the front of the house
and in the press the occasion passed without a ripple.
The play was an incredible stew called *The Red Falcon*,
produced at the Broadhurst Theatre, and so insignificant

was I that I played two bits and dressed in the flies.
The theater is one business where you start at the top
and work down. The smaller the part, the more flights
you climb to your dressing room. It is only when you
are a star that you reach stage level.

In *The Red Falcon* I was very versatile. I played an
Italian maid—the old Mott Street training with Stuart
and the pink cotton rose stood me in good stead—and I
also played a nun. The scene was fifteenth-century
Italy, and in rehearsals we were told to shriek loudly
when the ravening barbarians thundered at the convent gates. I asked, "What do we shriek: Goody, goody?"
The cast laughed, but the director was more staid and
thought it indicated dubious morality in one so young.

I was enchanted to be playing on Broadway, but it
had been a close shave—I almost didn't get the job.
Carlotta Monterey, who has now been married for
several years to Eugene O'Neill, was the leading woman,
and she had black hair and dark eyes and so did I—
I was also taller. It has long been an axiom in the
theater that the heavens will fall if two actresses of the
same coloring play a scene together, and sometimes the
most absurd devices are resorted to lest this fatal en-
counter occur. I have yet to hear one member of one
audience remark it, and I think it is an illusion in-
digenous to producers and fostered by actresses themselves, who wish to appear unique. In *The Women,*
cast and audience both had to put up with what they
could get, as there were thirty-three of us, and unless
the ladies dyed themselves blue and purple, like early
Britons, what were we to do?

The producers of *The Red Falcon,* however, were
die-hards and kept whispering to Carlotta that, of course,

they wouldn't engage me if she didn't want me. "Good
God," she snapped at last, impatiently, "the kid has
six lines and I'm playing the lead. If I can't score with
that setup I might as well leave the stage. Certainly
engage her—why not?" I had been standing tense
throughout this interview—embarrassed and desperate
—so that when they said yes, tears of excitement splashed
down my face, and I was more embarrassed than ever.

Carlotta and I became great friends. At that time she
was married to Ralph Barton, the artist. Later on they
were divorced; he married the French pianist and com-
poser, Germaine Taillefere, and eventually committed
suicide. Ralph and Carlotta's life together was stormy
and passionate, and she would arrive at the theater in a
seething emotional turmoil and pour her misfortunes
into my willing ears. As she was very beautiful, Ralph
was not the first man who had made her unhappy. She
had a small, exquisitely poised head, a delicate profile,
and superb dark eyes. She was short, with capable hands
and feet, and always dressed rather dowdily, but everything was expensive and of the finest material, and her
shoes were made to order of special leathers at great
cost. She was the most immaculate creature I have ever
known, and while other ladies were burying their noses
in striped and plaid and gaudy flowered handkerchiefs,
I never saw her use anything but sheerest, whitest
linen. From the neck up Carlotta looked Javanese or
Russian, or something mysteriously exotic, but her
sturdy little body proclaimed her Dutch and Danish
ancestry. Hazel Tauzig was her name, and even at
the time when she was sweeping New York as the
town's most sultry glamour queen, her apartment shone
like a fresh-minted coin. Her bills were paid on the

dot, she wore no jewels, and she dressed like a Dutch burgher's wife from the provinces. She was kind and funny, remarkably ribald, and she hated the theater.

She and Ralph Barton lived in a studio apartment, and I used to love to go there, because they had wonderful books and pictures and delicious little dinners; but they dined at half-past six even when Carlotta wasn't playing, and I never could understand why. It had something to do with their temperaments, I imagine; their temperaments were prominent, and everybody relaxed when they got a divorce. Just before the upheaval Mrs. Barton had given Mr. Barton a fur-lined overcoat, and she was furious when she thought of the expense, but she had to laugh when, in going around the apartment gathering up his personal lares and penates preparatory to Moving to My Club, Ralph had asked sheepishly if he might take his fur-lined overcoat with him. Not that he cared about the coat, he said, but it would be something to remember her by. Carlotta always thought he had hocked it.

It was several years after she divorced Ralph Barton that she married Eugene O'Neill. They lead curiously reticent lives in far places; at one time a château in France. Carlotta hated it, because the trades people, who were certainly not above gypping the native customers, fell gleefully to fleecing the naïve Americans. The day came when Carlotta could stand no more. "I got too embarrassed for them," she says. After the O'Neills had been back in New York for a while they went, at my suggestion, to Sea Island, Georgia, fell in love with it, and promptly built.

I visited them once for a few days. The house was quiet and exquisitely clean, with special boxes and bags to keep the mildew out of things and with little colored maids polishing like Dutchmen.

O'Neill wrote for several hours daily in small, beautiful longhand, and at meal times the food was put on sidetables, the maids withdrew, and we helped ourselves. Not being spied on was a kind of fetish with them. Personally, I feel that a cat may look at a king, and although I do not care for footmen behind chairs, once the lower classes have beheld you, it seems to me there is no *lèse majesté* incurred if they pass the soup.

In the evenings Gene played records of bawdy old songs, and his mind must have wandered far away from the tranquil island to the thick haze of Hell Hole where years ago, before he became America's most distinguished playwright, he had passed so many nights drinking, brawling, and carving out the great one-acters, *Bound East for Cardiff, S.S. Glencairn, The Long Voyage Home.*

Gene wrote in my copy of *Mourning Becomes Electra:* "To Ilka, who found our Blessed Isles for us, with profoundest gratitude." I cherish it, and hope to live off such distinguished literary items in my old age. Lawrence Langner, of the Theatre Guild, says he is saving the original O'Neill manuscripts for the same purpose.

After a time the Blessed Isles began to pall, the mildew penetrated even the little bags, and the O'Neills wandered westward to Contra Costa County in California, where they are now living. They rarely come to New York, unless for the production of a play or when the six-day bicycle races are on. The matter has a passion for them.

It must be a couple of years at least since I have heard from Carlotta, but at a time when I needed an understanding and not censorious ear, she was my dear friend.

A tall, dark, and fat man had come into my life—the last attribute one which the gypsies habitually over-look—and what with one thing and another, my existence was far from placid. Like every woman who ever lived, I yearn for gingerbread upon my romances, and gilt upon the gingerbread, but the gentleman's outlook was more streamlined: the shortest distance between two points and no loitering on the way. Tact was what he was not the soul of, although he was coached in certain of the more obvious gambits and would occasionally remember them. Flowers for instance: I was frequently the recipient of an enormous rose bush from Thorley's. They were rococo affairs, lush and burgeoning and easy to order by telephone. As March melted into April, I thought longingly of spring blossoms and I said one day, quite gently, I thought that I loved these simpler versions of Nature's handiwork. "What are spring flowers?" he asked suspiciously. "Why, you know, darling," I said, "tulips, freesia, jonquils——" My truelove's brows rushed together in a horrendous snarl. "So," he cried, "I suppose I haven't enough to do; I suppose I have to take a course in botany to please your ladyship." Really! The soul of a prickly pear.

I think he considered it effeminate to know anything about flowers, which is an odd point of view when you consider that with the possible exception of Miss Constance Spry, in England, the world's best gardeners are men. Look at Mr. J. P. Morgan and his iris.

This strange man, who would sometimes act like a boor of purest ray, not knowing when he was insulting, had gentler moods, of course, in which he compared my voice to dark velvet and called me his little child, but he also said that he delighted to look at Ina Claire, the actress, because she was so beautiful, and that beside her I was a mud fence. As they were both many years my senior, this made me seem to myself hopeless indeed if even youth could not weight the scales for me, and my heart felt pinched. But after Galahad had dealt me a smart crack upon the jaw—not without provocation, I admit; I had landed a verbal shot of my own which had galvanized his reflexes—I came gradually to the conclusion that the emotion we felt for each other couldn't be what the poets and composers had in mind when they penned immortal plays and wrote the symphonies, and so I decided I had better look further.

I was in luck, because about that time Henry Miller was taking a company to the Coast to do three plays in repertory, and he offered to let me do bits if I wanted to go along. I had recently met Gilbert Miller, and he wangled me the job with his father. I was grateful, as it served a dual purpose: it got me out of New York, which under the circumstances was a sound idea, and it got me into the company of a man who was one of the best directors we have ever had in the American theater, and he taught me more than anyone else I have ever worked for.

Of the men who have directed me, there are only three who have seemed to me outstanding in the sense that they could teach you how to act, who both understood the inner workings of a character and could give you the technical methods for achieving your effects. They were Stuart Walker in his calmer moods, Henry Miller, and today Otto Ludwig Preminger. George Cukor, although not so successful with men, as a tell-

ing way in his direction of women, but more because
he presents them at their feminine best than because
he elicits an outstanding job of acting. There are others
besides these I have mentioned, but it has never been
my good fortune to work with them. Most directors
are stage managers. If they get the actors in and out
the doors and across the stage without mishap, they
draw a sigh of relief and call it a play.

Actually Gilbert Miller, the town's most plush producer, has a shrewd eye for theatrical effectiveness himself and a packed storehouse of memory to call on, having for years watched the great actors of Europe in the
days when the Germans and French were theatrical
giants, earthy and authoritative, and the best of the
English were giving cards and spades to dukes in drawing-room behavior. At drawing-room acting the English
have no equals, and if they simmer instead of boil in
more arduous moments, that is doubtless because of the
well-known reticence of the English character. It may
be apocryphal, but I have heard that Mr. George S.
Kaufman, on his one fleeting visit to London, wrote
home—"I am well except for a slight cold caught while
watching Sir Gerald du Maurier make love."

Apropos of his early training, Gilbert Miller recounts
that in his youth he was once directing a play and
politely plagiarizing every effective bit of business he
had ever seen men like Sir Charles Wyndham, Sacha
Guitry, or his father employ. The elder Miller was
sitting in the darkened theater watching his son. At
a break in the rehearsal he called him over and, linking
his arm in his, walked him up the aisle. "You're doing
very well, Gilbert," said Miller *père*. "You'll go far, my
boy." His boy blushed happily, and his chest swelled

like Popeye's after spinach. "And when you do," added his father, "it will be the triumph of a first-rate memory over a third-rate imagination."

Well, the old man was partly right, and his son has gone far. Today Gilbert Miller, enormously fat, irascible, impatient with inferiors, bland and smiling with his peers, is a sound theater man with a quick wit and great taste. He will drive a shrewd bargain, but he is one of the few producers who has never descended to shoestring tactics, either through necessity or inclination, and when he says he will produce a play, he means he has the money and will do it, which is not necessarily what other managers mean. He is heartily disliked by many of his colleagues, who rightly consider him a snob (when he hurt his hand last winter Charles MacArthur remarked he had doubtless been goosing a duchess), and he is despised by others because he is no gambler. He rarely takes a chance on an unknown quantity, dealing almost exclusively with star names, be they actors or playwrights, and, if he can help it, never producing a play which has not already been a proven hit in some other country—preferably Hungary in the old days, although in recent years, until the outbreak of the war, he was more inclined to settle for London. He puts up a spirited defense on two counts, however, claiming that the *Welt-Urauffuehrung* (world première to you and me, dear reader) of Molnar's *The Play's the Thing* took place at Great Neck, Long Island, and that he first offered *The Constant Wife* in the exotic precincts of Cleveland, Ohio. This lack of pioneering on his part is extremely irritating to less glossy and more progressively minded managers, but as Miller says, he is in the theater not to experiment but to make money.

Like everybody else, he has failures, which he accepts
coolly, and he has a shrewd philosophy indispensable to
a theatrical career. "Do not be too downcast over a flop,"
he said once, "or too elated by a success. If you're spending your life in this game, what counts is your batting
average." His own is high, and though his method of
producing automatically excludes much that is lusty, ex-
perimental, and courageous in the theater, he almost
always presents his customers with agreeable cream puffs,
compounded of charm and gracious playing; and when
the plays are by Mr. Somerset Maugham, the added in-
gredient of trenchant writing.

Miller Senior was one of that great group of actor-
managers who died out for a while but who are now
coming again into vogue: such men as Orson Welles,
Eddie Dowling, and Maurice Evans.

Mr. Miller was old in the theater when I was young,
and he knew the technique of acting as a surgeon knows
anatomy. Testy, temperamental, and sarcastic, he would
take the trouble to show young people what to do and
how and why to do it.

Though no group of striplings, the principals of the
company which he assembled for the tour he was taking
to the Coast, soon after I met him, were notable: himself,
Elsie Ferguson, Basil Rathbone, Philip Merivale, Laura
Hope Crews, Margalo Gillmore and others. Every night
after the performance he would make a curtain speech
beginning, "Ladies and Gentlemen, I bring you the
flower of the American theater——" Some of his posies
were full-blown, but all had fragrance.

I played maids. I played more damned maids. In plays
today there don't seem to be so many; I guess it's the
Clifford Odets influence, but in a way it's hard to see

how beginners will get experience. They'll have to be cast as minor members of the family, and this may give them ideas above their station and upset the whole hierarchy. In my own case, the one time I didn't play a maid, there was nearly a crisis. Mr. Miller did a revival of *The Swan* in San Francisco and Los Angeles about two years after his son had produced it on Broadway. He played with great understanding, and some fumbling of lines, the part of the priest, Father Hyacinth, and I played Symphorosa, the maiden aunt of fifty. They costumed me in a rather startling affair of gold and crimson, which had hung in the wardrobe for years and which had once been worn by Blanche Bates. I was thin and Miss Bates was not, and so I had reefed it with safety pins. I had a gray wig which didn't fit and which swiveled about on my head; and as, even after a season with Stuart Walker and a few bits on Broadway, I was still shaky on make-up, in order to heap on the years I took a brown pencil and boldly lined my clock-smooth face—great furrows I had down my cheeks and across my brow. That the effect was distressing was attested to by Mr. Miller, who had not seen me complete with characterization—I was holding the best to the last—till the opening night in San Francisco. When I made my entrance and spoke, and he turned and saw me, I thought the great man would drop with apoplexy. In his efforts to control the shocked guffaw which rose from him at the sight of me, he turned quite purple, and actors went hurriedly to the wings for water, pretending all the while it was part of the plot. After that I was forbidden to use any make-up, and for the rest of the run played the part with my cracked character voice and a pan smooth if not dead. Until thwarted by nature, however, Mr. Miller was a great one for realism, and in the dinner scene in *The Swan,* when we were supposed to eat salmon, we were served real salmon till the night the boss was nearly suffocated by a bone in his throat; after that we had cake with strawberry sauce.

On that same tour the whole company escaped death by a whim. We were supposed to play Santa Barbara, but Mr. Miller suddenly decided that enough was enough. He canceled the engagement to the horror of his manager—we were sold out—and entrained for home. On the night we were to have opened there, the theater collapsed in an earthquake. After that I decided to take up fatalism. It is not a bad philosophy if you are in the theater business, as the ratio of failure to success is unduly high, although I suspect that even manufacturers of shoes and motorcars turn out duds too and take big losses, which they try to recoup with more popular models.

The most popular theater models eventually find their way into stock, and George Cukor's company in Rochester was no exception. I played there one summer, but although we had our share of tested successes, we were proud of the fact that we tried out lots of new plays as well.

Cukor is now a kind of pasha in Hollywood, and the Misses Garbo, Crawford, and Hepburn fawn upon him and cajole him with gifts of frankincense and pink quartz, which he likes in his house, that he may direct their pictures. But he is still a gay and ribald and infinitely kind soul, and it just goes to show that success does not necessarily change people, because he was the same in Rochester. The only difference is that now he is rich and gives Sunday luncheons which are eaten by

Ina Claire and Billie Burke and Aldous Huxley, and in the old days the luncheons were sometimes Dutch, but they were also eaten by Ina and Billie. Only Mr. Huxley was still in England and didn't realize the fun he was missing.

The summer I was in Rochester, Billie Burke and Louis Wolheim, who had been so magnificent in *What Price Glory,* came up to do the tryout of a new play, *Pardon My Glove.* They were very fine, and I was dazzled to meet such shining stars, but in the permanent company was one who far outshone them, Mr. Louis Calhern. I took one look at the tall, lean, and elegant Mr. C., and my revolving heart stood still. I had seen him on the stage when he played in *Cobra* with Judith Anderson and thought him the epitome of masculine attraction. On meeting him, I found no reason to change my mind.

Ours was a brief, passionate courtship; it was also an open secret, and the local press pounced upon it with delight; such goings on among the showfolks! I loved him and I longed for him to ask me to marry him. One morning he telephoned me and said, "Have you seen the papers yet?" I said, "No." He said, "They've got an idea, what do you think of it?" I looked and found that the press had decided that we were already married or shortly would be, they hoped. My heart sang. To think that I might really wed this marvel. That a procession of ladies had come and gone in his life I ignored; that he drank far too much I quickly glossed over. After all, why wouldn't he, the poor darling? He had never really loved any of the others, but life with me would be such that he would be drunk with happiness; what need would there be for other stimulant? The dread of long, lonely

years which at one time or another sweeps over every
woman, and which sometimes shoulders them into the
most unlikely marriages, vanished. I had a companion,
my darling, my love, someone who would be ever at my
side, someone who would never say, "Good-by, dear, it's
been a lovely afternoon. What are you doing this evening? Nothing? Oh, too bad. My wife and I are dining
out; such a bore, but we have to." He would be with
me in the evenings, a sort of perpetual escort—lovely! I
saw a full, happy life stretching ahead of us, a couple of
adorable children, hard work together in successful
plays: "Ilka Chase and Louis Calhern have done it
again. In their latest costarring venture this brilliantly
gifted couple . . ."; that would be Atkinson in the
Times. "As beguiling a performance as we will see in
many a season is that of Ilka Chase in the new play she
and Louis Calhern opened in last night. While perhaps
not so glowing as his wife, Mr. Calhern demonstrates
that he too . . ." the *Herald Tribune.* And then when
the work and worry and triumphs had faded, hand in
hand into the twilight rich in memories and currency
too. Ah well, it was a great life while it lasted. That it
lasted for seven and a half minutes in my imagination
made it no less good.

We drove into the country one night after the performance with Dudley and May Clements, who were in
the company, and Andrée, my mother's French maid,
whom she had lent me for the summer while she was in
Europe, as witnesses. The honeymoon hung low in the
sky, the groom was in his cups, and we had no ring. All
the way to the justice of the peace he kept muttering,
"Marry me, marry me, marry me." I was sick with love,
longing, and apprehension, but there was small joy in

the contract that night. We finally found the house we were looking for. It must have been two in the morning, but the justice of the peace tumbled into a pair of trousers, and we were married in his parlor while his wife stood by. The room was filled with lilacs, and when asked if he took this woman for his lawfully wedded wife, Mr. Calhern replied, "I do, I do, I certainly do."

The instant we were married I had a feeling of such revulsion that I rushed out on the porch and stood sobbing wildly. Lou followed me, slow and dazed, while little Andrée stood patting me, murmuring unhappily, "Oh, mademoiselle, madame, oh, madame, mademoiselle."

CHAPTER FIVE

Love and Loneliness

WHEN WE GOT BACK HOME—HOME WAS
the Sagamore Hotel in Rochester—the curious black en-
chantment was broken. We were together, and it was
sweet, but there was the realistic and ticklish job of
notifying our families.

Lou called his sister Emmy in New York, with whom
he had been living and to whom he was devoted. There
was, in fact, an extraordinarily close bond between them,
and it came as a terrible shock to her that he had married so unexpectedly and with no warning. Naturally
she took an immediate dislike to me. It was a shock to
us too, but we were shocked together and by our own
action, which is never quite so shocking. I had to send
two cables to Europe, one to my mother, and both extremely difficult to compose. I got two gallant replies,
but the atmosphere was strained all the way across the
Atlantic. Mother quite humanly wanted to find out
something about her new son-in-law, and so she cabled

Condé Nast and Frank Crowninshield, both of whom had known me since I was born, and asked them who he was. Condé knew Emmy Vogt—Lou's name was really Carl Vogt—I forget now why he changed it, but I think the reason was theatrical rather than criminal. Emmy told Condé that her brother was a darling, but she showed no enthusiasm for his marriage. Frank Crowninshield, always an angel and as eloquent an oil-pourer as the slick-paper group can produce, sent Mother a comforting cable and added hopefully that he understood Lou had gone to Yale. This was not true, but the myth consoled Mother for a while. She felt that an actor from Yale—she would have preferred Harvard—must be superior to a normal actor, a point of view a little hard to reconcile with the achievements of some of our alumni, but it must be said in defense of her opinion that that was before the boys of Groton and the major universities were really on their mettle. The stuff of which many of them were made had not become so transparent.

Lou and Emmy had both been born in this country, but their parents came from Germany—Bavaria, which sounded better, as everybody knows that southern Germans do not have those nasty Prussian traits.

The next few weeks in Rochester were very happy, even if there was no time for lazy honeymooning. We were both working hard, Lou especially, who, as it was a stock company, was playing a new leading part every week. He had to study next week's lines at nights after the performance, and I would cue him until I got too sleepy. I remember dimly through the years and the sleepiness that he would pick me up and carry me to bed when he was through studying.

We had a few skirmishes of course. After one of
them, I took Andrée and drove into the country. We
passed a flying field where for five dollars they took you
up in an orange crate. I decided grimly that I would fly,
and if I crashed, as seemed highly probable, Mr. Calhern would be good and sorry for his iniquities. Andrée
was game, and so I took her up too. Never in my life
again have I known such sheer terror. I think we must
have been with a stunt pilot, because the earth was
above our heads most of the time. I screamed through
clenched teeth, but Andrée was a much better sport, and
I think actually enjoyed it. When we got home I announced what we had done, and Lou said calmly, "I'm
glad you had such an exciting adventure." I said, "But
we might have been killed"; and he said, "But you
weren't." That seemed to end that episode with the
score one to nothing in his favor.

He took several vows to give up drinking, and two or
three times even did it. One Monday night, after an
opening in which I had had my first important part, he
said, "Well, darling, how would you like a drink? I'm
on the wagon myself, but you've been a good girl—let's
celebrate." I thought this was sweet, and also I had determined not to be a kill-joy or to try to keep him from his
old haunts and companions, and so we set off with my
dog, a wirehair called Naps, whom I had taken to
Rochester with me. Lou was devoted to Naps, and every
night after the performance would faithfully take him
for a walk before coming home. We fared forth, and,
after a couple of false starts and some indecision,
knocked at a little door in a back alley. "From Jim's
description, this must be the place," said Lou. "I've
never been here myself." Jim was his pal, one of the

stagehands, and a fellow who knew his way around the local speakeasies.

The little door in the big door slid back, and a sinister-looking party peered out at us. "I'm a friend of Jim's," said my spouse loudly. "I have my wife with me. How about it?" The sinister party opened the door. Naps leaped ahead of us up the steep flight of stairs, and we followed close on his heels. We came into the bar, and two or three of the men standing there gave him a pat and a "Hello, old fellow. In for your nightcap?" He made his way briskly among the tables to one in the corner and sat beside it, his tail thumping loudly, a happy smile of achievement on his face. There was a pause. Lou looked coldly at man's best friend, and I looked at Lou, and then we both burst out laughing. Every night when he and Naps were taking that health-giving walk before turning in, they had stopped for a couple of quick ones just to take the curse off being on the wagon.

Naps gave me to understand that Lou later addressed him with a few succinct phrases, but I gathered it was pretty rough talk—nothing he could repeat to the mistress. Naps was a wacky character, but quite a lad. When he was a puppy, Grandma, who had ideas of her own about canine hygiene, would take him walking enveloped in a Turkish towel. It was an odd sight to see a little bundle waddling down the street on four tiny feet. The day he came to man's estate and left behind all that sissy squatting business, he pranced up to a fire hydrant, sniffed around it, and gravely lifted his front leg.

We stayed in Rochester—Lou, Naps, and I—till the end of the season, and then went to spend a few days in

Maine with Carlotta Monterey and Elisabeth Marbury in the latter's house. It was a simple old farmhouse on the edge of a lake. After Elisabeth Marbury's death, Elizabeth Arden bought it. She has modernized, enlarged, manicured, and shellacked the old place beyond recognition, and installed smoothly efficient, discreetly made-up operators who distribute fruit juices and pummel the hell out of weary society women, who go there to rest from their pleasures. The place is called the Maine Chance, but whether for the clients or Miss Arden is not clear, and you get a very fine rest for $400 a week.

When Lou and I came back to New York we went to live at the Hotel New Weston until we could find an apartment, but things could not be said to be hunky-dory. I was alone a good deal of the time and got to be very friendly with a mouse who lived in our room. Normally, I am terrified of mice, but this one did not scurry in that alarming way, and I would bring him bits of cheese, and he would sit up on his haunches and eat it, his beady eyes shining at me. When we moved into an apartment, I missed him.

I guess it is true that the first year of marriage is the hardest even under favorable circumstances, and we were an ill-matched pair; incompatible, that was us. My groom was at that time much in the company of some of the town's leading tosspots, but as he was ten years older than I, I kept expecting he would soon settle down. He soon settled down in what I could not but consider the wrong groove, but he enjoyed the society of his cronies, he felt that our marriage was a great mistake, and, I think, he wanted to get it off his mind. We had been

married in June; by Christmas time it was apparent that
the crack-up was at hand.

Lou had gone away for two weeks to Muldoon's, one
of those men's health farms where they get them up at
six in the morning, run them ten miles, and boil
them for hours in electric cabinets. They're supposed to
come back with the tissues renewed, but something happened to Lou's. They broke down between the time he
got off the train and the time he came swaying home for
dinner. To celebrate his return, I had gotten tickets for
Broadway, the season's smash hit. We went to it with
heavy hearts, and after the performance drove home in a
taxi. I sensed that something terrible was about to happen to me but I didn't know what until we drew up in
front of the house, when Lou said, "I'm not coming up."
I asked him, not very brightly, what he meant. He said,
"We're through. What's the use? You go up to the apartment; I'll go to the Lambs or some place," and he did.
That was the end of our married life and the only
Christmas Eve we ever spent together. It always seemed
odd to me that my romance should have ended in a taxi,
where so many of them begin. I filed suit for divorce and
on the seventh of January sailed for England with my
mother and stepfather.

As Mother planned to be in London all winter, working on British *Vogue,* she and my stepfather had taken
a house in Park Crescent. The Crescent was a gracious
and decorative group of buildings, and most of it now
lies in ruins, attesting the superiority of the Master
Race. Because of illness in the house we couldn't move
in for several days, and the English *Vogue* staff, thinking to do the helpful thing, had engaged rooms at an
ancient and crushingly respectable hotel in the neigh-

borhood. We had left Uncle Dick in Southampton to cope with the car and drive it up to London.

Mother and I got off the boat train at Waterloo Station alone. The night was black and cold and dripping; we took a cab, one of the large, rattling, musty ones, and arrived at the hotel at the bleak hour of ten. Eight o'clock is a good time—you are just arriving for a dinner party or setting off for the theater, or settling down with a detective story. Nine either skims by unnoticed or is made eventful by the squawks of the thirteen-year-olds being shunted off to bed. Eleven is grand: the theaters are breaking, streets are crowded, and you're going to a party, or you can have a nightcap or think about going to bed. Even if you are alone, it's no admission of defeat to go to bed at eleven. After all, the back of the evening is well broken, and by the time you've undressed and brushed your teeth and opened the windows and read another chapter, it will be twelve, and you *should* be in bed by twelve. But what in Heaven's name are you to do with ten o'clock? It is an awkward hour at best, and at our hotel it lay embalmed in gloom. The lobby was lofty, dim, and, at that hour, deserted, but through double doors which opened off it came laborious music, and we caught glimpses of dancers and a great deal of bunched pink taffeta bespattered with rosebuds.

"Well, darling," said Mother, "wasn't it nice of them to celebrate our arrival with a ball?" She was trying to be bright, though her own spirits were ebbing through her toes, and she was more accustomed when in London to stopping at the Savoy or Claridge's, which were not county, but they had steam heat and Americans. I said nothing, owing to the constriction in my throat.

We went to the reception desk, and there was no one

there, but finally a bleak specimen of the undertaker's art emerged from the shadows, and we registered. This same gnome, like some hapless creature obliged to expiate his crime in subterranean darkness, corralled our luggage as best he could. We stepped into a large cage and ascended, creaking, into deeper gloom. After a long, tortuous route over miles of red carpet, he took out a large brass key, unlocked a chocolate-colored door, and ushered us into our suite. It was vast and crepuscular, and the chill of death lay upon it. The grate was empty, the high windows were wide open, and the icy January rain blew in gusts through the Brussels lace and musty velvet curtains. Two or three wicker baskets lay on chairs; we opened them, and they contained masses of pale spring flowers, beautiful but tubercular, with a kind of Burne-Jones *fin de siècle* air about them. Mother and I tried to fly to close the windows, but our feet seemed weighted as in a nightmare, and we moved slowly. Finally we managed it, and Mother turned on the gnome.

"Look here," she said, and the dank air shivered with her vitality. "What's the matter with this hotel? Why can't we get any service? Why isn't the fire lighted or even laid? Why aren't the beds turned down?"

"I'm sorry, madam," said the creature in sepulchral tones, "but you see, madam, it's the night of the annual staff ball. That would be the gaiety you heard downstairs, madam. I'm the only one on duty."

"What about coal for the fire?" demanded Mother in her brisk editorial voice.

"I'm afraid, madam, it's quite out of the question at this hour."

"Well, then," retorted my frustrated parent, "what

about a drink? If it's so damn gay down there, surely you can get hold of a bottle of whisky."

The gnome looked dismayed, hesitated, said he'd see, madam, and was swallowed up by the endless corridors.

"You know what we'll do, baby?" said Mother, as she looked at me mute and forlorn. "We'll get drunk."

It had such a nostalgic ring that my tears, which had been seeping over the levees all evening, gushed in cataracts. "There, there, darling," murmured Mummy, taking me in her arms. "You know what I think of Calhern," she continued, looking thoughtfully around the room, "but there are times when I can understand why he does it."

Hours later the cadaver shuffled back with the Scotch. We each took a great whopping pull and slithered into our shrouds, or "beds" as they are known in England.

Hostelries of this sort are the concentrated essence of English county life and are inhabited chiefly by retired colonels, the colonels' wives, wearing long strings of beads, and their fading spinster daughters. Many of them make these hotels their permanent homes, but some only come up to London for a bit of the Season, of which they must surely see very little, as they dine regularly in the hotel restaurant and play euchre in the cardroom after dinner. It is a dreary life, but expensive. How these morgues charge what they do and get away with it is a mystery. It is hard to see what you get in return for your guineas. The service is slow, the surroundings dismal, and the guests should be cited for valor when eating the food. There must be some quality, however, which appeals to the natives, as these hotels are as ancient and enduring as the fogs.

When we were finally able to move into our house,

life took on a brisker tempo, although the house, too, had little idiosyncrasies. As it had been semi-remodeled with an eye to renting to Americans, an extra bathroom had been installed in what was originally a small conservatory. I fell heir to it. Halfway up ran a solid wooden wall, but from there to the ceiling all was glass. When I sat in the tub, I had a modicum of privacy, but when I rose like Venus from my bath, I was as exposed to the public gaze as Mr. Botticelli's lady standing in her cockle shell. I could look upon the neighbors in their gardens, and they could look at me. In the course of the winter I developed into a fairly able contortionist.

About the heating system in that house it would be kinder not to speak. The bathroom, being an afterthought, had none at all, so that we had to use what the maid referred to as, "the dysy, madam." The "dysy" was one of those electric "daisies," a concave copper shield with an electric coil set in the center. When you plug it in, it gives a seering heat within a radius of three feet and as high as the knees. From there up you may freeze into a stalagmite, but daisies don't care.

The rest of the house had central heating. It was called central because a pipe ran down the middle, and if you put your hand on it, it was sometimes lukewarm. The drawing room was supposedly heated by an enormous fireplace, but because of some oddity in construction, the bigger the blaze the greater the draught which swept down the chimney, and if you lay on the sofa with your feet pointing toward it, your ankles froze and you had to cover them with a cushion if you planned to use them again. It is easy to understand the affection of the English for their whisky and splash. It wards off pneumonia. The only wonder is that they don't use it in lieu of morning tea. Personally I enjoy tea in the morning and never drink anything else, but I can get along all right if they don't wake me at seven to give it to me. When I ring for my regular breakfast is time enough. That was another Americanism which scandalized the "staff." When Mother had rented the house, she agreed to take over the three servants, and they showed stalwart bulldog spirit in staying with us, though we must have tried them sorely. The butler was named Eels, and he looked like something from Central Casting, with snowy hair and a striped waistcoat. He hated us. He hated making cocktails, but we banded together and stood firm, and countless were the sidecars he shook, using disapproval instead of ice to chill them.

English servants eat all day, and we frequently had to answer the doorbell ourselves, because they were having tea or "elevenses." "Elevenses" are hearty meals they sandwich in between breakfast and lunch. Naturally most of the afternoon is devoted to preparing, eating, and disposing of tea and the peeling of the boiled potato for dinner, and so it is obvious that there is little time left for housework.

I always felt that the boiled potato, not the tudor rose, should be the national emblem. Frank Crowninshield once said that the bidet was the emblem of France, as chicory was its national flower. The potato, it must be boiled, is the great English staple, and even rich people, who could have asparagus if they wanted it, cleave to the tasteless spud. I was once taken through Lady Sackville-West's house in Ebury Street by George W. Plank, the artist, who was her great friend. The Sackville-Wests own Knole, one of the most beautiful and ancient of the great country houses, and the dining table in Ebury Street was a slab of lapis lazuli the size of a sarcophagus, but I don't doubt they ate boiled potatoes off it three times a day.

Another English idiosyncrasy is the climate, but it is so notorious that I will heap no further infamy except to say that we congealed. If our vision of life that winter was distorted, it was because we gazed out upon the world through a block of ice formed by our own breath. That frozen maiden at the World's Fair was the number two company—we were the original exhibit. Many the fine new evening frock no one but the fitters and I ever saw, because though I would wear it when dining out, it was concealed by layers of jersey jumpers, velvet jackets, scarves, and odd bits of fur, till I resembled a bedizened crone after a fruitful forage in the junk shop. I was grand though, and went to all the best places, and twice bumped into royalty. On both occasions the blue bloods were busily injecting red corpuscles into their systems via the pleasant method of elbow bending, and their efforts were crowned with conspicuous success. One night in the Café de Paris the face of H.R.H. the Prince of Wales was quite scarlet from his endeavors, and another time, at the opening of the Russian Ballet, who should be battling his way manfully to the bar in the intermission but His Most Catholic Majesty, the King of Spain.

When spring at last came, far behind, I went walking one day in Hyde Park. Although the flowers were still tentative, the park was riotously abloom with babies, nannies, and eager citizens waking from hibernation. A watery sun shimmered through the clouds, and I blinked incredulously when I saw one cautious soul raise her parasol against the grueling rays. I must say she was exceptional, because while the English claim they love their climate, I have observed that the most ardent sun-worshipers on the Pacific Coast are the English actors. They luxuriate in heat like salamanders. Who are the great colonials, the boys who thrive in the tropics? The English, by Gad, sir. They probably credit it to gimlets and the old school tie and the fact that, although they deal with the natives man to man, they don't have them in their clubs, but I say different. I say it's the heat itself that engenders their success. They thrive on it. Given three or four people of different nationalities, all sprinting for an open fireplace, your Englishman will come in well ahead. Lifelong training counts. My husband once told me that one warm July night in London he was walking home late from a party and came to a place in the road which was being repaired. The night watchman had a little fire going and was basking happily in its glow. "Pretty warm night for a fire, isn't it?" asked Bill. "Oh no, Guv'nor," came the reply. "Makes it more cozy-like."

Well, it's a cozy-like country; for all the great parks and sprawling cities and sweeping marshlands, it's a small place, England—almost as small as on the map. I found that out when I went on a motor trip. No matter how far we drove, we couldn't get more than eighty miles from London. Phyllis Povah, the actress, was in London the same year that I was. She had recently closed in a play and was at a loose end too, and so Mother suggested we take a little trip.

"I'll lend you the car and chauffeur," she said, as neither of us could drive, "and I'll pay for him. Maybe a change is what he needs." (He certainly needed something—a new head would have done as a starter.) "But the rest is up to you." Phyllis and I at the time were suffering from genteel poverty, but we thought that as we wouldn't have to pay for transportation, we could manage nicely by going to out-of-the-way little inns. Just as we were about to start off, Mother decided that Andrée, whom she had brought with her to London, looked peaked and needed a holiday, and so she came along too at Mother's expense, but with firm instructions that she was to rest and not do any packing or unpacking or looking after us. Actually, *we* were only in the car on sufferance, but the general effect was de luxe, fatally so, as we discovered when we picked up the check for the first day's luncheon and realized that such grandeur was a definite detriment. It was then that we hit upon our scheme. As we drew near to what we decided was to be the night's lodging, we would leave the car, with Stotts and Andrée, in the lee of a hedge and walk humbly on foot up to the door in our simple tweeds. We would say we wanted a double room for the night and haggle over the price. Then, when we had hit rock-bottom low, we would run to the door and signal to the chauffeur, and he and Andrée would roll up in style and unload the luggage. This made the landlords very angry indeed but saved us precious shillings, and we returned to town much rested and re- freshed and quite under the spell of the beautiful coun- tryside and the colorful little inns.

I traveled a good bit that year, what with one thing and another. I returned to New York for three days, ap- peared in court to get my divorce, and sailed im- mediately back to England.

A day in court is supposed to be a traditional in-

stitution dear to the American heart, and it has been
the dramatist's stand-by from time immemorial. But it is
not a pleasant experience, and my advice would be to
settle out of court if you possibly can. It is always
frightening, and in divorce cases it is sordid.

My lawyer knew me well enough to be apprehensive,
and most of his fears were realized. I gave a poor performance in the courtroom. What I had to do was not
very difficult, and he coached me over and over again,
but I was the parrot who forgot. "For God's sake," he
said, "if you're uncertain, pretend you didn't hear. Give
yourself time to think and ask them to repeat the question, or in a real pinch, cry. The judge doesn't want to
waste time on an open-and-shut case like this, so they'll
hurry through it if they see you're going to blubber all
over the place." He needn't have worried about my
tears, for I exceeded his most optimistic expectations. I
was a jelly. My imagination soared, and I was terrified. I
had visions of crowds of reporters and blazing flashlights.
Ordinarily if you are in a business like the theater—
where the more people know you, the better your livelihood—such a vision is delightful, and you are vaguely
disappointed and sometimes good and sore—especially if
you are paying for it—when the boys do not turn out.
But there are times when keeping clear of the papers is
a neater trick than achieving headlines, and I think
divorce is such an occasion.

Fortunately we got by with singularly little publicity.
The case was on the docket as Vogt versus Vogt and
passed unnoticed, whereas our professional names would
have inevitably attracted some attention. Lou was lucky;
he didn't have to show up, but I was the plaintiff and
did. I dressed carefully for the occasion, bent on achiev-

ing a combination of chic and feminine charm which would melt the judge's heart. It was spring, and I wore a sort of toast-colored dress and hat, and barely any lipstick. My lawyer is a New Englander with his own ideas of what is brazen.

The procedure of the New York divorce courts must be as distasteful an example of law as exists anywhere. I was unnerved to such an extent that when the judge asked me in what year I was married—it had been in 1926, and we were then in 1927—I replied shakily, 1928. Judge and lawyer looked at me in despair and shook their heads. The witnesses were called, among them the colored elevator boy from a cheap West Side hotel, the sordid questions about bedding and the degree of undress were asked and answered—imagination has no place in court, the delicto must be graphically flagrante—and the case was over.

Since the sovereign state of New York sees fit to grant divorce for one cause only—witnessed adultery—public humiliation of law-abiding men and women who no longer wish to be married to each other is the obscene but legal procedure. I think no one who has ever been in love can sit in a divorce court and not feel quite sick to see the wretched ending of that which was once alive and sweet and bright with hope.

Our marriage was so brief as to be almost stillborn, and yet its death was sorrow. How much worse it is for those who have lived through years together and who share a thousand memories. Even when they really wish to be divorced, either because they are unable to form a working basis for the marriage they have or because they are eager to contract another, married people must still feel a tug when it comes to the definite break. Few are immune from that deep sadness which pervades the heart when we come to the end of the road and realize we have failed.

And if the divorce court only were an ending; but so often it is the beginning of loneliness for women who used to have a husband and a home. I never feel sorry for divorced men or bachelors. They are single; but women are alone. The man doesn't live who can't find some woman, frequently an attractive one, who will give him companionship and often affection, but women who may at other times have two or three gentlemen eager for their favors can undergo periods of famine. I know, because the winter of my divorce was the winter of my discontent. Travel is frequently advised as a method of getting one's mind off a broken heart, the idea being that new sights and new faces will superimpose upon the old, and of course you may, by a fluke, take a long voyage and meet a dark man, but on the whole it is better to stay on familiar ground where there are friends. My own miseries were intensified by my going to foreign parts where I knew hardly anyone. During my stay in London I was lonely and unhappy. I had few friends and no work.

I tried to get a job on the English stage, but with rare exceptions, the great Tallulah being the most notable, the English do not feel cordially toward American actors. The admiration Americans have for English performers has never been mutual, and yet, curiously enough, American women and English men get on very well together, but that doesn't work so well the other way around either. My trouble was that I didn't have an Englishman or an American or Frenchman either, and I was in a deep sentimental depression. Two or three years afterward, in Hollywood, Sidney Howard and I spoke of these emotional lows in one's life, and he said a penetrating and true thing about them. "You know," he said, "if people break a bone, or are desperately ill, it takes them a long time to recover, and they and everybody else understand that and expect a slow convalescence, but people undergo great emotional stress or suffer loss and are amazed and alarmed when they have not recovered in a week. Those wounds take a long time to heal."

That is one reason why the loss of men in wars is a desperate twofold tragedy, not only for the young who suffer and are killed, cheated of their lives, but for the women who must live on without them; the bitter loneliness of women who must live out their days without love, companionship, and children. That is why a Hitler is a monster. He is a biological sport. He curtails and diverts into channels of destruction the natural creative impulse. Because of him not only do millions of people die but millions will not be born. The great reforms, and the great inventions, the books and music which should have come from the next generation, will never be, because the next generation will never be. Instead of begetting their children, the young men are lying dead by the thousands, burnt up in planes, rotting at the bottom of the sea, crushed and suffocating in overturned tanks. The destruction and appalling waste which those who remain must somehow make up are staggering, and one wonders if even the Germans themselves, as they go heiling and goose-stepping, killing and dying through the world, don't have fleeting moments of doubt. Does no German mother ever ask herself what she has gained when even the censors can no longer keep from her the news that her son is dead? What do German girls think when first one and then another and then a third young man fails ever to come home again? No matter how hysterical the young ladies' attachment to him, it is not the Fuehrer who will be their life's companion. To think that you have crushed Czechoslovakia must be a cold substitute for a pair of arms around you and a warm mouth on yours, and it is odd that nations of slaves a thousand miles away are not so satisfactory as one free man by your side. Perhaps you will find you have no need for the *lebensraum* he killed and died to get. It would do you no good to go into those conquered countries in search of young men; their own women would be there looking at you with stony eyes, and neither the men nor the women would understand that you are a member of a superior race. Sometimes you forget just why you are, but you know it is so, because Der Fuehrer said it.

If you are a young German girl and you look at a map of the Third Reich, spread like a cancer over Europe, surely a little cold flame must lick at your heart when you think of the hundreds and thousands of other girls who want men too, who want to live a woman's full life, but who are likely to find when the heiling dies away that the only ones left are the old and the maimed or those with minds brutalized by the new order or twisted by torture and privation.

CHAPTER SIX

Land of Promises — and Options

PREMEER! KILL THAT BROAD! SANTA CLAUS
Lane! Bury your loved ones in Well Drained Ground!
It's in the Can! When it's Option Time in Hollywood,
I'll see you in New York! Palaces by courtesy of RKO,
MGM, and FHA. The fabulous city, folks, the promised
land, where they await a telephone call from Central
Casting more desperately than they ever awaited a
lover's voice; where they live for seven days on oranges,
if lucky, and where they walk off the end of Venice pier
in black despair more often than they attain stardom,
swimming pools, and cheesecake photos in movie magazines. But why be a kill-joy? It's not constructive, and
the Chamber of Commerce will be pained. The way we
figure is, these things show up the dark side, and that's
not good for the Industry. Now we don't want to blacken
the Industry, do we? Hollywood's a pretty fine place, lot
of regular folks, lot of rich ones. Sure, some people get
tough breaks, but what the hell, that's life, and this

seamy side you talk about, it's not glamorous, gives the public the wrong idea. It might hurt the boxoffice, and God knows, the boxoffice has been walloped enough.

It also causes talk and tiresome little inquiries, and people who don't understand are apt to suggest cutting executives' five-figure weekly salaries instead of the stenographers'.

Although it's true that you have to live in Hollywood to know it, just as you do most towns, there are few places, I think, where the surface is so indicative of the core. The sordidness, the cheapness, and the naïveté are revealed at a glance. So is much that is gracious and charming.

The architecture is telltale, characteristic of the local mentality: buildings in the shape of brown derbies, windmills, frozen custards, and bulldogs. Cute. There is also Bullock's-Wilshire, a magnificent store, and the Jack Warners' house with its Grecian columns and one of the most beautiful rooms in the world, brought from Europe; made entirely of pale thirteenth-century Gothic paneling. Smart magazines yearn to bedeck their pages with its splendor, but the Warners shy away from published photographs when they think of the stockholders' reaction. There are row after row of bastard-Spanish bungalows in rough concrete with arched picture windows and red velvet "drapes" hanging from iron rods. There are the lovely houses in the hills done with subtlety and taste, and there are awful oaken playrooms with beetleware plates and cups and German beer steins for decoration. There are brown-stained bungalows set among frowzy palms, housing the fortunetellers, masseuses, and religious sects which pullulate in the year-round warmth.

George Cukor, the director, and I arrived in Hollywood at about the same time, and despite my brief trip to the Coast with the Henry Miller company, it still seemed virgin territory. George and I used to browse around in his Buick, a risky business, as he was just learning to drive and was full of originality and enthusiasm but short on skill. It was a sedan, and I would sit in the back seat and the instructor would sit beside George in the front. One day the student stripped the gears with an earsplitting screech. "——!" he exclaimed loudly, and then, turning swiftly to the young man beside him, apologized with the most charming smile. "I beg your pardon," he said graciously. To me he said not a word—what the hell, we were old friends. We went cruising around the town agape with amazement. We thought it affected, but rather elegant, the way they prefaced everything with "LA"—La First National Bank, La Figuroa Market, La Monkey Farm. It was several days before we caught on to the fact that "LA" stood for Los Angeles.

I think the climate is largely responsible for some that is wacky and much that is shoddy in southern California. They say you go to hell in the tropics, and I remember Lewis Milestone, the director, once observing that Hollywood is semi-tropical, so that it takes you twice as long, but you get to hell in the end. It is perhaps because my own roots are deep in the East that I personally find the vaunted climate enervating. It's all right in the summer—it's supposed to be hot, but when you are routed out of your bed at six-thirty by the demands of the film industry on what should be a crisp October morning, it is a letdown to find the air like milk instead of cider. There is no tang in that country. How can you tell it is spring when the lilacs never bloom and the jonquils never come trooping through the grass? What kind of fall is it where only a few dusty palm fronds rattle to the earth, and no glory of crimson and gold crowds the hills? Life itself is in the turning year, and there the days slip by in monotone, no less monotonous for being fair. And though, to be sure, they have drenching mists and a month of May which is a disgrace, it is all heavy-footed and tropical, with none of the delicacy and sparkle of American seasons. The temptation to regard California as an outlying colony is hard to resist, as even people who have spent years there will testify. Mr. Charles Brackett, whose name adorns many a successful screen comedy and who is a pillar of New England conservatism, went to a newsreel the night of Roosevelt's emergency speech in the summer of 1941; the President's picture, thrown on the screen, was received with apathy, but when Lindbergh appeared there was wild applause. Mr. Brackett turned to Mrs. Brackett and remarked coldly that it might be a good idea if California joined the union.

Not only the point of view but probably much of the outlandish garb worn by the natives may also be traced to the influence of climate. I am not speaking of the gleaming movie queens draped in splendor and sweltering in silver foxes, although that is outlandish enough, but of those whose connection with the glamour factories is indirect—the customers. Seeing is believing, but the costumes in which they go about their homely tasks are incredible. Men and women ride in streetcars and go shopping and draw up for a snack at the Colonial Nutberger in outfits any ambitious costumer would give his eyeteeth to have thought of. The first rule for gents is no tie. A kind of porous short-sleeved shirt, wide open at the throat, with tufts of dark hair sticking out as from an ill-stuffed mattress, and bright plaid trousers held up by suspenders are the next vital requisites. Either huarachos or suède shoes may be worn, and occasionally a coat, but only if the plaid is different from the trousers. The ladies are even more inventive. They are always barelegged and resort to either high-heeled, cracked patent-leather shoes and socks or multicolor canvas beach sandals for street wear. The head may be wrapped in a bandanna, although the younger natives prefer shoulder-length, rigidly waved, brass blonde locks. Shorts or slacks tight across the backside are *de rigueur* for both young and old. These are generally crumpled and worn with a silver-fox bolero. Such *dégagé* dress among the natives naturally makes it difficult for the colonials to maintain their standards, and the fact that the bunting of Bergdorf Goodman, Falkenstein, and Sophie Gimbel still flutters is greatly to their credit, although there is an ugly rumor that the men of the English colony have occasionally slipped up on the white tie for dinner.

Much as one may deplore it, one must be realistic, and it is, alas, probably true, because many social customs undergo a sea change on the Pacific Coast. It is customary, for instance, for the women to dress for dinner and the men not to. Gentlemen throughout the country will probably inquire with envy how the beaux of the cinema get that way, as they themselves are forced resentfully into the soup and fish, and I can only say that the male population of Hollywood has turned the exigencies of its job into a very neat excuse for itself. They say they have been working late at the studio. Often they have, because though the cynical may raise an incredulous eyebrow in view of much of the output, the pressure of work is stupendous. Even if there were less quality than there is, you have to account for the quantity.

Hollywood turns out some 450 pictures a year, or more than eight a week, as the more astute Einsteins may figure out, and there is rarely any quarrel with the physical production. It is slick and accomplished, and the technicians of the picture business are the nicest people in it, unassuming, honest, and expert in their jobs. That is because they have to deliver the goods and cannot pass the buck. You can't talk your way out of a bad shot or a garbled sound track, and to turn in good ones requires knowledge and experience, whereas a picture executive's job is ambiguous. If the arch-producer berates the super-producer, this victim vents his spleen on the producer, who in turn belabors the assistant producer, who casts about for *his* whipping boy, and as justice is not to be foiled, the blame eventually lands squarely where it belongs, on the shoulders of the casting director's stenographer. It is this ferreting out of guilt which takes time and makes movie people late for dinner.

There is some excuse for the delinquent guests, however, as, after you have been in Hollywood a little while, you come to realize that dinner is always served an hour and a half later than the time for which you were invited. It is a vicious circle, like the opening night of a play. The producer advertises that his curtain will rise at eight-forty but doesn't wish to ring up on an empty house, so, as the audience doesn't arrive till eight-fifty, he waits till nine for everyone to be in their seats. After a couple of doses of that, the few who believed the ad and arrived promptly don't get to the theater till nine o'clock the next time. But the producer, having been

fooled, and the cast driven to distraction by the late
mass entrance at the last opening, the curtain is cannily
held up till nine-ten, and so it goes. It's the same with
Hollywood dinner parties—the late working hours and
the great distances are so often legitimate excuses that
it gets to be a habit, and even those who are between
options and live next door will murmur absently, "So
sorry to be late, darling, the studio, you know, and the
long drive."

There are other curious customs too. Although the
idea is fading, the wistful hope still lingers in the public's breast that maybe a Hollywood orgy will crack the
press wide open. I used to hope so myself, but after
countless visits to the Coast, lasting anywhere from four
weeks to two years, I have come to the reluctant conclusion that the orgies are apochryphal. To begin with,
an orgy presupposes men and women in close juxtaposition, and traditionally drunk. Except for the usual isolated cases, which are to be found in any community,
the drinking is restrained. The only difference is that
in Hollywood the isolationists are such magnificent
topers as W. C. Fields and John Barrymore. And as
for the juxtaposition, it's remarkable that there are as
many babies in Hollywood as there are, because the
ladies and gentlemen lead widely divergent lives. The
studio separates them all day, and at night social usage
drives them further apart. After dinner they never talk
to each other. The ladies sit on one side of the room and
discuss their hairdressers, and the gentlemen sit on the
other and discuss the Industry and Communism. It is always referred to pridefully as the Industry, as if it were
the nation's number-one concern. Actually, it's fifth on
the list, but the moguls give scant heed to steel, oil, and

the cloak-and-suit. A little more to the cloak-and-suit, maybe, as it is the source from which many of them stem.

Besides the segregated conversations, another social pastime is gambling. They play personalized bridge for enormous stakes, and one night at the Sam Goldwyns', Bill played his hand while Sam retired briefly, and in ten minutes won him $2,000. Bill thought it would have been more piquant if they had been shooting craps. The stakes are alarming, but it's all kept on the books, which are settled only when a nice balance has been achieved all around. The boys understand this, but they play a lot of poker too, and this sometimes undoes them. I am told that the frail Miss Constance Bennett, after a twenty-four-hour session, has wrenched cries of "Hold, enough!" from such tycoons as Zanucks, Warners, and Schencks. It is further reported that the gentle artiste is more interested in cold cash than in fancy bookkeeping, and her opponents have had to dig painfully into their jeans to meet her winnings. There are also singed victims who observe acidly that that brooding look in the eyes of France's gift to American womanhood, Charles Boyer, has less to do with sex than with doping his chances for a royal flush.

Their extracurricular activities sometimes land picture producers in spots where they are, so to speak, whirling in circles, holding tight to their own tails. There was the classic instance of the writer who stayed on the Paramount payroll for years because the boys were so far into him at poker that their only chance for a settlement lay in continuing to pay his salary. They would also make little side forays and buy his old manuscripts off the shelf, but they got stung on that deal, because while they were paying him with one hand and eagerly reaching for it with the other, his wife would nip in between and use the money to pay outside debts. This the boys did not consider cricket, but they were hog-tied.

The other local evening pastime besides gambling, not counting the universal one enjoyed both in Keokuk or Hollywood, and rather less in Hollywood, is looking at pictures. They make them all day and look at them all night, and the magnates vie with one another in the ingenious concealment of their private screens and projecting machines. Sometimes a whole paneled wall slides away; sometimes the floorboards rise before your astonished eyes, forming the top of a sheetlike expanse; from behind you shoots a ray of light, and the filming is on.

Occasionally there is a bright spot when they piece together tag ends of scenes which have been muffed in the shooting, generally because of actors blowing their lines and in their annoyance substituting a few pungent Anglo-Saxon phrases. The ladies are frequently more eloquent than the men, Miss Bette Davis, for one, having a modest edge on the field. Aside from these few light moments, running pictures makes for a dull evening, and one wonders why they subject themselves to it, as tough-minded tycoons are given to stating loudly that they don't know what the hell their rivals are driving at and that the picture stinks. Pictures are either great or they stink; sometimes both, for I remember Miss Marlene Dietrich neatly encompassing the range when she once remarked sympathetically at a private showing of *Wuthering Heights* that it was a prestige picture, which could only do poor, dear Merle irreparable harm.

They must have stumbled across *Wuthering Heights* by accident, as the wealth of storytelling literature in public domain has never been seriously mined. When the production bosses read at all, it is something called Treatments, digested synopses of current books and plays, compressed into a few pages, and they read those as little as possible, preferring to listen to them. Life in the picture colony has a kind of Alice in Wonderland quality, and through long afternoons grown men sit in their offices and are told stories by other men. Almost as hard to find as the stories are the titles, and bitter battles wage and huge sums are squandered while the boys scramble for box-office bait. Jed Harris was once the smug possessor of a highly regarded title, *Out of This World,* which he'd gotten from a play which he hadn't produced but which he graciously agreed to cede to Sam Goldwyn for two thousand bucks. Charles Brackett and Billy Wilder, who wanted the title for a story they had just written for Goldwyn, explained the situation to the boss, who was righteously out- raged by what he considered the snide tactics of Mr. Harris, but campaigning to catch his fly with honey rather than vinegar, he called Jed on the phone.

"Hello, Jed," he cooed. "How are you? I didn't know you were in town."

"That's funny," replied Jed coldly, "considering you saw me on the lot half an hour ago and wouldn't speak to me."

"He had me," Sam later admitted to his writers. "What could I say? I'd done it."

"Well," said Wilder, "you might have said, 'Yes, but then I didn't know you had something I wanted.' "

The picture was released under the title *Ball of Fire.*

The workings of big business must ever seem curious and wonderful to outsiders, and the ways in which magnates arrive at their grave decisions are instructive.

Stanton Griffis is chairman of the executive committee of Paramount Pictures, deeply and still profitably involved in Wall Street, and a singularly perfect example of the popular idea of a Financial Figure, except that his paunch is small and his sense of humor engaging. He occasionally cocks an eye at me, gives a deep sigh, and says, "When I think of the thousands you cost Paramount!" Considering that I once did a tiny bit in a Paramount picture which must have set them back all of two hundred smackers, I was baffled by this till the master explained.

A few years ago I read a play of Edwin Justus Mayer's, which I was enthusiastic about. It was the story of Davy Crockett, it was beautifully written, and he had called it *Sunrise in My Pocket*. Mr. Mayer has many shortcomings, he is woefully unpunctual, and for a man of letters a singularly poor correspondent, but his is the most aristocratic mind I know, and the all-too-infrequent product of his pen has a wit, taste, and incisiveness matched in the theater by only the best of the seventeenth-century writers. He told me that *Sunrise* was under consideration at Paramount, and so in speaking to Stanton about it I said, "You must read it, Massa." We had christened him "Massa" because he is always doing kind things for people and giving lovely parties on yachts and in general behaving like a rich, generous gent and a patriarch. Well, it seems Massa took the script to bed with him, but the California air closed his Eastern eyelids—no reflection on the play, he explained hastily—and he read no more than one scene.

The next afternoon at the studio the minds were in meeting assembled. They had been discussing various properties all day, and checking lists of tentative purchases. Just as they were good and weary and beginning to long for a drink and the tender ministrations of the little woman, their own or another's, *Sunrise in My Pocket* was hauled on the carpet.

"Then, there's this," continued the foreman, a glutton for punishment, with no sense of when enough is enough. "Should we buy it, or shouldn't we?" Opinions were laggard and varied, and no one seemed to know much about it.

"Come, come," continued the gimlet, boring into them. "If we're thinking of buying it, surely some of us must have read it." There was a muffled chorus of "Well, you see, old man," and "I've been too busy to read," etc., etc.

"What the hell," thought Stanton. "Maybe it *is* good. Ilka's no worse judge than these guys." He debated with himself but an instant. "It's a great story, boys," he said briskly. "The very thing we need."

"Really!" they all cried, relieved. "Say, that's fine. Let's tie it up." The vote was taken, the ayes were unanimous, and the meeting adjourned. Stanton claims that the reason they never made the picture is because now we're good neighbors with Mexico and the final scene is the Alamo, and the Alamo places the lads from below the Rio Grande in a light that you couldn't call favorable. "And," he adds, "we've headaches enough without political censorship."

So I nod understandingly and say, "Yes, of course, Massa." But privately I think they've never produced it because no one has read it from that day to this.

Another interesting thing about the moguls aside from their illiteracy is their nepotism. Nepotism is a ten-dollar word meaning to stow your relatives in a soft berth. This the boys are expert at. Relatives have to live —though why some of them must is a moot question— and the boys figure it's better to have them working than sitting around being supported. Thus it happens that every niche in a studio is occupied not necessarily by the man best equipped to fill it but by the most ubiqui- tous relative. It may be that Uncle Benny, bland as junket, two-faced as Janus, and a hard man with a nickel, has the very qualifications for a super-supervisor, but we must recognize the fact that Cousin Max is a total loss and set him beyond the pale; so beyond the pale he goes. He is the gatekeeper. That there might be better supervisors and better gatekeepers at less money is a little thing for the stockholders to worry about, and let us have no meddling, see, or the heat will be turned on where it will do the most good.

These relatives, however, are all too much in evi- dence—the real Hollywood mystery is the Case of the Hidden Kin. It is possible in this wonderland to know a prominent star or executive or writer very well indeed, to have been to his house many times, and yet never to know that hidden away upstairs is a sister, mother, or half-witted niece. Talk about Jane Eyre! Sometimes these appendages of the great slip wraithlike through the room. The visitor, skeptical of his own vision, does a double take, whereupon the favored darling may say with an apologetic little laugh, "Of course, you know Mother," or, "I don't believe you've met my sister." It generally develops that these nearest and dearest serve as housekeepers. It may be presumed that their reward lies in having a roof over their heads and the fun and excitement of reading about their astronomical relatives and hearing accounts of the gay parties they have been to. It is a bitter twist, with sisters especially, who often look very much alike, except that one is beautiful and the other is not. I remember Mother telling me that years ago the superb Dolores came to pose at the *Vogue* studios. She was the most radiant woman of her day, and came accompanied by a mouselike creature whom Mother took to be her maid until Dolores introduced her as her sister; and, said Mother, the fantastic thing was that once you knew it was her sister, the likeness was striking, though Dolores was a beauty and the other girl a drab and homely counterpart.

The first of the mystery relatives I met in Hollywood was Lilyan Tashman's sister, Kitty. Kitty lived with Lil and Ed Lowe, but I never knew it until one night as a great concession—there must have been an extra man or something—she was allowed to come to a party with us. Lil was a robust, lusty, generous creature, but, like many successful actresses, jealous of her own accomplishment and determined to shine alone. Kitty came down the stairs swathed in ermine and obviously delighted with the effect she was making.

"Why, Kitty," someone exclaimed, "how nice you look."

"She ought to, for Christ sake," put in Lil. "It's my ermine coat she's wearing."

Kitty stopped dead. I never saw the light go out of anyone's face so quickly.

In Hollywood a fur coat is almost more of a sign of success than a swimming pool, and when I once complimented Constance Bennett on her new minks, she said bitterly, "My God, they ought to be good. They set me back five thousand bucks."

La Tashman was a colorful belle who grabbed at life with both hands, and it is good to remember that she did live so wholeheartedly, because in a way it enabled her to cheat her premature death. She ate and drank copiously—the food she served in her house was incomparable. She dressed beautifully, and at what must have been vast expense, for I never saw her in the same dress twice. She never read a book, and she was no actress at all. There was much that was sordid and some that was scandalous in her life, but she was generous and she had wit and beauty and abounding energy, and three weeks before she died, consumed by cancer, she was the loveliest thing I have ever seen: she had been appearing at a benefit in Madison Square Garden and she came into a party at Stanton Griffis' house—pale as a fairy-tale lady in fragile white organdie, a sable cape about her shoulders, and her golden hair gleaming.

Lilyan Tashman was one of the famous group of Follies girls, all of whom were beauties if not actresses, who had gone to Hollywood while silent pictures were still in their heyday and who had harvested the hay: Billie Dove, Tashman, Marion Davies, Dorothy Mac-Kaill. Then came the talkies. When I first went to the Coast, some of them were still big names, though slipping, but they talked so entertainingly of their Ziegfeld days that they sounded like a glamorous group of ex-debutantes from a super Junior League, and I used to listen enviously and feel afresh that all those finishing schools and coming-out parties which I had gone through had been a deplorable waste of time.

The best part I ever had in a picture was in a Marion

Davies supercolossal epic called *The Florodora Girl,* in which we both played members of that famous sextet, and Bill still recalls fondly the scene where I explained to Marion how to get and hold a rich man.

A job in a Marion Davies picture was considered a plum, as time meant nothing, and your salary was apt to continue for weeks and weeks. It was rich in experience too, for if Marion liked you, you were for the duration of the shooting drawn into the orbit of that fabulous existence where the life of the Renaissance bloomed again.

Almost all big stars have apartments or little cottages by way of dressing rooms, but Marion had a two-family Spanish *palacio* on the Metro lot with enough kitchen and bathroom paraphernalia to equip a hotel. Sometimes she would ask me to lunch with her, and I accepted with pleasure. Mr. Hearst was almost always there, and I remember one day, when he didn't arrive promptly, she called him on the phone in Louis B. Mayer's office. There was some slight discussion as to whether he would come or not. "Oh, c-c-come on over, W.R., and I'll give you a b-b-big k-k-k-kiss," stuttered Marion. That cinched it; he must have said he'd come at once, because she hung up, satisfied. "The old b-b-bum," she observed pleasantly. Sure enough, three minutes later in walked the lord of San Simeon.

There may have been others, but one of their eternal feuds that I knew about was the battle of the orchids. Marion was irked and eloquent on the topic. Because of some quirk of economy, Hearst, although he wanted orchids blooming in the halls of the Santa Monica beach house, refused to pay for them, and insisted that that particular expense should fall to Marion. I found their domestic bickering over the orchid budget piquant, but I was on Marion's side. You couldn't know her and not be, for she is a darling. Unduly devoted to luxury, perhaps, but she gives as good as she gets.

There was a beach sequence in *The Florodora Girl*, most of which was done in the studio, but one afternoon we went to the shores of the Pacific for the reverse shots. The scenes were done in front of Marion's house, and the close-ups were taken in the pool, for that is one of the peculiarities of the cinematic rich: they build their houses twenty feet from the high-tide mark of the Pacific Ocean, and between the house and the ocean they put a swimming pool.

Marion was the perfect hostess, with buffet tables heaped with food and drinks set out when the sun had gone, and she showed a handful of us who were interested through the house. The cellars were particularly entrancing, as shining and well kept as those ads for oil burners, where you see a happy American family playing ping-pong and serving toasted-cheese sandwiches in what was, till the advent of the oil furnace, just a grimy old basement. The Hearst-Davies mansion has a system of oil burners and waterpipes to knock your eye out, and even Marion, to whom they must have been an old story, looked at them in awe and murmured, "T-t-t-t-terrific, isn't it?" She has an engaging way of blinking when she stutters, and though you think sternly of lilies of the field and the worthy poor, it is hard not to feel a warm affection, pied with only the gentlest laughter. She also has a huge bedroom facing the ocean, with a bathroom at either end. This is the kind of thing which haunts one when waking up in the middle of the night, and

brings hazily to mind the story of the donkey who
starved to death between two bales of hay.

While we were working on the picture I dined once
or twice at the Santa Monica beach house. It abounds in
portraits of Marion in all her roles, and there are also
portraits by the Messrs. Holbein and Rembrandt, but
no one looks at them much, being more engrossed in
pictures by Metro, Paramount, and RKO, which are
invariably run after dinner. Mr. Hearst watches them
too, surrounded by movie actresses and pansy decorators,
but he has been known to commit acts of *lèse majesté*
and leave in the middle of the second reel. Once, when
in search of surcease myself, I stumbled over him in the
pantry, drinking a glass of milk and reading the next
morning's *Herald-Examiner*. It may not sound like much
of an improvement, but at least the *Examiner* was his
own baby.

They run pictures at the ranch too, and when I was
there, the theater was not yet complete—the plaster was
still wet—so an immense pile of fur coats was heaped at
the door and each guest picked one at random and enveloped himself before entering. The regular seats
hadn't been installed, so we sat in wicker armchairs;
there was one wicker sofa, which was tacitly understood to be reserved for Hearst and Marion. They
would sit close together in the gloom, silhouetted against
the screen, and bundled in their fur coats, they looked
for all the world like the big and baby bears. Although
there was an occasional interloper, most of the pictures
shown at the ranch were Marion's, which put a slight
strain on the guests' gratitude.

Mr. Hearst is a strange man, and his vast power lends
a curious implication to some of his lightest remarks.

One night, after dinner, when the others were in the drawing room, I walked back through the dining room to get to the lavatory. The dining room was enormous, and deserted, or so I thought until I came to the end, and there in the shadows stood Hearst and his lieutenant, E. B. Hatrick, discussing some song they wanted for a picture. "I'm afraid, Mr. Hearst," said Hatrick, "we won't be able to get the rights." Hearst is a big man, and he stood teetering back and forth on his toes.

"Well," he said in his thin, high voice—it is the voice in which an elephant might speak, thin for all his great bulk. "Well, I'm afraid that will be regrettable."

I cannot describe the chill which went through me as I heard it. There was something so sinister in that light tone and the pale, gleaming eyes. One thought involuntarily of the dark rumors which swirled about his name, of the ruthless qualities attributed to him. Woo! I scuttled back and gulped some champagne.

I was invited twice to San Simeon. The first time a special train pulled out of Los Angeles in the evening, crowded with guests and all fares paid, and when we arrived at the little station of San Luis Obispo, a cavalcade of motorcars waited to drive us to the ranch, where we arrived at about two in the morning. I was ushered to my room, and I drifted to sleep in one of the most beautiful beds I have ever seen; it once belonged to Cardinal Richelieu, and his hat is carved in the headboard. All the old furniture at San Simeon gleams with a patina like satin, and Mr. Hearst's housekeeper told me that the secret is to rub it constantly with your hands. It is the touch of the human hand on ancient wood which keeps it shining and alive.

I had no sooner got to sleep when I was startled

awake by the loud and vicious roar of what sounded like a lion under my window. The window was low, and I lay quivering in terror. When I finally screwed up my courage and crept over to peer out, there, sure enough, was a lion; only he was behind bars, and there was considerable yardage between us, but his voice had remarkable carrying powers. In the moonlight I could dimly make out a huge round cage divided into pie-shaped pieces, in which wild animals padded back and forth. I believe the San Simeon property covers something like 240,000 acres, and psychiatrists might well be interested in why William Randolph Hearst kept wild beasts cooped wretchedly in narrow cages. He would go to watch them with his pale eyes, and they would look out at him with hatred and frustration. He had at that time an enormous ape who gripped the iron bars and screamed in frenzy whenever he caught sight of him, and in another cage an eagle sat hunched all day long, the creased gray skin of his eyelids lifting from time to time to reveal his glittering yellow eyes.

While I was living in Hollywood, Mother came out to visit me, and while she was there, Marion called me from the ranch to ask me for the week end. It so happened that I couldn't go, as I was working on a picture, but I told her Mother was with me and asked if I might bring her up the middle of the following week. There was a long wait, during which I presume Marion went to ask Hearst if he would care to have the editor of *Vogue* in his house—the woman who for years had made the magazine he was always trying to imitate in his *Harper's Bazaar* but whom he had never met. The *Vogue* folk laughingly refer to their rival as "*Harpies Bazaar.*" Hearst, moved probably by curiosity, said yes, and

Mother and I set off in my car. It is a beautiful drive; the last thirty miles of the road borders the Hearst property, and as we turned in at the unpretentious wooden gates and started the seven-mile rising drive to the house, we passed hundreds of wooden boxes scattered on the beach which held the ancient Spanish monastery Hearst had had torn down and imported piecemeal from Europe with some vague idea of reassembling it under the California sky. He never did, and at the present writing it is on sale at Gimbel's along with most of his vast collection.

CHAPTER SEVEN

My Night with Gary Cooper

WE ARRIVED AT SAN SIMEON IN THE AFTER-
noon and found Hearst and Marion on the tennis court,
Hearst playing in ordinary shoes and a high stiff collar.
As it was the middle of the week, the Sunday exodus
had already taken place, and there were only four or
five other guests and ourselves. I remember that Ruth
Taylor and her husband, Paul Zuckerman, were there:
she was the girl who had made such a hit a few years
before as the devastating Lorelei in the picture version
of *Gentlemen Prefer Blondes*. There was also Sadie
Murray, a vague relation of Mr. Hearst's by marriage,
and Marion's hairdresser, Esther, to whom she was devoted. I know of no place other than Hollywood where
such a strong bond exists between ladies and their hairdressers. It is quite touching, the manner in which
world-famous stars confide in their humbler sisters;
shows they're human after all. The hairdressers play the
role of the confidante so ubiquitous in the French class-

ical drama, and into their sympathetic ears are poured tales of romance, sex, and the more odoriferous skulduggery of the studios. Their ears are open, but their lips are seldom sealed, which is why they are in such demand by ladies other than their immediate mistresses, and why the mistresses, once they have found the rare and happy combination of deft fingers and a sympathetic personality to whom they can let down their metaphorical as well as actual locks, rivet them to their sides with bolts of gold.

Constance Bennett, whose reputation was on the stony side, was pliable as a reed with hers, and Miss Katharine Hepburn found the entente with her Emmie so cordial that she promptly made her her secretary, and they are inseparable. After her sudden marriage to Jack Gilbert, at that time King of Glamour, to whom did Ina Claire rush to recount the glad tidings? To her hairdresser. And on the male side, if we are to believe the movie magazines, who was it who briefly squired the popular Miss Joan Crawford, who put out of joint some of the highest paid noses of the picture colony? None other than Mr. Sydney Guilaroff, hairdresser extraordinary of Metro-Goldwyn-Mayer.

With this tradition, it is no wonder the Davies hairdresser was one of San Simeon's most constant visitors.

Mother and I were given a suite, not in the castle, as it is accurately called, but in one of the guest houses, simple Renaissance dwellings, rich in tapestries and rare objects, built to shelter eight or ten in luxury. As I recall, there are three of these baby *palazzos,* and all the countless bedrooms of the big house, so that Miss Davies and Mr. Hearst are nicely fixed in the event that they should get lonely and wish to have a few friends in.

That we might not rattle around like peas in a barrel, Sadie shared our quarters with us. She did better than that; she shared a bottle of Scotch, for one of the peculiarities of the house was that though cocktails were served before dinner and champagne flowed like wine, Mr. Hearst was violently opposed to any drinking between meals. Sadie would wait till her gimlet-eyed host was out of the way and then call the big house for ice and soda.

"He'd be mad as a hornet if he caught the butler bringing it over," she confided. "But what the hell, it's a free country." We felt like conspirators, and every drop was delicious. Actually Mr. Hearst's opposition to a twenty-four-hour license was understandable. The place frequently swarmed with actors and newspapermen, and as everyone knows, theirs are the thirstiest professions. Also it was during prohibition, and the liquor bills for that place must have been noticeable even with the Hearst income. Marion herself was quite a girl for the golden wine; it matched her hair, and she would get hold of a bottle after dinner and snag two or three cronies and withdraw to the mirrored ladies' room off the dining room for a pleasant aftermath. I was once or twice in on these festivities, and I remember Marion remarking how nice it was to have a few friends. "One night," she said, "there was nobody here but W.R. and old sourpuss C-C-Coolidge and Brisbane. They didn't pay any attention to me all through dinner, wouldn't even join me in a little champagne, so I c-c-came in here all b-b-by myself and looked in the mirror, and I remember saying, 'Marion, you p-p-poor kid, it's a shame, they're a bunch of d-d-dull old bastards!' " Moved by the pathos of this tale, I asked what they had been talking

about. "Their G-G-Goddam circulation," she cried. My
heart went out to her. Having been brought up in pub-
lishing circles myself, I, too, knew those eternal conversations of circulation, policy, and advertising rates. Although Condé Nast never owned a newspaper, he and
Hearst have been rivals for years, because Nast's *Vogue*
has always led the field of high fashion, and Hearst
runs an eternal second with *Harper's Bazaar*.

In line with his lifelong policy of always raiding the
other fellow's staff instead of building a good one for
himself, Hearst from time to time made forays into the
Nast fold and did snatch off some of their good people,
together with some very fine lemons. However, the plum
he really wanted, Mother, never fell into his hands.
Many emissaries would from time to time broach the
subject to her, but to Mother the Hearst school of
journalism was anathema, and her reaction was about
as cordial as Mr. Churchill's to Mr. Schickelgruber.
However, she was a woman and human, and she had a
natural curiosity to see the man who was forever trying
to find an editor who could make another *Vogue*.

Their meeting the afternoon of our arrival had been
brief; it seemed probable that the first real conversation
would come at dinner. Certainly the dining room of the
ranch is a fit setting for historic occasions. It was once
a Spanish church and is equipped with choir stalls,
leaded panes, war-torn banners, and tapestries. There
are two magnificent Gobelins, belonging to a set of six,
four of which hang in the Louvre. I understand that
the French government, anxious to collect the masterpieces under one roof, offered to buy his pair from Mr.
Hearst, but he replied in his thin, light voice that if the
French wanted the six tapestries together, he was per-

fectly willing to buy the other four and hang them in
San Simeon. There is a tremendously long refectory
table, ancient and beautiful, down the center of the
room, and high-backed brocaded chairs. The food and
drink are epicurean, but set at intervals along the tables
are groups of Worcestershire, chili sauce, and catsup
bottles, alternating with stands for paper napkins; and,
when a little surprised by the anachronism, you ask
why this modesty in the midst of such splendor, they say
it's because they want to keep the place simple.

As the only dinner guests that night besides ourselves
were the Zuckermans, the hairdresser, and Sadie—who
was, after all, a relative—when we entered the dining
room, Mother, as the oldest, and at even a modest esti-
mate the most distinguished woman present, gravitated
vaguely toward Mr. Hearst's right, expecting, naturally,
that that was where she would be placed. Not at all.
Ruth Taylor and Esther shared the host, and Mother
was shooed off somewhere below the salt. Our eyes met,
Mother's feathery brows lifted ever so slightly, and her
mouth twitched. We could hardly wait for dinner to end
to discuss this interesting titbit.

"What I am dying to know," she said, "is whether it
was malice or just an original form of *Bazaar* etiquette."
We never did figure it out, and the two or three days
we were there, Mother never did sit at Mr. Hearst's
right, and when they strolled on the terrace they talked
only of the beauties of California and never of the dif-
ficulties of editing.

William Randolph Hearst is surely one of the most
curious and complex figures in America, and many
books have been written by people who hate him, and
with ample reason. My brush with him was so fleeting

and superficial that I had no reason for personal hatred, but I found him alarming. It may have been his reputation working on my imagination, but he scared me to death, especially in the swimming pool, where he looked like an octopus. One day he dived in and came up quite near me, and the sight of his long head with the white hair plastered down over his brow by the water, and his strange light eyes gleaming on a level with my own, sent me thrashing to the far end of the pool.

Of course by now there is something legendary about him, and he is regarded more objectively than in the old days, and I remember that Condé Nast, who certainly had cause to dislike him, was deeply angered by the exposé which *Time* published in March 1939. He thought it unscrupulous to attack an old man, especially, he added candidly, an old man who was still so powerful.

From the feminine point of view there is much to be said for William Randolph Hearst. Power and ruthlessness in a man have ever appealed to women, and whatever his shortcomings, he has certainly loved in the grand manner and he has forced the great of the earth to accept his mode of living and the lady of his heart. He has enveloped her in luxury unique in our era, and her jewels are the talk of a community where the Koh-i-noor would rate no more than a passing glance; everyone has twenty-carat diamonds, but Mr. Hearst's lady, in line with his flamboyant patriotism, sports among other bijoux an American flag tastefully done in diamonds, sapphires, and rubies. He has heaped her with more fame than infamy and has disbursed fabulous sums that her artistry might be well spoken of, although the pathetic thing about that is that had her pictures been produced with less money and more intelligence and taste, Marion might well have developed into an enchanting light comedienne.

For some reason, an interesting psychological one, no doubt, she did not stutter when playing a scene; and when Hearst kept his finger out of the pie, things went very well. Harry Beaumont, who directed *The Florodora Girl*, devised a simple and ingenious trick for keeping the boss from underfoot. When the red light is on outside the door of a sound stage it means a scene is shooting, and God Himself can't come in. Harry posted scouts at all the approaches to the stage, and as Mr. Hearst advanced upon it, he would promptly order the doors closed and would then rehearse his scene in peace while the mighty one cooled his heels. There was one sequence, however, where this ruse failed. The "Tell Me, Pretty Maiden" scene was shot in *glorious* technicolor, and because of the blazing lights the stage got so hell-hot the doors couldn't be kept closed longer than five minutes at a time, and in would nip old Nosey Parker. Despite his newspapers, his storehouses packed with treasures, and his vast real-estate holdings, one always felt that Marion was his primary concern, which is very complimentary to a lady, as most gentlemen have difficulty concentrating on their heart interest, even when their business is no more momentous than a hot-dog stand. He was deeply devoted to her, although so many years older that there must inevitably have been a good deal of fatherly affection mixed up with his more conventional reactions to her blonde charms.

While at the ranch, Mother had made a great hit with Sadie, who invited us to a party at her house shortly after we got back to Hollywood. We arrived rather late, as I was at that time under contract to Fox and had had to go to an exhibitors' convention. I would sooner go to a convention of amalgamated plumbers, as the plumbers I have met have been a cheery lot who remembered their tools and did their jobs expertly and with dispatch; also they were sober, none of which could be said for the exhibitors. Maybe it was something in the air that particular night, because when we arrived at Sadie's house the door was opened by one of the weavingest gents I have ever seen.

"Come in, come in," he cried convivially as, looping and swaying, he led the way to the drawing room. We laughed and skillfully countered his excessive ministrations with the social aplomb of women of the world. We finally shook him off, but he reappeared a few minutes later with a tray laden with champagne and, by that time, even more in the spirit of things. He barged into our little group, took one look at the most famous face in the circle, and with a delighted whoop of "Hurray! It's Colleen!" crashed headlong, champagne and all, into the unwillingly receptive lap of Miss Colleen Moore. It turned out that he was the butler, and Mother was still further intrigued by the quaint native ways.

She also found unexpected and piquant the greeting of the young daughter of the house, who, when she saw Mother, extended her hand in the most cordial gesture and said warmly, "Jesus, Mrs. Chase, am I glad to see you!" I later explained to Mother that even for Hollywood such good fellowship was rare.

Hollywood parties can be the best fun in the world, full of spontaneity and awash with the famous, which makes everybody happy. The less celebrated are delighted to be in such lofty company, and the celebrated are delighted to be there too. It bolsters their ego, which, though flamboyant, is insecure. But sometimes the parties are bad ones, with barefaced self-promotion the motivating factor, and flattery rich as eggnog, and as sickening, dished up with the caviar and wild doves. Hollywood hostesses should write Miss Elsa Maxwell's famous dictum ten times in their diaries before retiring. Said that robust and forthright lady, "The way to have good parties is to ostracize the bores. Don't mix dull people with gay ones just because you have to repay an obligation. If you owe a bore a dinner, send it to him." Of course the difficulty is that in the Industry there are bores in high places, and such ruthlessness would send a shudder of horror through the finely attuned Hollywood mechanism.

There is one particular party, however, that I recall with fondness: a little thing of my own, which I refer to in my book o' memories as My Night with Gary Cooper. Although nobody could be said to have furthered his companion's career at that soirée, the guests felt no pain, and in my role of hostess, from strolling through the garden in the course of the evening, I can vouch for the fact that the good-neighbor policy was in full swing. Along about three or four o'clock people began pulling themselves out of the warm bushes to go home, and I at last shut the door on what I thought was the ultimate guest, but when I went to close the french windows opening on the garden, what should I see but the recumbent form of a gentleman in a long chair beside the swimming pool.

I tiptoed out and gazed down in rapt surprise upon the sleeping countenance of Mr. Gary Cooper. Mr. Cooper has long been the nation's dream man, and I follow right along with the herd. It was indeed a scene to send a thrill through a maidenly heart—the quiet garden, the waning moon, the small creeping chill of dawn, and, stretched at ease, that lank and beautiful creature. Perhaps he has cared all along, thought I, and has adopted this ruse, the clever darling, to tell me of his love.

"Gary," I whispered, touching him ever so gently, "wake up, the party's over." But still he slept. Was ever conscience clearer? "Oh, Gary—oh, darling." He slumbered on. "Hey, Gary!" I shook him, and I suspect the slightest edge crept into my crooning. Dream prince or no, the thing was getting oppressive. I looked around the deserted garden. There was enough evidence to indicate to the normally alert that the festivities had run high. Apparently the tide had washed unchecked over my unconscious hero. "Gary——" This time the tone rang definitely sharp even on my own ear. I gave a mighty heave, but for all he is so slender, it will please maternally minded ladies to know that Mr. Cooper is solid, a veritable Wheatie boy. With a deep sigh I gave up the struggle. It is hard on the feminine ego, but sometimes men just don't care. I went into the house and got a blanket and covered him carefully, protecting my interests against a future day, which, alas, never came, and retired to my lonely bed. When I woke around noon and went to the window, the bird had flown, leaving his little nest of pink blanket trailing in the pool.

When I had acquired that pool, I was tremendously proud. It was my first, and, I strongly suspect, my last; and during the hot summer afternoons there was always a group of varyingly prominent celebrities idly dunking. I remarked happily to George Cukor that it was nice to be so popular, with an endless stream of friends immersing themselves impartially in water, Scotch, and gin, but George said, "Honey, don't kid yourself. Wait till the first cold snap—the place will be a desert." He was pretty nearly right too. But while the warm spell lasted, we had some cheery afternoons, and I can still smell the rich, burning odor of the Tashman silver foxes the day she carelessly draped them over the electric-light bracket in the bathhouse.

But though there were many parties, there were lonely times, too, and on more than one occasion I escaped the empty house to go strolling through the streets of Beverly Hills looking into other people's windows. It is perhaps because of my own prowling tendencies that I suspect them in others and am a great stickler for drawing the curtains as soon as the lamps are lit, for though nothing interests me more than looking on unseen, I hate the sensation of being watched. Others apparently do not mind it, as witness the lack of walls between one house and another all through America. As a people, we pass our lives rocking on the front porch, watching the world go by, and not averse to being watched. To me, privacy is vitally important; but it is not a national trait. I think the mushroom communities—Rainbow Homes, Hi-Lands, Park-Vu, etc.— would be less dreadful if the houses were flush with the streets, leaving as much of the plot as possible to make a little courtyard or enclosed garden, but as people like what they are used to, my community would probably languish till the walls buckled and the doors flapped on their hinges while the Joneses and the Browns relaxed in happy exhibitionism on their open front lawns. Watching them there is no fun. It is when nature more closely approximates the theater that it becomes enjoyable. Indoors, seen through a window, people become characters on a stage. That is the only reason to bemoan the current passing of the elevated trains. They are terrible, roaring monsters disfiguring the city, but New York affords few pleasures comparable to riding on them and gazing into the windows of the third-floor flats at eye level. Of course in Beverly Hills more footwork was involved on these tours of inspection, but the enjoyment was about equal. It is not that people do anything very interesting with the lights blazing and the curtains open; they eat dinner or play bridge or trim the Christmas tree; they read and listen to the radio or romp on the floor with the baby; but it is life, sometimes entertaining and always a little sad, and it is a picture book for the solitary. When you are not riding the els, even this solace is hard come by in a city of apartment buildings, and I think the most grinding loneliness in the world must be that of girls going home from offices and stores, from libraries and telephone exchanges, going home in subways to supper in the drug store and a furnished room.

In Hollywood, if you are working and earning a good salary, the loneliness is more de luxe, but it is still there. You may have a beautiful house to go home to, and a maid and a butler to serve your dinner, but you pass the evening by yourself, and it is a blessing to be working, because then you are so tired and you are getting up so early in the morning that you have to go to bed immediately afterward. The worst times for me used to come toward the end of a day at the studio, when I had no engagement that night, or the next, and knew, too, that I would not be working for a couple of days.

Sundays and holidays I hated. It is never fun to be
between beaux, but in Hollywood it is particularly bad,
and the social setup being what it is, even when you
have a beau, he is not necessarily your exclusive property, though it is only fair to admit that community
rights are indulged in elsewhere than on the Pacific
Coast. In the picture business the most charming and
beautiful women sometimes become the mistresses of
very dubious gentlemen indeed, and across the country
there is amused laughter or raised eyebrows as the gossip
seeps and gushes in columns and on the radio. There are
shrugs and murmurs in the drawing room, and mutter-
ings from the Church, but it may gratify the smug to
know that frequently the ladies think as little of their
choice as do their critics, only it is the best they can
get, and the alternative is sitting home alone night after
night. Getting used to solitude is a bitter lesson, but one
which, given time, we have no choice but to learn.

William Percy has a passage in his book, *Lanterns on
the Levee,* in which he describes his loneliness in
Europe as a boy, when he was terribly poor, and he says
he became accustomed to it, and he adds, "What must
be learned at last had best be learned early." I think that
is wise. In my Hollywood days loneliness was my frequent companion; I came to know it well, and though it
is not an endearing presence, it is a familiar one, to be
endured without alarm. As it is one of the greatest
ordeals we experience, once we have met and faced it
over a period of time, other things are bearable. Loneliness is the ultimate sorrow. Not that loneliness is to
be confused with being alone—within limits that can be
distinctly pleasurable, and there are times when most
of us find our own company infinitely preferable to that

of any available companion. It is just that solitude, like
a piquant sauce, should be used sparingly and with discretion.

I suppose I am a feminist in the sense that I believe in
careers and votes and independent incomes for women,
but I still believe that, for a woman, life without a man
is no life at all. Not that life with a man is one glorious
summer of song. Men get tight and are either bellig-
erent or maudlin, they cling to their ancient haber-
dashery, they repeat their old stories, they sleep with
other women, they play golf or bridge or gin rummy
while you languish alone, and they always want the
crossword puzzle. They lose the rent money at roulette,
and when they have a headache they carry on so that
you think at least Athene is about to issue forth. Most
of women's heartaches come from them, and they
are indispensable. Aside from our emotional and sexual
needs, they are vital to us socially. Women are bound
round with taboos and traditions, and in the case of
famous women these are all emphasized. A woman can't
go into a restaurant alone unless it is a dreary spinster
tearoom. The gay cafés are out. A movie by oneself is
possible, but a theater is more difficult and not much
fun. An ordinary woman would feel conspicuous; a lone
movie star would be ridiculous. If a famous man chooses
to go out with another man, nobody thinks it's because
he can't get a girl; on the contrary, there is something
gala about it, and women are all envious as they think
of such fine material going to waste. But if two famous
unmarried women go out together, everybody knows
perfectly well it is because they either can't get escorts
or don't feel like paying the way of the available
pansies and gigolos. If they are married, it is not so

bad, as the onlookers may suppose that their husbands are away on business or acting in a play or in the army, though, as the army will probably be a long-drawn-out affair, a substitute escort is desirable. Actually, people think little of a woman going out without her husband, provided it is common knowledge that she has one, but to be single after girlhood is a nuisance, to say the least; one's activities are so curtailed. Travel alone is deadly, for what pleasure is there in taking a trip to foreign parts if you must gaze at the Aztec ruins in splendid solitude or watch the moonlight shimmer on the Nile in the company of other ladies and a rickety guide?

A single man, however, unless he is a lighthouse-keeper or alone in Nome with the serum, can always find companionship. In drab little towns, where the only warmth and light come from the theater and saloons, he can wander into the latter and find a crony, and in urban centers, Nature, in her witless way having created more women than men, their society is at a premium. In Hollywood it is at more than that. To be able to walk and talk, if you wear pants, is to be immediately a rare and desirable item, fought over by some of the richest, most beautiful, and most famous women in the world. It is a strange society, and the unpopular girl has the bleak consolation of knowing that many of her more alluring sisters are equally swainless.

For every eligible man there are easily five girls. Frequently beautiful, sometimes intelligent, and most of them cakewinners. But unattached men are few and far between. Half the attractive ones are married, and the unmarried are more securely hobbled than the most uxorious husband. The rest are galloping through the field like stallions, which makes any kind of permanent relationship unlikely, unhealthy, and unattractive, and the remainder are effeminate. Under such circumstances, it is small wonder that if a couple is seen dining together twice in succession, it is taken for granted by the gossip writers that they are sleeping *à deux,* and they probably are. It creates a more cozy atmosphere for work, though the myth that having an affair with a producer is the same thing as a picture career has long been exploded. The exigencies of picture work, the easy camaraderie, the dearth of men, and the extrovert tendencies of actors inevitably tend to make love in Hollywood a catch-as-catch-can affair in many instances, and high-pressure publicity blazons it to the world. As legalized love, smoothly running, has scant publicity value, the countless happy marriages, with one or both partners working hard and leading the dull life of a small town outside working hours, are not thrown in the public's teeth.

For don't think that Hollywood can't be dull, even when one is beloved. If you enjoy sports—tennis, golf, yachting—it's a good place to be, but if the theater, night life, a press that doesn't make you retch, awareness of the rest of the world, varied conversation, and a change of pace—in short, a cosmopolitan life—are necessary to your happiness, you'll find short shrift on the Gold Coast. In the credit column are three or four very good restaurants, and the shops are some of the best in the world, so that that beef which held till three or four years ago is no longer legitimate.

Also, music, of which there once wasn't any, flourishes. Since the scoring of pictures has become so important, many first-rate musicians have migrated to Hollywood, and sometimes in the evening they get together and play for their own pleasure, and for yours if you are invited to the party or are passing by. The most charming concert I ever heard was at about two o'clock one morning the last time I was in Hollywood. Edwin Justus Mayer, the playwright, was bringing me home from a party, and to get to my cottage in the Sunset Plaza we had to pass Al Newman's. The most lovely noises floated from his windows, and so we stopped to listen and watch, as he had generously left the curtains open. Walter Damrosch was at the party, and Deems Taylor. Al and several top men were playing for them—piano, cello, and violins—and Eddie and I sat on the coping of the swimming pool in the starlight and listened to the music. I told Al about it a couple of days later, and he said, "You great goose, you knew everybody in the room. Why didn't you come in?" But I said, "No, it wouldn't have had the same quality," and I think I was right.

I cannot with any honesty, however, bemoan the shortage of Philharmonics in Los Angeles, as I am totally unmusical. I don't even recognize what I like until Bill says to me, "That's the Sibelius you were so crazy about last time," and right away I begin to love it again. But the ordinary concert hall leaves me cold. What I really enjoy is stacking symphonies on the Capehart and lying by the fire to listen to them. I like wandering around too, and knitting to music, or pouring an occasional drink, a procedure frowned on in Carnegie Hall.

I am glad, though, that I sometimes hear music in the orthodox manner, because it was during an unexpected quest for culture that I met my husband. I was

living in Hollywood at the time when, late one afternoon, Ina Claire called me and said, "Listen, kid, Jack
and I have had kind of a row, see, but I've got a pair
of tickets for the Horowitz concert, and I'd like to go.
Will you come with me?" Ina and Jack Gilbert were frequently rowing; it was the perpetual jousting of two violent egocentrics, who also happened to be violently in
love, and that marriage was about as turbulent and short-
lived as my own had been.

Gene Markey, an old friend of Ina's, muttered once,
"That Jack is a dope. You've got to learn to duck those
haymakers Ina lets fly, let them whiz past. Jack takes
them on the chin." I'm afraid that before it was all over
Ina got in a few lefts to the jaw herself, because she
was terribly in love with him, and at that disadvantage
which those who love the more invariably suffer. She
was hurt, angered, and unable to cope with a passion
which had so roughly intruded itself into her poised and
self-sufficient world.

It was my good luck that she and Jack had had a
falling out that particular night, for I went to the concert with her, and in the intermission, while we were
strolling about, talking to everyone we knew, she suddenly called to a middle-sized nice-looking chap, "Why,
Bill Murray, what are you doing out here?" Mr. Murray
and I were introduced, and that, kiddies, is how Granny
met Grandaddy. I invited Ina and him and several
others whom we had picked up at the concert to come
back to my house for a drink, and he asked me to dine
with him the next night, which I did. We had caviar,
which did credit to his palate and gallantry, but I
learned afterward that it dented his purse.

I was impressed by Bill because he knew all about

music and could read Greek, which seemed to me intellectual, and I thought it very nice of him to take an interest in me, as I couldn't have been much stimulus for the academic mind. He stayed in Hollywood a couple of weeks, and I went with him to the train when he left for New York, and that seemed to be the end of that—which just goes to show that life is full of surprises.

CHAPTER EIGHT

The Sexes, and What to Do with Them

I WAS FIFTEEN WHEN I LEARNED ONE OF life's important lessons. It had to do with dancing. As a child I had taken ballet dancing and aesthetic dancing and just plain dancing, and I had quite a lot of expensive theoretical equipment, but I never learned anything so practical from high-priced instructors as I did from a girl at school who was two or three years older than I. Sometimes we had parties in the gym, and the girls would dance together. Nora, my most frequent partner, was older and taller than I, so that she would do the leading, but I was strongminded about my dancing and full of initiative. One evening, irked by what she felt to be not only lack of co-operation but actual competition in our partnership, she said to me, "Look, all you have to do to dance well is to relax like a rag doll." It was simple, invaluable advice, and I have been grateful to her all my life, for dancing is great fun if you do it well, and by dint of remembering the rag doll I have had good times at parties.

Another useful lesson I learned at a tender age was not to express myself in such a way as to leave no room for difference of opinion. I was a dogmatic child, lacking in tact, so that when I was right in an argument, my little companions naturally enough nursed a smoldering grudge. One day a committee waited upon me.

"We have come to tell you," they said sternly, "that you ought to put 'I think' in front of things. You make remarks as though they were the law, and we don't know whether they're facts or just your own ideas."

I didn't think it politic to point out that murder was gotten away with by just such tactics, but I must have sensed obscurely the science of modern propaganda used with such telling effect by the gentlemen of the Third Reich—say something loudly enough and often enough, and the most preposterous lies, gagged upon at first, will eventually slip down smooth as oil. I vaguely apprehended the principle, but prudence urged capitulation to the popular demand.

Since then I have always said, "I think." You might as well; it makes you more popular socially. I occasionally point this out to my husband, who is a boy to get his teeth into a fact and categorically state his case, with none of your weak-kneed, "Well, it seems to me," or, "In my opinion." His sort of candor takes more moral courage than I possess, and besides I am frequently fuzzy about the facts, and if you adopt those tactics you must be either very accurate or very glib.

The third lesson I learned took more doing, and I was older, sadder, and wiser when it finally came home to me: that there is no more humiliating experience for a woman than trying to hold a man against his will. I was fortunate in that the man I learned it from was of only temporary importance to me, which even at the time I knew. It was a good example of what I call my negative luck. Blows fall upon me, but they strike obliquely, so that I am spared the full force of direct impact.

When I was a small child they dropped acetic acid into my eyes by mistake instead of boracic. There was pain for me, and panic for my family, and the doctor said that had it gone a hairbreadth deeper, I would have been blind. But it didn't, and I can still see Catalina on a foggy day. Herbert Agar canceled his appearance on my radio program on the Fourth of July. He wished to speak more freely than commercial candor allows, and I was dismayed, as I had announced him the previous week. But for the only time in the history of our show we were kept off the air by a senator from one of the Carolinas, who ate up our time as well as his own, so that the listeners never suspected the disappointment in store, and I was spared the embarrassment of twiddling my thumbs with the prominent Mr. Agar for a sterile half hour.

The night the stove gets out of order, the guests phone they can't come anyway. The gentlemen who have trampled on my toes have been transients in my life. My clouds have at least pewter linings. Indeed, the professor from whom I learned the above-mentioned lesson was something of a mug; but it was chilly consolation. A lady likes to assume that she is devastatingly attractive to even the most unattractive man whom she would happily spurn, but you can't spurn someone who ignores you. It was driven home to me then that the enforced physical presence of a person who would rather be elsewhere is a bitter ersatz brew when the heart calls for the heady wine of spontaneous and mutual desire.

I have never been able to understand women who berate men, who blackmail them, who say, "You'll stick to me, or else——" What reward can be conceivably great enough to compensate them for the hatred, the indifference, and the deception, sly or open, which will be visited upon them by their victim? Naturally, circumstances dictate the mode of procedure, and if a man and woman have lived together all their young and middle years, if she has no capacity to earn her own living, if she has been honest and kind in her marital dealings, and yet the husband seeks a divorce because he falls in love with a young girl—and there are plenty of such cases—then that man is ignominious who does not provide for his wife financially, for even a generous settlement is inadequate compensation for the affection and companionship an aging wife has the right to expect. It is lamentable that so many aging husbands choose to make goats of themselves, staggering from crag to crag after some nimble gazelle. But even with these sad and ridiculous examples before us I think the average alimony laws in this country are shocking.

A young, able woman can get her grappling hooks into a man for the rest of his days merely because they have experienced the frequently dubious joys of one another's bodies in an atmosphere thick with licenses and wedding guests. In the majority of cases, when the marriage sours, the wife is as culpable as the husband. Why should she sit back for the rest of her days, raking in the coin when, if she hadn't married, she'd be on her own, making her living anyhow? Most people have to work in life. The years you don't are exceptional, and generally dull, so that if you find yourself back in harness, what is there to beef about? All women should learn a trade, but for those who sprang from the convent gates or the Ritz ballroom into the nuptial couch with no time for training, there should perhaps be some years of grace. Five might be a good average in which to get a footing to learn to support oneself while banking the ex-husband's weekly check, and after that, it seems to me, the gentleman has paid for his indiscretion and the lady has profited neatly from her original stake in the partnership.

There should be a financial cleavage. There is, of course, a difference between alimony and contributing to the support of one's child, about which there should be no argument whatsoever, unless the mother is just naturally rich or is working and making much more money than the father, and even then I see no reason why Daddy should not sweeten the kitty as far as he is able. But the alimony law is predicated on the theory that some of our most astute felines are curly, helpless kittens who, it seems to think, should be encouraged in their helplessness, and in the words of Mr. Bumble, "If the law supposes that, the law is a ass."

To me, the good women in life are not the chaste ones, nor the most secure, but those gay and able ladies who may love frequently but who are not tawdry, for there is nothing mean in their make-up; they are free of spirit and have talents or brains which they turn to practical use.

I don't mind tarts, and I don't mind ladies, much, if they are bona fide, but I can't stand the socially impeccable darlings with the cheap little souls, masquerading as moral virgins and pulling tricks an honest whore

would blush at: the ones who marry solely for financial
security and contribute nothing which would justify
the deal; the ones who are stupid and extravagant housekeepers, and when their husbands murmur, burst into
tears and say they are not strong enough to cope with
the marketing or the servant problem; those whose egos
are such that they are sullen and ill-tempered when they
are not the focus of attention. I know a gentleman who
knows Hollywood well, and when I was remarking one
day about the peculiar phenomenon of the beautiful
menless women of the picture world, he erupted with
mighty oaths, the gist of which was that it was small
wonder those dames sat around alone of an evening;
they damned well should; what self-respecting man
would put up with their tantrums, shenanigans, and
twisted egos? "God," he added feelingly, "the poor bastards have to endure that crap in the studio all day;
naturally they don't want a further dose at night.
Heaven deliver me from actresses," he continued, snort-
ing and growling. "They can't bear the truth about
themselves, but themselves is all they want to talk
about." He is a director, and so he spoke from the heart,
but it is his misfortune that the actress doesn't live who
doesn't fawn upon him, and the more horrendous his
indictments, the more slavish her devotion, for he beats
a better performance out of her than she ever gives
again; he is hilariously funny and, as he is so violent,
fatuously thinks he must be kidding. But he sincerely
thinks actresses are bitches, and some of the ladies he
has directed certainly are.

For my own part I like actresses as well as other
women, but I can almost always get along with women
who are good at their jobs. I purposely don't say work-

ing women, because there are some who think they are
working the tail off a beaver, but they accomplish nothing beyond their dizzy arabesques. They are the simon-
pure amateurs who get no results.

They work in shops, but when they can't make
change they giggle. They are frightfully palsy-walsy, to
show they too are ladies, but they know nothing about
the stock and bring you countless dresses to try on and
are amazed when you swim in a size eighteen or burst
from the seams of a ten. They take up interior decorat-
ing, but the curtains don't fit the windows and the lamp-
shades come unstuck. They are life's ditherers, sometimes temperamentally, but more generally because of
lack of training or owing to the unacknowledged idea
that it is feminine to be inefficient; and the backward
ones are perhaps troubled by the deeper and more
atavistic notion that real ladies shouldn't be in trade,
but they may cherish the warming thought that arch-
dukes and duchesses these days work at the most
menial tasks, because they have to eat too, only they
eat rather less than the common people, because they
aren't so efficient. If we are self-supporting, we can be
either grand or well-fed, but if we are on the side of
the vitamins, we have to deliver the goods.

Among women who work there is one category particularly which is full of surprises, and that is the
Southerners. The I-declare-honey-sugars, with their
pretty, dowdy clothes and soft, husky voices can do yeo-
man service in the clinches. They are accurate, inventive, and conscientious, and it comes as something of
a shock to Northerners, who think they have a corner
on efficiency. And yet if we stop to analyze it, it
shouldn't be so surprising. In the old days the well-to-do

Southern woman was forced to develop brain, heart,
and stamina. She lived on great estates in isolated communities, and she was in a very real sense the servant
of her people, who looked to her for food, clothing,
shelter, and medical attention. It is the descendants of
these capable and busy women, transplanted into commerce, who have a shrewd eye for a penny and the wit
to turn a pretty one.

And they perhaps keep to a greater extent than their
industrious sisters their clinging charm; they are more
willing to maintain the illusion not exactly of helplessness—no executive wants a helpless secretary, no producer wants a helpless actress—but of femininity. They
are charming and sympathetic, and though those qualities sometimes get lost in the rush of our daily lives,
they are still the great feminine stand-bys. It is absurd
and dangerous for women to drift carelessly into the
attitude of mind which presupposes that as they are
financially independent they no longer need their
femininity to get along in the world. Their financial
independence frequently derives from the men who
head organizations, but even that is not the primary
reason, for whether or not she appeals to the boss personally, an able woman can usually command a job
through sheer ability. In their careers they get along,
but I never heard of any woman, no matter how busy
she was, who didn't need a man in her private life in
order to be happy. Love is very, very important to ladies,
and I can see no reason for not admitting it.

As there are all kinds of ladies, so there are all kinds
of love. Some prefer the same good man from the altar
to the grave; some crave variety, and seek it themselves;
others have variety thrust upon them either through

widowhood, divorce, or the transient trade. I believe it was Madame de Stael who once made the sage remark that there is no happiness for a woman without marriage, and, although the feminists will balk, I think it is true. The only moot questions are, when, how long, and with whom? Some argue that it is desirable to spend at least one's youth in fun and frolic, with as changing a panorama of gentlemen as charm and luck attract, and then, in middle years, gracefully to infiltrate oneself into the marital state with a suitable companion and quietly enjoy autumn's mellow glow. Others contend that the smart thing to do is to establish a background early, embark on marriage and motherhood at a fairly tender age, and, having salted away the domesticities, reach the variety stage in the full flower of womanhood. Both these viewpoints are understandable, but to achieve the perfect balance at the moment we want it is a neat trick and, to be candid, one which is rarely accomplished. All too frequently when women don't marry early it is because nobody asks them, so that they are relieved to take what they can get before it is too late, or if they have married young, by the time it occurs to them that there are other men in the world they are so bogged down by habit and responsibility that they have neither the inclination nor the façade for romance.

There are those who believe that the dream setup would be a husband, a lover, a son, and a friend. Then all the facets of a woman's personality would sparkle like a revolving prism in affection's steady glow, and I must say it sounds an abundant life if one has the time. But one would have to be strong and expert or it would preclude other forms of endeavor, and one would be lucky to get in an afternoon's shopping let alone attending to a job or indulging in charitable works. Still I now and again do meet ladies, those with jugglers' blood, who pretty nearly get away with such legerdemain, and very attractive they are too, and sometimes even hardworking in other fields as well, which only goes to prove that the more you do, the more you can do.

They are kind and generous, these ladies, and they have loving hearts, which I think is important, because how can you love mankind in the mass if you don't love man individually? They are generally regarded with acerbity by other females, who consider that they have more than their share of the available man power, but they forget, these censorious ones, that those ladies go to a good deal of trouble to please their gentlemen. They sincerely wish them well, and will go out of their way to prove it. They get up at ungodly hours in the morning and stay awake at night helping their friends and planning treats for them. They furnish their apartments and do their shopping; they pull wires to get them citizenship papers; they help them plan dinner parties; and they read manuscripts for them, they go to the movies to try to unearth talent for their next production, and they devote afternoons to taking them to Chinatown and Hammacher Schlemmer's when their ships put into port for repair. They buy presents for their small nephews when they have their appendixes out, and they see a man about a job. They recommend doctors and they have the prescriptions filled; they can only pray that he takes the medicine. In the meantime they take their own children to the dentist and get to the office on time. They are superwomen, and they deserve super-rewards in the form of a loving husband or steady, affectionate beaux who are free with proposals of marriage. It may fleetingly occur to these ladies that they are taking more trouble than any man on earth would go to for them, but when a woman loves, imagination and labor are part of the service. Affectionate, appreciative, and desirous men in her life is the reward which is warmer than virtue. When one has given so much, it is quite natural to give oneself, or if that is putting the cart before the horse, when one gives oneself, the rest follows easily if the choice has been a happy one. That is the best and most natural way, though of course carnal relations are sometimes entered into, but rarely maintained, for casual reasons, the most common being that men seem to expect it.

It is remarkable how much some men think they are entitled to in exchange for dinner and an evening at the theater. If the lady is similarly inclined and fancy free, I suppose there is no reason for foregoing mutual indulgence, but more than one woman has said to me with a shrug, "What can I do? I'm not particularly interested, but it seems only courteous to give in—they make such a fuss and bother." I suppose the majority of women are in love with their lovers, but what with the pressure of modern life, and the emphasis on sex to keep us normal, many have affairs as a kind of prophylaxis. "At last, I'm in love," murmured one of the most sophisticated comediennes of the New York theater, "and it's heaven. I was getting sick and tired of doing it just to keep my skin in condition."

By which comments, culled from real life, it may be seen that camping out doesn't make for happiness perhaps, but done with tact and discrimination, it can make for understanding and afford one many a chuckle as well as heartache. I don't know why it is, when one considers masculine shortcomings, but the stark fact remains that those ladies are more lovable who have been schooled by men. For the most part it's the college of hard knocks, all right, and they may consider themselves lucky if they get by with nothing worse than bruised pride and a heart only delicately veined with cracks like old china; but if they are nice ladies to begin with, they develop an earthy charm and a sense of humor which stands them in good stead all their lives. Of course, they are sometimes made to realize that the price of tuition may be loneliness, for lovers are not necessarily companions. Love can take a shorter time than one might think, and there are the hours in between to be filled, and children to be born, and a home to be built, which is why marriage is a far more satisfactory arrangement. A really clever woman mixes her romance with respectability, so that her life has both aroma and body, like well-blended tea. Unless one has some standing in one's own community, existence can be cruel indeed, and unless one has a good deal of money, irregular liaisons are for the most part sordid. It is one thing to sin in charming surroundings after a delicious dinner with dry champagne and a crackling fire and the Hungarian gypsy records playing softly on the gramaphone and quite another to resort to cheap hotels and the parked car.

Amusingly enough, what lends charm to the life which has come to be regarded as *la vie de Bohème* is the quality of domesticity which, contrary to general belief, usually emanates from it. Women who have many lovers are frequently those with a strong homely streak. They like a man in the house. A pipe, a companionable toothbrush beside their own, a tube of shaving cream, the loved one's movie camera—such things are comforting.

A woman's nature may deepen and mellow in the wake of love, but it is the trivialities which she accumulates that bring the secret reminiscent smile. The bits and pieces which become part of her life, those morsels of driftwood and shell and seaweed which cling to her long after the tide has gone out: a special brand of coffee which one continues to use, a brand of cigarettes, a toilet water, the habit of going to a certain shop for leather goods, a rare white wine, a fondness for a particular sports writer—in time they become so much a part of a woman that she forgets from whom she caught the habit, just as, when we have known people well for a long while, it is impossible to remember how we first met them.

In considering love outside the bonds of matrimony, it is interesting, I think, to reflect on the social censure, if any, attached to it. Certainly today in a great city Mrs. Grundy's disapproval is negligible, and I think society's attitude resolves itself down to this: if a woman lives by her love affairs, she is still measured pretty much by the old standard, and that slight rustle you hear is the drawing aside of skirts, and whispers, ranging from "demi-mondaine" to less polite words, trail after her as she passes by. Nine times out of ten, I should imagine, these ladies are completely indifferent to what the socially secure ones are thinking. But these latter have at least more justification for disapproval than in the old days, as, in normal times, the social and economic standards are now such that, has she any brains or ability, a woman can gain a fairly decent livelihood without entering the oldest profession. Indeed, since the installation of the SEC, the chances are that she will make not only good but better on her own than by seeking a keeper and a gilded cage. Let her remember that he can't even get aluminum. If, however, a woman's primary profession is a legitimate one, her amorous life causes little comment and is of only the most casual concern to her friends and neighbors, provided she manages matters tastefully. Indeed, in many communities it is devoutly to be hoped that, if unmarried, she will have either a steady companion or a ready choice of men, as, goodness knows, it's hard enough balancing a dinner table under the most favorable circumstances.

It is remarkable how often women are the offenders against discretion in love affairs. I think they babble far more than men, because no matter how relaxed our social standards, the man who blabs of his conquests is still considered to be letting down the old school tie. I don't know what goes on in their clubs, of course, but it's rather pleasant to think that peppery old colonels would still regard him with choleric if alcoholic eye and rumble through white mustachios, "Egad, sir, you're a cad." Ladies' powder rooms are the standard depositories of their secrets of the boudoir, but in my research work I have been told that such is not the custom while gentlemen are powdering their noses. As a matter of fact, say my informants, the whole thing goes on in stony silence, with no sociable interchange of the latest scandal. Sounds dull. Still, there are some ladies who would do well to emulate, if to a lesser degree, the great silent chiefs.

Although in the United States it is far from routine, one occasionally sees traditional standards flouted with signal success, and there are couples who sincerely believe in a tryout before the New York opening. They feel it is only common sense to know what they are getting, as they consider a pig in a poke an unnecessary risk under any circumstances, commercial or matrimonial, and it is piquant for their friends who are sometimes witnesses to heated arguments as to whether they went to that quaint little inn before or after they met up with the preacher. I do not say this custom is to be condoned, and the success of those who indulge in it is rightly distressing to moralists—who should be respected, because they act as society's corsets and keep it from billowing over in a formless, gelatinous mass, but I do say it is true that more than one lady has taken a lover without bell, book, and candle, that he has subsequently proposed, and that they have been married and lived happily ever after.

Once, in an open forum where this custom was under discussion, it greatly aroused the ire of my old friend, Mr. Stanton Griffis, who claimed that we and our friends in New York and Hollywood were a small sophisticated group who did not understand the mass of the people. He, he said, did. We said that he seemed quite sophisticated to us, and how was he qualified to understand the mass of the people, and he said it was because he had once raised apples in Oregon. The implication being that apple-raising was a simple, earthy pastime, and himself a son of the soil. He doesn't look the part very much, an *en-tout-cas* tennis court on Sunday mornings being about his closest contact with Mother Earth, but he talked learnedly about smudges, and at that it was kind of interesting. Smudges are little pots of burning coal which apple-growers set under the young trees when the frost is in the ground. I gathered from Massa that there was nothing like a smudge for putting you wise to human nature. But I don't blame him for being nostalgic about his crop-growing days, for remembering the tart, crisp taste of red apples and the still cold twilights of his youth. As I have said elsewhere in this book, I am overly sensitive to weather myself, and I am probably the only person in the United States outside of farmers and sailors who listens enraptured to the radio weather reports.

Radio and sex seem to me in a curious way not unalike. They are both enormous hidden empires, so to speak, existing all around us, but we only see their manifestations. How different nations and societies cope with sex is interesting, and nowhere are the individual methods more clearly indicated than in their literature and drama, including motion pictures. As we all know, the Hays office regards any suggestion of sexual intimacy, marital or otherwise, as highly indecent, and if we relied on American movies for our information, we would have to assume that it really must be the stork who brings babies. European-made pictures are more candid in their acceptance of the facts of life; they admit that a man and woman do sometimes share the same bed, and it doesn't seem to them something shocking which must be kept from the eyes of any stray minors who might wander into a movie without the consent of their parents. They don't gear their pictures to adolescent consumption, and if adolescents see them, they probably figure they already know it anyhow, or it is high time they learned.

On the other hand American pictures have always been a good deal more free to lambaste politics than have European ones, even before the war. I suppose those aspects of its life which a nation censors are significant, but American love isn't that bad, and recently I have noticed that the nation's manhood seems to be stirring in revolt. The ads are beginning to intimate that even the clean-cut, average American man and wife sometimes see their mates other than fully dressed for a football game. Quite recently a gent in shirt and shorts was complaining to the little woman, who was attired only in her slip and a Maiden uplift, that one of his garments wasn't pre-shrunk, and Beautyrest mattresses are running advertisements showing a couple just before the lights go out. She is lying in bed discreetly covered up, looking frightfully placid and neat, and he is about to raise the window, clad in both parts of his pajamas, a mode which, because of my sheltered life, I assumed had gone out with the night shirt. Even so, it seems to me a healthy sign, and I am sure we may rely on Anglo-Saxon good taste not to overstep the boundaries.

That, however, is what I like about French novels. There is less taste. Love scenes in English and American romances follow to a greater or lesser extent a familiar pattern. After the wedding ceremony Beth and Gordon drive away to the little cottage set in the old-fashioned garden which Aunt Patty has lent them for their honeymoon. Old Hester has prepared a delicious dinner, and afterwards they sit in the starlight, drinking in the fragrance of the night-blooming cereus, along with coffee and liqueurs. Finally Gordon kisses her tenderly, and Beth withdraws to the chintz bedroom, with its sheets smelling sweetly of lavender, whither, after a couple of cigarettes and a stiff slug, Gordon follows her. And that, if you please, is the end of the chapter. Just as we get to know and love this couple, just as we are aquiver to share their rapture, the door is slammed in our face.

The next time we see them it is the morning after, the birds are singing, and the happy pair is rollicking over Hester's waffles and sausage after a brisk invigorating swim. Not so in French novels; there the author has the reader's interest at heart. We are allowed to share the secrets of the alcove, we know right away whether the chances for future happiness are firmly grounded on skill and co-operation, or whether frustration, boredom, and resentment are to be the lot of Monsieur and Madame. In this way the reader fosters no ill feeling against the writer, and is almost sure to buy his next book. Of course there are exceptions in American literature, Mr. Hemingway being perhaps the most notable, and it was a lucky thing for all of us that he put in those sleeping-bag sequences in *For Whom the Bell Tolls,* for to my way of thinking it is an overlong tale with an arbitrarily unhappy ending, but once having picked that title, the hero damned well had to die, whether the story called for it or not. Perhaps at that it was a good idea, for I couldn't help but wonder if the earth would continue shaking after they had been married a few years and settled down in that college town.

It is, I suppose, humanly impossible to maintain the high exaltation we experience when love is new, but one good way to shield the bloom a little longer is not to take each other for granted. This requires doing, and there will come times when the effort seems too deliberate and rather foolish, but I think it is worth it just the same. A couple may complement each other, but they are still two distinct entities, and to think you possess another individual is to tread on dangerous

ground. Men who do it are fantastically shortsighted;
they cheat themselves out of a delicious harvest by fail-
ing to sow a handful of seed. A thoughtful gesture, the
smallest gift, a few I love you's, and a sensitive woman,
provided she loves at all, flowers before their very eyes.
Flowers are charming and lend graciousness to living.

Women who are possessive are embarrassing and evil.
They have a coy yet predaceous manner toward their
men, and if another woman is agreeable to them, such
ladies hide their furious resentment under playful insults and exaggerated and deadly compliments. Their
contortions, if they suspect their prey is wriggling from
their clutches, are not pretty. But perhaps it is their
means of survival; perhaps it is natural for them to
raise such hell at the slightest quiver that only the very
strongest male will face the horror squarely and get
away.

And yet, in spite of these unpleasant examples, men
and women do fall in love; the good people of the world
do sometimes get together in harmony and affection.
May I suggest, as a conclusion to this little treatise
on the not-so-gentle passion, that we keep our wits about
us and try to recognize the real thing when we see it.
There is nothing so sad and so wasteful as those who let
the rare chance slip through their fingers.

It would be a happy thing could lovers think with
their hearts and feel with their heads, and not neglect
their bedroom manners—for they are indicative of a
general outlook on life, and selfishness, greediness, and
gross lack of courtesy are wretched giveaways. I once
heard a bitter story of an unhappily married lady who
was having an affair with a man to whom she was
devoted. He was fond of her too, for specific reasons

and in a limited way, but terrified of complications. One night, as they were dressing to go home, he launched forth into a warning about how she might as well know the truth: he had no intention of getting involved in matrimony, and they had better be damned careful, as he would certainly not take the rap; if her husband got suspicious, he would categorically deny all desire for and responsibility in the affair.

"Of course he had the merit of frankness," she said sadly, "and I had known his attitude all along and accepted it, but I felt he chose an inopportune time to state his creed."

Protect yourselves, gentlemen, by all means, but surely a little tact can do no harm. Simple courtesy will not be misconstrued as love eternal; if you have chosen wisely, your lady will not pinion you because of a gentle word and an understanding smile.

CHAPTER NINE

Why I Married My Husband

I MARRIED MY HUSBAND FOR A VARIETY
of reasons, but two of them were that he can open train
windows and he is wonderful at getting taxis in front
of a theater on rainy nights. I have known him ten
years, and I have still to see his record equaled. Also,
he can read Greek and Anglo-Saxon, and though this
leaves me out in the cold, as I am the type who plods
slowly along in my mother tongue, whispering the
words as I go, it impresses me, and I think it is healthy
for married people each to have some accomplishment
which baffles the other. Makes for respect. Also, he has
great musical knowledge and plays charmingly. Strictly
classical, but on him it's becoming; and as these private
concerts are rare, they are greatly appreciated by his
audience of one.

We acquired a Capehart as a wedding present, and
thinking to make of our married life one glad harmony,
I started collecting records. Melody surged for about

the first six weeks; then, as it takes longer to listen to a symphony than the layman realizes, and as we both seemed to be very busy, the concord of sweet sounds grew fainter. I solaced myself by explaining to Bill how pleasant it would be for him to lie in the living room of an evening while I was at the theater, alternating between Homer and Bill Corum, the *Journal-American's* sports writer, and listening to Sibelius. He said yes, he guessed it would be—but a note of doubt predominated, and in all our married life he has never touched the Capehart when I am not in the house. It frightens him, and he regards it with cold suspicion. Our particular one is a capricious instrument, hurling from the turntable such records as it doesn't like with a fury and discrimination alarming in an inanimate object. It is like a wonderful servant who can accomplish miracles but is subject to dark and murderous rages.

Bill and I were married on the thirteenth of July in 1935, but before that there was a five-year period of marking time while he waited for his divorce. I suppose you might say we were engaged. We spent our evenings together and were invited to the same parties in New York and Hollywood. Only a few in Hollywood, because, though we have both spent considerable time there, we have rarely coincided. But Bill is a demon with the long-distance telephone. Another agent, Mr. Leland Hayward, has had much publicity about his love affair with the telephone, but I resent this, as Bill Murray bows to none in his affection, loyalty, and ingenious use of Mr. Bell's invention. He has located me in a country house in the wilds of Ohio when he had no conceivable means of knowing where I was; and while I was fishing off the Florida Keys, the master's voice has called out to me. In Nassau it was a comparative cinch for him to spot me, as I was in a diver's helmet at the time, admiring the undersea flora. And once having tracked his quarry down, Mr. Murray is not a boy to be satisfied with those picayune three minutes. No sir; having gone to that effort, he settles down to a *Kaffeeklatsch* and a fine gossipy time is had by all as the news of the day is exchanged and the charges soar. He has had to be forcibly removed from the instrument in the midst of a violent political argument, and when Mother was in Europe at the outbreak of the war, and we telephoned from Long Island to see if she had been able to get passage home, Bill had his arguments marshaled for persuading her to a quick return and expounded at length the more abstruse theories of the German High Command; foretold with some inaccuracy but great zest the fate of Warsaw, the Balkans, and France; painted lurid pictures of bombardments; and expressed grave fears for the island of Bali. Mother came home.

Although she gets a little annoyed when we tease her about it, and says that it is all nonsense, that in her role of international business woman, cablegrams and transatlantic phone calls are part of her daily routine, the fact remains that Mother has the thrifty soul's mistrust of the urgent, expensive message. She does not send jokes by telegram, and when called long distance, her initial reaction is one of alarm: first, that I am dead; second, on hearing my voice, that I must be involved in a murder; third, when assured I am calling from three thousand miles away just to talk to her, that my mind, about which she has been nervous for years, has finally given away. Much further along in the conversation she begins to glow with pleasure at the idea that it was nothing more sinister than a desire to hear her voice which prompted the call.

She annoys William because she keeps reminding him of the expense, and he claims he could be telling her wonderful things in the time she consumes with these exasperating remarks.

Bill called me one New Year's Eve when I was in Pittsburgh with the pre-New York tryout of *The Animal Kingdom* and he was someplace in Jersey. He had promised to call at midnight, but I didn't put great stock in it, figuring that while I would have been giving a performance, he would have been getting well under way with the celebration. I maligned him, because he called on the stroke of midnight, but from a pay station, which seemed odd. I could tell it was a pay station, as I caught the mellifluous tone of quarters dropping in the slot and, from time to time, the operator's musical request for, "Another fif-uty cents, pul-leeze."

"And another little quarter won't do us any harm," caroled the prince of my dreams, squandering a week's wages as the coins cascaded into the box. We discussed the play, wished each other a tender New Year; Bill confided to me that he had no use for the people he was with and hung up. Then he went out and joined the Army. It was a good three weeks later before I heard of his military prowess. Apparently his enlistment came as quite a surprise to him too. He says he knew nothing about it till New Year's morning, when, on opening his eyes to the horrid sound of a bugle and doing a double take as his surroundings penetrated the haze, he realized he had spent what was left of the night in a barracks. Two pairs of friendly and quizzical eyes watched him from the flanking cots, and their owners, when they could control their mirth, enlightened him as to the night's events.

Seems that soon after telephoning me, determined not to go back to his uncongenial friends, Mr. Murray, with time out for further celebration, had roamed the highways and byways, finally meeting up with a band of mercenaries, to whom he confided his sad plight. Moved by this tale of friendlessness on a night which should be abounding with the auld lang syne, they suggested that he return to camp with them. As there was no crisis in those days, there were several empty beds, and the proffered hospitality, which might be frowned on today, apparently went through without hitch, although it seemed more prudent to all concerned to muster him out before roll call.

Another New Year's Eve, memorable for sheerly sentimental reasons, was the night I was in Boston, with what play I no longer remember. A party of merrymakers had repaired to Stanton Griffis' house in New Canaan and were having a lovely and convivial time, as opposed to New Year's Eve at the distant Ritz. Although I was not present, I remember the festivities well. My imagination was fertile, and in my mind's eye, Horatio, I saw the crackling fire, the happy group gathered round, and Walter, Mr. Griffis' terrifying German butler, fierce of eye and bald of head, bearing the pungent smoking mulled wine. Bill had taken my dachshund, Noodles, up to the country for the holiday. Noodles was black and powerful and had acquitted himself with such magnificence in plowing through snowdrifts ten times his height that the house party had awarded him an ancient iron cross, excavated from God knows where, which dangled pridefully from his collar. Won by these manly virtues, and fancying himself as a country squire stalking the roads, his dogs at heel, Massa offered to take Noodles on as a lifetime pensioner. He subsequently bought him a wife, but I fear with his eyes closed and one hand tied behind him, as shortly afterwards the Griffis property was overrun with oddments, in which Mr. G. took great pride, and he laughed indulgently when he recounted Noodles' wedding. There had been a palpitating and expectant bride, but, overcome by novelty and excitement, the conquering groom retired to a corner and was sick. However, nature quickly triumphed, and he sired as large and varied a clan as ever waddled down a Fairfield pike. Miss Teddy Griffis, smitten by his charms, took Noodles to Cornell with her, where he caused a furor in academic circles, but one day he was run over by a student momentarily bemused, but whether by culture, liquor, or love was never clear, and after a brief space in the infirmary, where, as Teddy's father is a trustee of the university, the attendant physicians applied the combined sciences of the Mayo boys and Johns Hopkins, Noodles passed to the Elysian fields, where I hope he still is sniffing trees and chasing elusive rabbits.

In New York it is difficult to keep in constant touch with one's friends, but there are some who run like a bright intermittent pattern through the tapestry of one's life, and Stanton Griffis is such a one. Sometimes we see a great deal of each other, and there are large parties and small dinners in quick succession; and then again months will pass and, diverted by travel, business, and other people, we see each other not at all, and it is only through casual reports and stray bits of gossip and the columnists that contact is maintained; but when we do meet up again it is delightful. Out-of-towners are right when they say New York is not a neighborly place. We have five good friends who live in our block, only one of whom we see with any degree of frequency. Indeed, Stanton lives directly across the street, but I do not suppose it is once a month that we glance at each other's windows to see if the lamp is lit or if a silhouette falls athwart the light. Such a system makes for independence and seclusion, but it also breeds indifference and selfishness, and one realizes with sadness the swift passage of the days.

For a gentleman of wealth, and I can hear his hollow laughter if he reads this phrase, Mr. Griffis lives simply, but his one real luxury is his yacht, to which he is much attached. The rich always seem to run either to horses or yachts, but personally I could own every emerald in India and have eighty billion dollars after I'd paid the taxes, and nary rowboat nor pony would I own, though if I could find a milk-white unicorn I would be glad to give him houseroom.

Non-yacht owners always think the life of yacht owners must be wonderful, with Lana Turner popping out of every hatch, and witty, good-looking men and mellow old salts more than eager to accompany the skipper on tropical cruises, but in my limited experience I have found this is not so. Getting guests onto a boat is hell's own job. Getting them off is just as bad, so that gathering a congenial group requires a firm hand not too thickly encased in velvet.

As nothing sounds more sumptuous than idle days at sea, this is perhaps hard to understand, but to begin with, unless all the yachter's friends are in his own

financial brackets, they have to stick on their jobs with
very little time out, and if they are rich they have to run
like mad to stay in the same place. This automatically
eliminates long cruises to the Caribbean and the South
Seas and, incidentally, lowers the death rate, as any
group cooped up together for weeks tends to become
homicidal. Week ends are easier to manage, although
Mr. Griffis' more truculent friends sometimes balk at
those too. This seems ungrateful, and there is no doubt
that they cut themselves off from a great deal of pleasure.
On the other hand they sleep in their comfortable beds
at night, and they can sleep late in the morning, for
I have observed that no matter how grandiose the
master's quarters, the guest cabins are apt to be cramped.
Then there is marine plumbing. It is loud, so that the
more intimate functions are no secret, and it is stiff, so
that you have to pump your arm off to get results.
Added to it all, to maintain this luxury Mr. Griffis
has to be in Wall Street at nine o'clock on the dot of
a Monday morning in order to plunge into pools or
corner wheat or whatever he does, which, as the boat
has always been anchored in the Skagerrak on Sunday
night, necessitates starting up the engines at 5 A.M.
Monday if we hope to make the New York Yacht Club
in time.

But at least when he steps into his waiting limousine
he waves farewell to that batch of friends and has no
further worries until he hits Wall Street or tries to get
a new bunch for the next trip. It is the gladsome holidays which prove the headache, when the master an-
chors off the Flamingo docks in Miami, and the trick is
to pry out the current incumbents so that a fresh group
may slide into their grooves.

In his capacity of chairman of the executive committee of Paramount, chairman of the board of Madison
Square Garden, Wall Street tycoon, owner of Brentano's
bookstore, etc., etc., and entertaining human being, Mr.
Griffis has at one time or another played host to most
of the biggest names in finance, sport, and the arts. Edna
Ferber and Katharine Cornell have sailed the high seas
with him, and one of our more unexpected romances
blossomed on his boat when Mr. Floyd Odlum, who
carries the Atlas Corporation on his shoulders, and Miss
Jacqueline Cochran were smitten by Eros. That Miss
Cochran is an enterprising lady, and Mr. Odlum a
gentleman of discernment, is evinced by the fact that
they got married and Miss Cochran is today the fore-
most American woman flyer.

Of course not all of Mr. Griffis' guests are limelight-
personalities, sometimes they are the Powers behind the
thrones, and sometimes they are just nice people, and
sometimes they are not; but muttering and grumbling,
Mr. G. continues happily playing the role of Mine Host.
A party of us were once complaining loudly about the
food and service and saying that things would have
to improve around there or we would leave, and Massa
asked, with the eager gleam of one who can hardly
believe the good tidings, "You mean Griffis faces guest
strike?" He didn't get the break just then, however.

I had been spending ten days in Nassau and flew
over to join the party and get a little sleep. I had gone
to Nassau at the end of an arduous and unsuccessful
season, having rehearsed, opened, and closed in three
or four flops in a row, but found no rest on the coral
isle because of the noise. The bands played and the
cocks crew all night long, and it was impossible to close

an eye. The boat seemed, and was, a haven of refuge if not exactly peace.

Winkie Thomas was there, heavenly Winkie, and Jane Grant and Margaret Case, and a few gentlemen of passage, and Rocky and Gary Cooper came down, Gary sweet and quiet as usual, and Rocky absolutely silent, with curving crimson nails and a sullen, bored, beautiful face. She never spoke, and she never smiled, for fear of cracking it I suppose. Her mother was with us for a while too.

We went to the jai alai games and we went swimming every day at the Bath Club, and all the little debutantes surged like schools of minnows as close up to Gary as they dared, and Rocky continued to look bored and beautiful. When the silent Coopers went away, we broke loose from our Flamingo moorings and went for a fishing trip off the Keys. For three days we left the *North Star* before dawn in a special fishing boat Massa had chartered. Jane Grant refused to go, because she said she would be seasick. I said I would be too, but I went and I was.

Those boats are frightful little tubs, but their hiring costs a fortune. Our boat had a crew of two, and all kinds of elaborate tackle for deep-sea fishing, but no place to lie down out of the wet when you were sick. I would fish, eat the superb picnic the *North Star's* chef had provided, lose it, and fish again, and by about three in the afternoon I would be good and bored.

I would distract myself as long as I could by watching the enormous turtles who swam just under the surface of the water, floating at ease in the long swell which I found so inimical. About once every three hours there would be a sudden brisk tussle when one of us had a strike. If it was me, I would hang on grimly, the men would shout advice, I would pray for a sailfish or a tarpon, and out would come a barracuda. On all that trip, with the exception of one measly mackerel, we caught nothing but barracuda. Their nasty teeth would grin maliciously, and the sailors would toss them into a big box with an inadequate cover, where they flopped convulsively. I had alarming visions of their bursting out and snapping off my leg and of me stumping about for the rest of my days like John Barrymore in *Moby Dick*.

Stanton would grumble and swear mildly and suck on his pipe, and Winkie would comment appreciatively on the glory of the blue sky and the refreshing breeze and refer to the absent fish and what they were doing in lieu of biting in lewd and pungent terms, and I would strive endlessly to retie my bandanna so that it formed a little shelf over my nose, which I could see burning bright in God's sunshine. Along about five-thirty Stanton would remove his pipe, scratch luxuriously, and say, "How about it, Queen? Shall we go in?" I would say, "Yes," refrain from adding, "And high time, for God's sake," out of affection and courtesy— after all, this dubious pleasure was costing him fifty dollars a day—and we would chug for home. The nicest part of the fishing trip was the evenings, when, after a hot bath and change of clothes, we wandered about the streets of Key West and dropped in at the bars.

The bars were friendly and highly informal. One of our evenings we strolled down a side street and passed a small shabby bungalow with a lantern swinging from the veranda. It seemed singularly unvicious, but it was the red-light district. Through the open door we glimpsed a little bar, and inside someone was playing a guitar. It had a hospitable look, so we went in. There were three or four girls giggling and chatting, a couple a little on the dark side—Cubans, no doubt—and a fat, greasy old party with violently black hair, who was the Madam. A lanky, sandy man in a striped sweater, like a French sailor's, was draped over one end of the bar, but he seemed bent more on sociability than business.

We asked for drinks, which the giggling girl who had been playing the guitar poured into jiggers, but it was during prohibition, and Stanton muttered to me, "Don't touch the stuff." The girls were gentle and friendly, but not very pretty, except for the youngest one, who must have been about eighteen or twenty, and with whom Stanton struck up quite a friendship while Winkie and I were talking to the others, because he remarked afterward that she had said she was a virgin.

Winkie hooted, "I suppose you believed it?"

"Well," Stanton said lamely, "that's what she said." Winkie was delighted.

"Massa's wonderful," he observed. "He goes to Newport and meets all the debutantes and says it's terrible the way these society babes carry on, but when he meets a girl in a house he gets all dewy-eyed and assumes she's doing it to put her little brother through college."

I have been lucky in my dealings with daughters of joy, as the French have it, in that the few episodes have had a kind of rakish charm. It may be said with justice that I have barely scratched the surface, but that seems to be all a woman who is accompanied either by her husband or his friends can scratch. The Key West experience was one occasion, and another was in Copenhagen, when Bill and I were taking a trip through Scandinavia. We were in the Trocadero bar, a gay and crowded spot, when I glanced across the narrow room at a rather attractive woman and happened to remark that she had been sitting a long while by herself and her fellow was certainly taking his time in the John. Bill gave me a slightly incredulous stare and then said, "Darling, you're a big girl now, take a look around." Ranged against the wall sat single women with glasses of orange juice or small untasted beers before them. The interesting thing was that they were all attractive, not exactly pretty, but with that clean, healthy look that people in the north countries have. Everybody in Copenhagen rides a bicycle, and you felt that they had pedaled energetically to the evening's work. There were several good-looking men at the bar, mostly upper-class Englishmen on diplomatic missions, unencumbered by family, their lean frames upholding the Empire in flawlessly cut suitings from Savile Row, their morals left at home for safekeeping. They glanced at the lonely ladies, the ladies smiled at them, and the oldest game was under way. Bill and I began to lay bets as to which one would bag her quarry first. We backed our entries heavily and defended them hotly, and finally, as the men drifted from the bar, all along the banquettes engrossed couples were making halting conversation, and advances less tentative, and most of the beers and orange juice had been metamorphosed into champagne.

Prostitution is a sad trade, but in this clean little country, among these healthy-looking people, it seemed less sordid; there was even an air of gaiety. But it must be said that Copenhagen was the peak. Three nights

later, at the Folies Bergères in Paris, I emerged from
the Ladies to find my William swamped by a crowd
of bedizened, shrewish old harridans who clawed and
ogled him and through whom he was battling his way
with the strength of a desperate man. "My God," he
gasped, as the horde, on seeing me, fell away resentfully, "don't wives know enough not to leave their husbands alone and defenseless in a Paris music hall?" The
denizens of the lobby were not pretty, and I thought
to myself that the members of the Hays office would
smile an oily smile were they to see the price of shame.
In Copenhagen it had seemed gay and sociable, and
that night in the shabby bungalow in Key West the
atmosphere was lighthearted and had a quality of casual
grace like a thin gray cat.

We told Jane all about it when we got back to the
North Star, and we proudly showed her our fish. The
barracudas had hardly seemed worth lugging home,
but we had nurtured our one mackerel with tender
care. He was a pretty sight, but not impressive in scale,
and when she heard what the junket had set the boss
back, she observed mildly that if Stanton had his heart
set on mackerel, it would have been cheaper to have
ordered it at the Flamingo Hotel, even at their prices.

Stanton finally decided that the life of the millionaire
sportsman was all very well in the glossy pages of *Spur,*
but on the open deep it took a little too much out of
you, and so one afternoon, immediately after lunch, we
sailed for Miami. The trip was so rough, it made any
storm at sea cooked up by Mr. Conrad look like a
celluloid boat in a bathtub. All hands were below except Stanton and me. I was stretched on the sofa in
the saloon, too ill to move, even if locomotion had been

possible, which it wasn't, on account of the turbulent
waters. All I could do was hang on, grit my teeth, and
pray. I have never been conspicuous for my bravery,
and for three hours, while the storm raged unabated,
I was in mortal terror. I would have been afraid had
it been the *Normandie*, and I looked on the *North Star*
as a pleasure craft at best and no fit shell to be tossed
by the elements. I prayed to God, but I also prayed
for a glass of champagne, which I felt would be of
more practical use, but as it hadn't been served in all
the time I had been on board, I assumed there was
none. And I am always shy about asking for champagne,
even with my richest friends, as it seems to me the
most lavish and gala of drinks. I am aware that the
really subtle palates scorn it, preferring fine wines and
rare brandies, but me, I like champagne. Mr. Griffis,
however, is strictly a Scotch-and-water man, and of
water we already had an abundance. As the horizon
rocked beyond the portholes, I felt no need of Scotch
either. Occasionally I opened one eye and peered greenly
at the Master. He was slumped in an easy chair, his
pipe clenched between his teeth, an open book on his
lap, and now and then he turned a page. At first I
thought it a gesture to bolster his own pride and stomach,
but as the afternoon wore on I realized he was reading,
impervious to our peril. At last we came into calmer
waters, but wreckage was strewn about us. Two vases,
all the books, the phonograph, and dozens of broken
records lay on the floor. Once or twice Stanton had
stretched an imperious hand to the bell, but it was a
vain gesture. We were lucky if the crew were able to
stay chained to the engines, let alone reel up the stairs
for domestic service.

When at last the *North Star* stopped leaping and plunging like a bucking horse and settled down to long, shuddering rolls, John, the steward, appeared, wan and shaking, in the doorway to inquire if there was anything we wanted. Mr. Griffis said grimly that he would have a Scotch and water and asked me if there was anything I cared for. The grave was the only thing with real allure, and through my mind flashed a rather touching picture of the ceremony as they lowered my flag-en-shrouded body into the sea, but I said weakly, "No, thank you," adding as an afterthought, and more like Oswald asking for the sun than because I thought the request could be granted, "I don't suppose there's any champagne on board?"

"Good God, kiddie, of course there is," said Mr. G. brightly, the host in him leaping like a war horse to the bugle. "Why didn't you tell me you wanted the stuff? I always keep it on ice, but I never drink it and it didn't occur to me you would either." How do you like that? It didn't occur to him I would either. I gently corrected this misapprehension, and from then on Mr. Griffis and champagne have been practically synonymous in my life except for one plebeian and never-to-be-forgotten occasion when we dined in a small Italian speakeasy in Philadelphia and Stanton ordered half a bottle of white wine. The waiter looked at us strangely and disappeared for a long time. He finally returned with a quart wine bottle half full.

All this happened several years ago, and as I look back now on those parties and excursions it seems to me people never had such fun. I think of two friends particularly who were often on the boat, Clarita and Phillipe de Forceville. They are now in France; Phillipe was for months and months in a German prison camp. I believe he was finally released largely through Stanton's efforts. Clarita was at the château in Abbeville when the Germans swept through, and she walked all the way to Paris, arriving with her shoes worn through and her feet bleeding. She has gone back there now and is farming the place by herself, and Phillipe has a job which brings him sometimes into the unoccupied zone, and once in a while we get a letter asking how we are and what we are doing.

Stanton eventually sold the *North Star* and bought the *North Wind*. She was twice as big and with not half the charm of her predecessor, but before the *North Star* went under the hammer Bill and I were married and Stanton had given us a wedding breakfast on board her. We had a gay wedding day, if I do say it myself, with the celebration beginning early in the morning and lasting all day long.

As Bill and I had both been divorced in New York State, there were complications about being married there, and we had to go to Connecticut for the ceremony. Mimi Rand, she was then Mimi Martin, gave a dinner party for us at her house in Oyster Bay the night before. Stanton had brought Bill and Winkie and several others down from town, and they were anchored off the Seawanhaka Yacht Club and all came ashore for dinner. After dinner we sat for a long time in the garden under the summer stars. I went home early with my mother, as seemed only fitting, but apparently the joyous wedding guests returned to the yacht in fine fettle and continued to toast the bride till dawn, some of the more flighty well-wishers plunging with abandon into the salubrious waters of Long Island Sound, from whence

170 *Past Imperfect*

they were hauled by the first mate, who regarded them
with a fishy eye. It sounds like a fine party, and I still
burn with resentment when I think that I missed it.
Bill slept on the boat, and the next morning Mother
and Uncle Dick and I went on board for the trip over
to Greenwich.

Hattie Carnegie made my wedding dress; it was full-
length white organdie, and with it I wore a green suède
belt and a large green straw hat. The dress was charming but much too long, and Mother and I spent the
entire trip across the Sound cooped in a cabin, cursing
out dear Hattie and reefing up the skirt.

We anchored at Greenwich, and as we drew away
in the launch everyone threw rice and confetti, and for
a moment we were caught to the *North Star* by hundreds of bright streamers.

We drove to the justice of the peace—Mother, Uncle
Dick, Mimi, Winkie, Bill, and I. The actual wedding
ceremony was brief; Winkie maintains the quickest on
record.

Somebody said, "Winks, it's hot in here, open the
window."

"I did," says he, "and when I turned around you were
married."

I was shaking, and Bill held onto my hand very
tight, but I couldn't see him clearly for the mist in
front of my eyes. As soon as we were married, and
everybody had kissed everybody else, we left the court-
house. The reporters were waiting on the steps, and one
of them, somewhat mixed up by the family names,
Mrs. Chase, Mrs. Newton, Miss Chase, Mrs. Murray,
said please, could he have a picture of Mrs. Chase.

My sentimental mood vanished as I thought of the publicity. Winkie claims that I said, "I'm the bride here, by God," as I stepped briskly into focus. I'm sure I didn't; I'm sure I hung on Bill's arm and said, "Darling, shall we let them take our picture?" but when I ask him about this, he only grins. Actually the press stories were all very pleasant and gratifying, though I didn't care so much for the one that said, "The groom's age is so and so; the bride *gave* her age as such and such." The one I liked best was Nancy Randolph's story, headed "Ilka Chase Yachts to Altar." It had a rakish sound, like "sliding for home."

When we got back to the boat, all our Greenwich friends who were coming over to Oyster Bay for the reception were on board—John and Carly Wharton, Armina and Lawrence Langner, Ina Claire, Arthur Richman, and lots of others. Ina is a charming-looking woman and a brilliant actress, but she is engrossed in Ina. It is the topic nearest her heart, and she likes to talk about it all the time, and for a few minutes there was quite a scrimmage as to whether we would talk about Ina or something else. I determined that my wedding breakfast was one scene she was not going to steal. We are both forthright, so that there seemed no sense in beating about the bush. I just said, "Shut up, Ina, and drink your champagne. This morning we will talk about Ilka and Bill." Which we did for the most part, although now and then, wafted on the breeze above the chatter, I caught the familiar phrases, "So I said to Gilbert when he was drawing up my contract," and "And on the opening night, that little bitch had done her hair exactly like mine." Ah well, people marry and are born and die and the world spins on. I think Ina

would come to my wake, for she is a sociable soul, and
clear and firm above the organ I would hear how she
broke Herman Shumlin down with kindness.

Massa had provided a Lucullan wedding breakfast,
and the scuppers were awash with champagne. When
we landed at Oyster Bay, a cavalcade of motors met us,
and we drove to Mother's house for the reception. We
were blessed with a day heavenly fair, the terrace was
abloom with flowers, and on the far side of the little
pond the tables were spread and the orchestra played.
More and more guests crowded around, congratulating
us, and our faces began to get stiff from smiling and
saying thank you. Dear old Alice Boughton came as
an astringent relief. She has known me ever since I
was a little girl and spent my summers in Brookhaven.

"How do you feel, Cully?" she asked.

"Why, very well," I answered in some surprise. As
a matter of fact I didn't, but everyone else had been
showering me with compliments. "Don't you think I
look nice?"

"No," she replied tartly, "you look mighty peaked
to me."

As it turned out, Grandma was the belle of the reception. She had on her party dress, lavender taffeta
with a fichu of soft lace, and a little lace cap on her
head. Winkie gallantly kept her glass filled to the brim
with champagne, and Grandma certainly showed that
the old Quaker stock can take it. She had a crowd
around her, and as the breeze lifted her taffeta skirt,
showing a peep of ankle, she cried happily, "Did thee
see what that pesky wind did?" and flapped her skirt
some more. She was always proud of her slender ankles
and little feet. Carly Wharton was entranced by her,

but says that I remarked darkly, "Beware, she'll drink your blood."

Bill and I finally slipped away about as inconspicuously as the usual bridal couple, up to the hubs in rice, and drove into New York. We were married on a Saturday and were sailing early Monday morning for Nova Scotia, and although we would far rather have spent the midsummer week end in the country, we had to spend it in the hot city because of tradition or something. Sunday evening we set out in search of a place to dine, but the restaurants were all closed. Twenty One, the Starlight Roof—all the cool and pleasant retreats. Wandering disconsolately around the Plaza at Fifty-ninth Street, we bumped into Arthur Schwartz, who was in town finishing a score, and hot and hungry too. We fell upon one another with glad cries and finally discovered the garden of the Park Lane. There was a table of four or five men, all of whom Bill knew, and so we joined forces, and they all toasted me, and I felt like the Queen dining with her regiment.

In the morning we sailed for our honeymoon in Nova Scotia. Nova Scotia is rural and mighty primitive. We did see a stag at eve and two beavers building a dam, whom Bill said were the old folks, who had turned their own quarters over to the youngsters and were starting afresh, but they did not quite make up for fried eggs three times a day, which was all the guide could cook. Of the bunks I will only say they were hard as rocks. It was with no regret that we bade farewell to the beautiful north woods and returned to Bill's comfortable duplex apartment in New York.

CHAPTER TEN

Certain Parties

THE APARTMENT IN FORTY-NINTH STREET
was in the remodeled private house of Robert Niles,
the architect, and had many things to recommend it,
but closet space was not one of them; also the kitchen
was a little too bohemian for practicality. Guests always
thought it was wonderful, because the living room was
charming; irregular in shape and flowing into the dining
room in an unexpected and pleasant way, which made
party-giving a delight. The back windows overlooked
the gardens of Turtle Bay, but the bedroom windows
opened on Forty-ninth Street, which is a noisy thorough-
fare, and I have never been able to manage Flents in
my ears, though I am a great one for the Black Night
Eye Shade; but stoppers in the ears make me uneasy.
I don't want to be as much of a recluse as all that; if
the house is burning down, I would like to hear the
warning crackles.

Also, though duplex sounds de luxe, the stairs were

a problem for Rosalie. Rosalie was Bill's cook, and she was such a type that people thought we had invented her. She was the comedy servant from a play, and the performance was flawless. I think now that she was really Mildred Natwick training for one of those character parts she does so brilliantly. Rosalie was Canadian French, and she and her half sister, Cora, had worked for Bill and stayed with us a while after we were married. Cora was rather quiet, but Rosalie was a rakish wench and debonair. She must have been about fifty, small and spry, her hair a grizzled mop of assorted reds and grays, and she applied her rouge with gusto. When we had company for dinner she added a dash of lipstick too, to lend a festive air, and she would occasionally put in a quip of her own while passing the roast.

On their day off, Cora and Rosalie went to public dances, and I gathered from Rosalie's unblushing accounts that she was quite the belle. She was hardworking, in a slapdash sort of way, and she had a light hand with soufflés and an unerring instinct for salad dressing. She was devoted to Bill and thought he did too much. She used to say to him, "Some day, Mr. Murray, you'll go out like a poof," and she would blow expressively as though extinguishing a candle flame. She had a kind of tough matter-of-factness about her, and an astringent humor. One day I was looking admiringly at some green-and-white flowery leaves which were shedding gently from a vase in the dining room.

"Look, Rosalie," I said, "aren't they pretty? It's called 'snow-on-the-mountain.'"

"It's also called pollen-on-the-table," she remarked tartly as she swept it off into her dust cloth.

And one time when I observed that I thought the

squabs we had had at a dinner party the night before were tasteless, she shrugged and said, "Mrs. Murray, what can you expect? Squabs are millionaires' food— millionaires' food never has any taste." After that we used to have stew *en casserole,* and it always had flavor, and the most highfalutin guests were satisfied.

Rosalie had once been called to testify in court along with five or six other people. She enjoyed the experience thoroughly and recounted it with relish, adding complacently that she was the star witness. She enjoyed life in the grand manner and told us that in their house in Maine no room had less than 116 yards of carpet. This properly impressed Bill and me, as we were at that time contemplating moving, but carpet for the new apartment was going to eat up so much of our budget that we weren't sure we could manage it.

But if you were sick, there were no flights of fancy. Rosalie was there with the possets and the Vicks, rubbing your chest, pinning on flannel bandages, and plying you with fruit juice. She told me that once in Maine, Cora had been very ill with pneumonia, and the doctors had given her up. "After they had gone," said Rosalie, "I sat up with her all night long. She was unconscious, but I said to her, 'You won't die, Cora, I am here.'" And as she said it, you felt that that tough, valiant little figure had looked death sternly in the eye and faced him down.

When Bill and I moved to our new apartment we parted with sorrow on both sides. Cora and Rosalie went to work in Jersey, but for quite a while afterward Rosalie would now and then drop in at Bill's office on her afternoon out before she went on to her triumphs at the dance.

When we were finally established in Fifty-seventh Street, where we still live, Bill loved it, and we are now burrowed in so deep I suppose we shall never leave except when carried out in a box. But the wrench from Forty-ninth Street was an ordeal for him, so much so that he would have no share in it and departed for Quebec, where Leslie Howard was handily arriving from England. When I told him in no uncertain terms what I thought of such ratlike dereliction, he explained that Leslie was an important client, a big radio deal was hanging fire, it was vital he get his signature immediately, and besides, he, William, trusted my sense of arrangement entirely—I would know just where to tell the men to put the furniture in the new apartment —and anyway, whenever they had moved when he was a child, his mother always told his father to take the day off, as she could do better without him.

Maybe she could, but perhaps Murray *père* was less cultured than his son. My husband is the bookish type, and thousands of volumes had to be packed. This I didn't mind so much, as I respect books myself, though tomes entitled *The Life and Works of Mencius* and Bergson's *Creative Evolution* leave me cold. There were also hundreds of musical scores, dating from the days when Bill was music critic on the Brooklyn *Eagle,* and as I packed alone at midnight, the temptation to stuff them in the fire and watch them frizzle, muttering lustfully to myself like Hedda Gabler, was strong. I solaced myself with the thought that in the Fifty-seventh Street apartment were fourteen wonderful closets where they could be stowed and forgotten. Bill was happy about the closets too. There are two big ones in his room, and he had visions of wandering happily about inside them, a man and his suits in splendid isolation, with no female fripperies crowding them out. I sometimes look back now, when I am counting his blessings for him, and remind him that the first few months *were* Utopian, but naturally, with the passage of time, a girl accumulates things, so that small encroachments have gradually been made on his preserves, but he still has a generous third of one of his closets for his very own.

. After we moved we had the familiar procession of domestics parading in and out of our lives, till we finally found Catherine from Austria, and my nightly prayer is that we may never part. Catherine is a wonderful cook, but her great sorrow is that we are not dessert-eaters. As she is from Vienna, pastry is her pride and joy and native talent. Bill and I seldom eat it, but, fearing a bad case of frustration, I give her her head at dinner parties, when, drunk with freedom, she sends in specimens which are masterpieces of the confectioner's art. I myself prefer a certain restraint in culinary decoration, but Catherine has an array of tubes and bags and pipes and brushes for performing excrescences on desserts that would shame the kitchens of Sherry's and Schrafft's.

The creative artist in her speaks, and crenelated peaks of whipped cream rise proudly from the deep purple foundations of a plum torte. Birthday cakes are her forte, and more things go on with the icing than Dali ever dreamed of. There are birds embowered in garlands of flowers, and tender mottoes and birthday greetings scrolled in pink and blue. Candles rise from the heart of incarnadined rosebuds, and the monument rests in a sparkling nest of spun sugar. A birthday tribute from Catherine is something of a milestone, and the good life for her would be a large family of her own, and the next best would be to work where there were lots of children, because they would adore her, and seven or eight birthdays a year would be just about right. At Christmas time we are crowded out of the house by the gingerbread men who come marching from the kitchen, and the nose of Miss Quinta, the dachshund, twitches for a week in advance from the pungent, spicy smells, and there are gingerbread dachshund puppies for her, with raisin eyes and pink icing tongues, and there is a fat Santa Claus with a terrific white beard and buttons down his front.

Catherine has a soul in flower, and birds and branches are stenciled on the kitchen walls, and the front of the window box where she grows herbs blazes with a lurid sunset reflected in a lake of improbable blue. She has the green thumb too, and thanks to her our plants and bulbs flourish like the bay tree. She also keeps a small aquarium with tiny transparent fish. As they say of the Chinese, they all look alike to me, but to Catherine they are distinct personalities and personal friends. She has a kinship with all animals, and last summer in the country she got very chummy with a small ailing bat she had found in the cellar. She kept him in a mason jar, where he clung upside down on a twig, and she spent hours trapping live flies for his dinner.

Like Rosalie, she is socially inclined and really enjoys planning meals for company. After we have discussed the menu, she will glance over it, and if she thinks we have done a good job, her eye lights up with pleasure, and she says enthusiastically, "Ach, Mrs. Murray, this tastes good"; and very nearly always it does. Her in-

terest in our guests is great, and when we have celebrities
like Frederic March or Bob Burns or Janet Gaynor, they
go into the kitchen to compliment her on her dinner,
and after that she is personally concerned for their
careers and always asks how they are getting on. The
Grand Duchess Marie has come to dine a few times,
and I sense Catherine considers that the ducal visits
have shed quite a glow on the establishment and she
could do with royalty at more frequent intervals.

Sometimes when Bill and I are both working hard,
our entertaining is forcibly curtailed, and then, like
many people, we find that the impromptu parties are
the most fun. I don't know how hostesses who plan
large formal dinners get through the strain, not of the
actual meal itself—although unsteady service and warring guests can age a lady twenty years, and her only
escape is to get tight as a mink and let the flood roll over
—but collecting the guests and setting the stage can be
a grim ordeal. The congenial people can't come on the
same night, the prize extra man drops out, and even
those on the C list have other fish to fry; the house is a
mess too. The spot where the pipes perspired through
the wall is only partially repaired, as the painters are
on strike, and the effect of subdued elegance is decidedly
marred by a glaring patch of white plaster. It is then
that the socially minded decide to take the veil and ask
themselves why in Heaven's name it ever seemed desirable to see their friends.

For several years we have had people in for New
Year's Eve, but the party has always grown sponta-
neously and has been a last-minute affair. This I find
most surprising, as I always think that everybody but
us has been asked to formal yet gay balls for which

they were engaged weeks ahead, if not indeed from year to year. The first time Bill and I had a New Year's Eve party we had not been invited any place, and so, thinking to cheat our loneliness, we decided to call up one or two close friends on the off chance that either they might be outcasts like ourselves, which we considered unlikely, or else that maybe they had bad colds and wouldn't mind just coming in for a little while after dinner for a quiet glass of champagne with old friends, and everybody home in bed by 12:20.

"You can try," said Bill glumly, "but you'll see— they'll all be at Mrs. Vanderbilt's party, or in the Crystal Room at the Ritz with tables of ten at fifteen bucks a head."

I tried. "Why, we'd be delighted," said the first couple eagerly. I called another number. "You bet," came the hearty response. "Count on us. We're free for dinner, too, in case you were planning anything." Spurred by my success, Bill went to his telephone and started calling up office friends. The upshot of it was we had twenty or thirty people, and good ones too, not just halitosis victims or lonely hearts who didn't use Kreml on their hair. Midway through the evening a batch of six came in together, and I greeted them cordially, thinking they were friends of Bill's. He plied them with drinks, thinking they were friends of mine; and they were very charming and gay. After a time, however, they began huddling in corners and eyeing us with perplexity. Finally the spokesman came up to me and said, "I'm terribly sorry, but I think we're at the wrong party. Are you the Manns?"

"Why, no," I said, "we're the Murrays."

"Oh," he said. "Well, we're having a lovely time. Is

it all right if we stay?" It was fine with me, but I feared the Manns' wrath when they heard we had commandeered their guests, and so I went across the hall to their apartment and told them. They joined us with more friends, and festivity ran high. We had champagne and Times Square on the radio and "Auld Lang Syne" on the piano and the windows open to let the New Year in and the gentlemen's faces splashed with scarlet from New Year's kisses.

We once had a gay Christmas party before Bill and I were married. It was in Mother's apartment, and there were about fourteen of us. George Cukor was in New York, and he played Santa Claus. George is now a wraith, but he was fat in those days, and it became him. Rosamond Pinchot was at the party, a most beautiful creature. Some years later she was to seek and find her death in a lonely garage on a winter's night, suffocated by carbon monoxide, but that night she was warm and alive and gay and she wore a coat of crimson velvet. George had put it on back to front; he had a formidable beard of absorbent cotton, and his horn-rimmed spectacles peered like an owl's eyes over the top. He delivered five-and-ten-cent-store presents from a huge basket, as comic and ribald a Santa Claus as never came down a chimney.

As I look back, all our parties seem to be in the winter. I can only conclude that heat makes us antisocial, or else we are away, or I am working, sometimes in Hollywood, occasionally in summer stock, and once in New York, during the run of *The Women*.

I had known Clare Boothe, the bland and lethal lady who in that little effort limned her sex in vitriol,

in an off-and-on casual sort of way ever since she had
been managing editor of *Vanity Fair*.

One day she called me up and asked me to have
cocktails with her at the Ritz—she had a part in a play
she wanted to talk to me about. When I met her, she
announced that Harry would join us shortly. Harry is
her husband, Henry Luce, and whether he joined us
or not was at that time a matter of supreme indifference
to me. I had met him only once, two or three years before, and we had had a violent row on the subject of
starvation in China. I forget the details, but I think
I said that millions of Chinese had starved to death,
and he said they hadn't, and he added that he ought
to know, as he had been born there. This seemed to
me a *non sequitur,* and I said so, and he asked if I had
ever seen anybody starve to death, and I said no, because if I saw anybody and knew they were starving,
I would damned well give them food. The clash occurred at a Sunday-night supper party on Long Island,
when we were both stuffing ourselves, and recrimina-
tion and hot dislike rolled across the table till the hostess
broke it up by withdrawing with the ladies in her wake.
But it was not the last time Mr. Luce and I dined for
starving China.

In the summer of 1941 he and Clare returned from
the Orient, fired by what they had seen of the incredible courage and durability of the Chinese people,
and this time he apparently thought that famine galloped fastest of the Four Horsemen over the beleaguered
nation, for he and his wife organized a large dinner,
which was immediately oversubscribed. The price was
seven dollars and fifty cents for a ticket for the meal,
which was too abundant, and what was left over after

paying the Waldorf cover charge went to China. Mr. and Mrs. Luce both made stirring speeches, but I thought it would have been more eloquent to have demanded seven dollars and fifty cents for the dinner, to have sent it all to China, and to have served a small bowl of rice or whatever it was that the vast majority of the embattled Chinese were subsisting on at that time.

That day at the Ritz, however, the Luces had still to discover China, and after we had settled down to our old fashioneds, Clare remarked with a sweet smile that Harry had never forgotten me, I had made him so angry.

"I envy you, really," she said with a little laugh. "I've never been able to make him mad."

"But you will, dear, I'm sure," I replied, my smile equally sunny.

After that, we got down to brass tacks. Clare told me about the part of Sylvia Fowler and asked me to read the script. My first impression was twofold: one, that it had the fetid atmosphere of a badly ventilated women's washroom and that if someone didn't open a window and let in a blast of fresh air, I would suffocate; and two, that it would be a hit. I thought Sylvia Fowler a harpy but a trenchant caricature, only, as she was so poisonous, it seemed to me imperative to play her for laughs; otherwise she would be a false note in the play, which, in spite of its curdled viewpoint and few touching moments with the child, was after all a comedy. Although I was certain that the script smelled box office, I was hesitant about accepting the part. It was the type of thing I was struggling to get away from, and I was just beginning to succeed.

I had recently played a light-handed adventuress in a lamentable bit of fluff from England, *While Parents Sleep*, and in *Wife Insurance* I triumphed for four performances as the irresolute and batsy wife who, however, got her men as neatly as a Mountie. Then, in *Small Miracle*, I was the alarmed, deserted, but sympathetic lady. I found I liked those parts, and I was leery of Mrs. Fowler, the Queen Bitch. But, reasoning that a successful play never hurt an actress, though it might condemn her for years to come to the same type of part, I signed the contract.

I had never cared much for Mrs. Clare Boothe Brokaw in the days when she was editing *Vanity Fair*, but during rehearsals of *The Women* my opinion did an about face. It is impossible for me not to respect a hard worker, and that she certainly is. The only thing which is exasperating about her is that no matter how hard she works, she always looks beautiful, her face clean, her nails exquisitely manicured, every blonde hair in place. In my own case this is not so. The instant I start work I begin to need a shampoo. Perhaps it's all those juices escaping from my brain. I eat off my lipstick, I looked tired and dirty, and I get runs in my stockings. Miss Boothe remains impeccable. I remember her sweeping in to rehearsal one evening on her way to a satin soirée. She was gowned by Hattie Carnegie, sabled by Jaeckel, and from her finger flashed one of Flato's larger ice cubes. The all-female cast of *The Women* sat about the dirty, bare stage, in the cold glare of the work light, in varying attitudes of despondency. We were tired and wished we were going to a party too, or we would have settled for a sable coat hanging in the closet when we got home. Miss Boothe went to the prompt table, handed to Robert Sinclair, our director, a few pages of revised manuscript; when he asked for some new lines for the scene we were working on, she scribbled in a couple of pretty funny ones on the spur of the moment and departed to join her eminent husband, who waited at the stage door in the Lincoln limousine.

Clare is quick-witted on paper, but I would not say that in conversation she tossed off witticisms and repartee at the rate of Dorothy Parker. I know Mrs. Parker very slightly, but judging from the few times I have been with her, I wouldn't say that she does either. Conversational wit is, I think, largely mythical. Bright people occasionally say extremely funny things, and from then on witticisms they may have labored over for hours and set down on paper with much travail are snatched up and bandied about as spur-of-the-moment inspirations. Anyone who has achieved even small fame as a comedian is forever being called on to Say a Few Words on a multiplicity of occasions, and when he protests that he has nothing prepared, the organizers of these horrid fetes laugh indulgently and say, "Nonsense, we just want you to toss off a few remarks in your inimitable style."

A couple of conferences with gag writers of radio scripts, as glum and dyspeptic a group as you will meet in a nine days' march, would cure them of the illusion that comedy is a funny business. I one day received a letter from a young lady in college, who said she often listened to my radio program and liked the "Robert Benchleyesque monologues" which I sometimes did.

"I have dozens of these stowed away in my desk," she continued, "which I would be glad to send you, because, as you know, they can be tossed off in five minutes."

I didn't know, and so, out of a depressed and morbid curiosity, I asked her to send me some. After I had seen them I sent them back with a little note saying: "Dear Miss ——: You underestimate yourself. After reading your essays I imagine you must have tossed them off in two minutes."

Clare Boothe really can turn out pearls though, if not in two minutes at least between the matinee and night performances, which she did continuously while *The Women* was trying out in Philadelphia. I think the myth has since been exploded, chiefly by the gentleman himself, that George Kaufman wrote *The Women*. Clare had plenty of enemies, for she was an easy target for envy, and people were only too eager to say that her husband financed the production and that somebody else wrote it, though their logic was not too clear, as why should he be putting up the money if his wife had nothing to do with it? The truth of the matter was that neither of them had a penny in it, but that George Kaufman and Moss Hart, because they thought it was good, each had a share, as they do in many Max Gordon productions. How much Max himself owned is anybody's guess, for they say around Broadway that he has a knack of going broke with his hits.

Clare wrote the play alone and unaided, but I suppose that after the Philadelphia opening Kaufman and Hart may have offered a few suggestions as to rewriting and rearrangement of scenes, all of which work she did herself. That kind of doctoring is a common or garden occurrence in the theater, where, at one stage or another in production, every manager who ever breathed calls in all his friends for their opinions and goes around with lumps of ice on the end of his legs instead of feet. They get producers' stomach and live on stewed fruit, like George Kaufman, or Scotch and soda, like Dwight Wiman, depending on their temperaments. Gilbert Miller shovels in ice cream, and Max Gordon invokes the Son of God in loud and anguished tones. Rumor has it that at a Cornell opening Guthrie McClintic fainted in the wings. Edward Duryea Dowling stays up all night every night for a week before the opening, playing pinochle with the stage crew, and Otto Preminger observes hoarsely and at half-hour intervals that it is obvious he should seek another profession.

Before the New York opening of *The Women*, Max was as usual in a tiz. "Holy Jesus Christ, I'm ruined; the God-damned show has ruined me; the bastards won't come in," he moaned, as Philadelphians stayed away in droves and the box office languished. I annoyed him bitterly, because I refused to be discouraged and went around saying smugly, "Don't worry, Max, the show can't fail." It is only fair to admit I have once or twice said that about other shows and been spectacularly wrong, but that time I was right, and a year later, when the road company played there, Philadelphia stood in line for the privilege of seeing what it had previously scorned.

We opened in New York to what you might call mixed but provocative notices. The critics, being men, were horrified that a woman should write so callously of women, but the spectacle had for them a gruesome fascination, and the tenor of the reviews was: "This is a horrible thing, but don't miss it." Mr. Watts was pained by what he termed the bathos of the scenes with the child, and Mr. Atkinson cut me to the quick when he referred to me as the mother of all vultures. I wouldn't have minded daughter, but mother! For the first two or three nights after the opening the public was a little uncertain about how to react to this strange stunt, then with a whoop they took us to their hearts, where we nestled snugly for a year and a half.

Of course, compared to *Tobacco Road,* seven years, and *Life with Father,* three to date, that's not so much; but it was nice going just the same, and we felt no pain.

Naturally, with an all-female cast, conjecture as to how the little women were getting on was rife, and columnists were continually calling the press agent in the optimistic hope that hell had broken loose backstage and that the days of the Amazons flourished once again. Unfortunately for the public prints nothing of the kind happened. I do not say that there was not now and again the quick spitting of cats, or that thirty-three sets of coral nails did not on occasion curve in swift, clawlike gesture, but it was no different from any other company who play together for a long time and who are subjected to the irritation and tension inseparable from the constant repetition of personal mannerisms, carelessly played scenes, and the hot competition for publicity. To be sure, there were cliques and squabbles, and during the struggle for Equity reform, feeling ran high, but in other ways we were singularly free from friction, as we had no sex problem. There was no leading man for whose affections we were contending, and there were, thank God, no actors' wives cluttering up the premises and making suggestions. Actors' non-professional wives are the theater's greatest headache. Bad ideas pullulate in their idle but fertile brains, and they drive everybody connected with a production crazy, offering advice and thinking up ways further to spotlight their heart interest at the expense of the rest of the cast. Some of the more intrepid managers, when they know from past experience or the gypsy's warning what they will have to contend with, insert clauses in the contract stating that the little woman is not to show her nose inside the theater until the opening night; but most of them are too craven for that, and so they just grit their teeth and bear it. The cast endures the ordeal with ill-concealed disgust, and the star's performance is highly inconsistent as he tries desperately to reconcile the conflicting direction given in the darkened theater with that which he gets in the darkened bedroom.

I must doff my cap to the male sex, as stage husbands are far less likely to interfere with their wives' performance, thinking tolerantly that playacting is women's work anyhow.

During the run of *The Women*, people used to ask us if we didn't miss not having men backstage, but the answer to that one was, "What do you mean no men? We can hardly make an entrance for having to fight our way through them." This was not, as the romantically minded may suppose, because we were deluged with gentlemen friends, but because we had a crew of twenty-one stagehands. It was a heavy production, and the boys were constantly shifting scenery, running baths, making coffee, and ringing telephones.

We played preview performances Christmas Eve and Christmas Night, and we opened the twenty-sixth of December, so that the following Christmas we had run a year, and some kind of celebration seemed indicated.

All those who were speaking to one another gave presents, and a couple of the more outstanding feuds were liquidated in the spirit of good cheer, and for two or three weeks beforehand we were wondering what the management would do. As it was a double celebration, and we were after all the fair sex, we anticipated something pretty handsome. Also, as soon seeped out, everybody was privately speculating on what that blonde, rich Santa Claus, Clare Boothe, would leave in our stockings. Clare, on the whole, came through nicely. She tried to give everybody something appropriate to her part, and in a few instances succeeded. As I was playing a cat, euphemistically speaking, she gave me a charming Currier and Ives print of two fat white kittens under a spray of lilac. Betty Lawford, who was Crystal and played the scene in the bathtub, received a sumptuous basket of bath salts, soap, talcum, etc. But when Clare came to Margalo Gillmore's part, she bogged down. What would be appropriate for Mary Hayes, who was the one pure woman in the play and a character Clare hated? She finally settled for a string of beads, and after that her invention ran out. Almost everybody else got cigarette holders. They were Zeus holders, six in a box, and expensive, but they were received with varying degrees of ingratitude by the several ladies of the cast who didn't smoke.

Christmas Eve, after the performance, the cast gave a party to the stagehands, and the next day we settled back to wait for the management. The management sent posies, but something less than orchids. One Mr. Al Cohen of the Gordon office had been entrusted with this flowery mission, and never a chap to throw the boss's money around—if the boss didn't, why should he?

—had hied himself to a subway flower stand, where, as the holiday was almost over, he was able to pick up a tidy bargain in wilting blooms. These he tastefully wrapped in newspaper and presented to the ladies of the ensemble. The collective reaction was instinctively to throw them back in his face, but I couldn't help laughing as a tired old bag of dead flowers was thrust into my hand. After that we were each given a bottle of champagne, I presume to assuage our feelings.'

Though it galled him, there came a time when Max could no longer close his eyes to the pitiable condition of our wardrobes. Willy-nilly, and it was the strongest nilly on record, he had to recostume the play. We had implored him for months, "For God's sake, Max, here we are a bunch of swell Park Avenue dames, and we're in rags!" Every quick change was a hazard, as the material was worn so thin you could put your heel through even a tweed skirt, and when Audrey Christie made her entrance into the ladies' room in the last act, she had to slither in sideways like a crab, as the seat of her brown sequin dress was worn through and her pink crepe de Chine bottom was exposed to the customers. Audrey is a fine, honest actress who will always play a scene directly to the person with whom she is acting, but there were a few weeks during the crisis when she faced dead front, as immobile as a caryatid, turning only her head ever so gingerly, her generally abandoned movements restrained as she backed and sidled about the stage, never daring to turn her back. You'd have thought the audience was royalty.

Max finally capitulated, but as we had played in our old rags for so many months, the night the new clothes worked for the first time, we were as nervous as if it had been an opening. It bucked our morale though, and even the stagehands rejoiced and felt so refreshed by the change of scenery that they gave us a fine party under the stage to celebrate the event.

In July 1938 *The Women* closed. I left two or three weeks before the end of the run, as I was dead tired and wanted to get away for a European holiday with Bill, who could leave then but not later. Also the play had been milked dry; we had made good money for seventy-eight weeks, which in the theater is a respectable record, and it seemed pointless to continue a routine which had become dreary, stale, and mechanical for the few dollars a week the management was willing to pay. The receipts had fallen to almost nothing, and they were only continuing at all because some of the cast were willing to work for the minimum, but as the final two or three weeks proved, even that was not little enough.

Bill and I sailed the end of June for what turned out to be an enchanting trip through Norway, Sweden, and Denmark, the lovely lands of the north, which perhaps never again in our lifetime will be as they were through that clear and shining summer.

CHAPTER ELEVEN

Vanishing World

I RECALL THE SUMMER OF '38 WITH TEN-derness because I did no work. We went to Europe and lived off the fat of the land and acted like gentry who never had to earn their bread, although after a couple of months of superlative Scandinavian food, simple bread began to look pretty good.

We sailed on the *Franconia*. She was a huge old tub returning to England from a round-the-world cruise, and she put in at every whistle stop. Not that I like to speak disparagingly of a cultural hub, but it was some-thing of an anticlimax after a gala New York farewell—with flowers, friends, and monogrammed eggs—to wake the next morning in Boston harbor. We dined that night on the roof of the Ritz, nearly missed the boat for cele-brating, but at last settled down to a nine-day passage. I am a poor sailor, and I was very tired, and so I slept and lolled in a deck chair most of the way and played possum whenever the games steward came around. Never one to indulge in the sport of kings on dry land, I see no necessity for participating in that gloomy substitute practiced so avidly at sea.

The passengers were all colonial British going "home" to England, many of them for the first time. There were couples from Australia and New Zealand, and colonels from Rhodesia. That is the striking thing about the British; the familiar types out of Somerset Maugham really do exist. My William is a gregarious fellow, and they all liked him, so that he played a great deal of bridge and got along fine. I don't play bridge; I think it's antisocial, and besides I've never been able to learn it. My inability worries me no little. I wouldn't mind if only the more advanced mentalities could cope with it—I know my niche—but I am alarmed to see that some of the stupidest people play with great éclat. Perhaps mine is a glandular deficiency.

We had boat drill and lessons on how to get into our life jackets, which were designed for 250-pound men. I kept falling through mine, and the petty officer in charge humiliated me by pointing me out as a signal example of how not to do it. But to compensate for such chastisement there were the long, pleasant evenings by the fire in the bar; I have crossed many times to Europe, but the *Franconia* was the only boat that I remember having open fireplaces. We docked at Glasgow and spent an enchanted week motoring through Scotland. To me it is the Romantic Land. I remembered it with nostalgia from my first trip years before. I remembered the rolling moors and the soft air; and that one evening the pipers had marched around the little inn where we stayed in Pitlochry, piping in the rain; and there had been a red-faced, red-mustached old gentleman at our table who took whisky with his breakfast porridge.

Bill and I hired a car and a wonderful chauffeur named Douglas, who knew Scotland like his pocket. We fell in love with him, but I felt untrue to our own Philip back in New York and had a guilty conscience— the Philip who once said to me, when I asked him why he was late picking me up, "I couldn't get across Fifth Avenue, Mrs. Murray, there are tanks going up and down." I must have shown considerable alarm, because he added reassuringly, "American tanks." And soon after the President had declared an emergency, on seeing a drove of fat pigeons on the sidewalk wallowing in grain, he remarked sadly, "Just think, Mrs. Murray, them poor little pigeons will soon be in the Army."

Douglas drove us through the most beautiful scenery and recommended the most comfortable inns. The one that won my heart was the hotel in the Trossachs, where, when you slipped between the icy linen sheets and stretched out tentative and quivering toes, you met the blessed warmth of a hot-water bottle. Our luck and Scotland's held, and for ten heavenly days the sun shone. Bill and I swelled with pride at what we considered our personal achievement and debated renting ourselves out to the British government to keep away the rain. We ate an enormous tea on the banks of Loch Lomond and peered for the monster in Loch Ness. We asked a farmer who was cutting hay beside the road whether he had seen it, and he replied kindly, "Aye, that I have." We saw Inverness reflected in its river, and silhouetted against the setting sun, and we tarried for an hour in the peaceful ruins of Dunkeld Abbey, with the sun falling in a pattern through the archways and the old gravestones crumbling through the centuries into the daisy-pied grass. We saw the island in Lochleven from which the ill-starred Queen of Scots disguised as her laundress tried unsuccessfully to escape, and we came to Stirling Rock, where on a December night in 1566 the candles blazed and the music played for the baptism of the infant James. The captain's garden within the walls of the castle is a sweet and sheltered place, and from the parapets one gazes for miles over Stirling Plain to the purple hills.

We spent two or three days in Edinburgh, and before luncheon on the Sunday we were to sail on our North Cape cruise we met Johnny Van Druten, the playwright, in the revolving door of the Caledonia Hotel. He had a young man with him, and the four of us lunched together and had deep-dish apple pie for dessert, and Johnny said wistfully, "Now do you think English food is so bad?" We had to admit that the apple pie was tops.

We sailed from Leith; it made me think of Helen Hayes and the first scene of Anderson's *Mary of Scotland*, out through the Firth of Forth, a temperamental strip, into the North Sea. The attitude of the North Sea is distinctly uncivil, and my stomach and I were not on what you would call a co-operative footing. Along about the middle of a chaotic night the captain had the charity to decide on the inner waterway, so that we were in the lee of the Norwegian islands, and they bore the brunt of the hostilities. God knows, they were better able than I.

Our ship was the *Viceroy of India*, broad in the beam, and very comfortable, with an Indian crew. They were picturesque in their blue cotton costumes and turbans, and the passengers used up countless rolls of film photographing them. I took thousands of pictures, mostly blurry, and Bill remarked mildly that perhaps I should aim more for quality and withdraw from the quantity handicap.

The passengers were predominantly English and Scotch, and we met a charming couple from Edinburgh called Turnbull, and when the boat put into the fjords and we took inland trips, we would share a car or a railway compartment. There was also an Indian potentate with his retinue. The men wore European clothes, but the women were draped in saris, thickly bordered with gold. On account of their religion they couldn't eat at the same table with the common people, which was all right on the boat but became complicated on the excursions, as most of the mountain hotels had long tables, like boarding houses. As the Scandinavian countries are democratic, they served us masses first, while the dark aristocrats looked hungrily on, waiting till we had risen and they could sit down uncontaminated to our leavings. I used to feel sorry for them, for nothing so destroys me as the pangs of hunger. Mother says that when I am particularly depressed, just as she is thinking how interesting it is to have a soulful child with dark, Slavic moods, it occurs to her that perhaps a steak will dispel the gloom, and she is always right. I could sympathize with the Indians, and I would smile encouragingly. Besides, I hoped the head man would take a fancy to me and toss me some emeralds, but he was impervious to my winsome occidental ways.

We went ashore at Narvik and Tromsö and Aandalsnæs, all the places whose names were to become so tragically familiar the following year. We saw the midnight sun, and didn't believe it; when we woke up at 2:30 A.M. and it was bright daylight, I said to Bill with some annoyance that his watch had stopped again, and why hadn't he had it fixed in Edinburgh. But it was the sun which was at fault: it had neglected to set. The next night we sat up till nearly four to get the second Louis-Schmeling fight on the ship's radio. What came through best were the Buick commercials.

We climbed the North Cape puffing and panting, and regretting every cigarette we had ever smoked, and were much humiliated by a seventy-two-year-old grandmother who sprinted past us like a gazelle, calling back that it was her third trip up. For my taste once is excessive. When you finally arrive at the top, drained of all strength, there is still a mile of nothingness to be traversed. The plain is bleak and desolate, like the landscape of the moon, and at the far edge, perched on the curve of the world, is a hut where they dispense hot chocolate and post cards. The wind from the North Pole whistles round you, and you long for the tropics, but you would settle for a straight shot of Scotch. You don't get it, because in Norway, while it isn't *exactly* prohibition, getting a drink is about as easy as getting a bar of gold out of Fort Knox. Of course on the cruise boats there is no difficulty, because that is His Majesty's territory, and they know what to do with a tot of rum.

Such grandeur as the barren scene possesses is marred by the thought that you have to climb down again and make your perilous way back to the ship through mountainous waves in a tiny launch. There is also the terrifying see-saw effect when you try to clamber up the rope ladder hung over the side, while the launch wallows in the trough of the wave and the mother ship rides the crest. The prospect was grim, but whipping ourselves on with cries of "Stout heart" and "Excelsior," we finally made it and fell upon a supper of ham and eggs, brandy, and coffee.

The whole Scandinavian trip was a saga of wonderful food. Even the English boat was exceptional, because, with her oriental crew, you could order excellent Indian curries, and I remember one inland excursion we made when we lunched at a spot called Videsaeter, high in the mountains of Norway, and ate a salmon that was a revelation. An hour before he had been leaping in the plunging falls, and bore about as much kinship to that yellowish stuff they give you in drugstores as ambrosia does to sawdust.

Just as the moors *are* Scotland, so the thousands of waterfalls cascading down the mountainsides, smoking and glittering in the sun, are Norway; the falls and the silent fjords, where the mountains rising to the sky eternally contemplate the mountains submerged in the dark water.

We were in Norway in June, but where the road wound through the heights, the snow lay banked twelve feet deep, and once we saw a fleet, lithe figure on skis swoop in breathtaking curves down the face of the mountain. The snow and the mountains we had expected; we were not prepared for the northern flowers, the enormous, beautiful flowers blooming in profusion. They bloom only during the few months that the sun shines, but then they make up for lost time, and the valleys ring with color.

Around Videsæter were many agile goats, with their goatees, and herds of reindeer, their horns encased in velvet, roamed like fairy-tale creatures through the snow with short fat Lapps in attendance.

Before going on to Oslo we stayed a night in Bergen,

one of the old Hanseatic ports. In Bergen it rains 365
days a year, and even the Murray magic, which had
worked so effectively in Scotland, was of no avail. We
went into a shop and bought rubbers and an umbrella.
We had no difficulty in making ourselves understood;
indeed the salespeople beat us to it and came rushing
forward with the merchandise as soon as we opened the
door. Besides, in all Scandinavian cities they speak
English. It is an intelligent and friendly gesture to
address the visitor in his own language; it makes him
feel at home, though a little stupid that he is unable
to show to this hospitable people the same courtesy. I
was shocked to find that the commercial attaché of our
ministry at Stockholm had lived in Sweden for seven
years and had neither the good manners nor the intelligence to learn Swedish. I was also shocked to realize
that my native land apparently does not consider foreign
languages an integral part of diplomatic training.

The night we spent in Bergen, Bill and I looked in
the papers to see if there were any theaters open. The
magnificent Opera House was closed, but there were
two or three others, and with the help of the hotel
porter we selected a revue, as we figured that even
though we didn't understand a word, they would bring
on the girls and music, and we would feel right at home.
The revue was charming, with imaginative, simple sets
and excellent actors. When I asked an usher how it
happened that in a comparatively small town in midsummer they were able to put on such a good show,
she looked at me pityingly and said, "But, madam, of
course the actors are good. They are the best in Norway,
from the State Theater. They play all over Scandinavia,
Ibsen and drama in the winter, and revues to amuse

themselves in the summer." They did it with great skill, and I thought fleetingly of Katharine Cornell doing a hot tap routine or Miss Ethel Merman reviving a bit of O'Neill and had to admit reluctantly that our team is not so versatile. One skit in the revue took place in a shop, and a man came in to buy something, already laden down with packages. He indulged with perfect timing the eternally funny business of dropping one, clutching wildly at the others, and in his endeavors to retrieve the first one, dropping the lot. He then proceeded to explain to the salesgirl what he wanted. Even in Norwegian the words sounded funny, and suddenly recognition broke upon me: he was doing the old Beatrice Lillie sketch about double-damask dinner napkins.

After the performance Bill and I went to what we had been told was the gayest night club for a bite of supper. In a little while a group of people came in and sat down at a table near ours. They were laughing and chatting, and we recognized them as the principal players in the revue. We watched them surreptitiously for a while, and then I could bear it no longer. I said to Bill, "Go over and introduce yourself. They're bound to speak a little English. Tell them we're in the theater in New York. When they hear you're from the William Morris agency they'll probably reach for their fountain pens, and maybe they've heard about *The Women*. Ask them if they won't join us for a drink."

It took a little prodding, but Bill finally rose like a noble trout. They turned out to be darlings. We shoved the tables together, ordered more champagne all around, and spent the gayest evening of our entire trip, with mutual compliments about the Scandinavian and American theaters floating back and forth like paper boats on the champagne bubbles. As I write this it is a dank Sunday afternoon in New York, but I feel the warm glow again when I think of how nice they were, and of the easy, happy camaraderie of artists the world over when they do not fear one another's competition.

They wanted us to go on with them and really make a night of it, but it was already late, and we had to catch the early morning train for Oslo. So with the hearty reassurances that we would soon meet again, characteristic of those partings which must inevitably be forever, we bade them good night. What has happened to them, I wonder? It is strange to look back on the events of one's life, after the future has become the past, and to foresee with belated clairvoyance in the light of our subsequent hindsight the events we never guessed at the time. It is a curious exercise in metaphysics and bears out those who maintain that time is not the past, the present, and the future, but concurrent and simultaneous.

In Oslo we presented a letter of introduction to Mr. Matiessen, the Norwegian representative of the Texas Oil Company, who had once spent some months in America. He promptly put aside his own business and personal life and devoted the next forty-eight hours to entertaining us. At the end of the whirl, as we sat at dinner as his guests in the Oslo Yacht Club, he turned to us and said enthusiastically, "You know what I love about Americans? They are so hospitable."

We did squeeze in one meal on our own, our first luncheon. We strolled into a restaurant at random about one o'clock and found a great many women, mostly pretty girls, lunching exclusively on cakes. It seemed a little odd, and I said to Bill, "Maybe in Norway the meals are progressive, the way they are at those country parties at home, where you eat soup at one house, the main course at another, and dessert at a third. This is probably the dessert restaurant." We asked Mr. Matiessen about it, but he said that while ingenious, that wasn't quite the explanation. It seems that our pretty young lunchers, were stenographers for the most part. They eat a big breakfast at home about 7:30 or 8, take a cup of coffee and a piece of cake for lunch, and at 5 or 6 have a heavy dinner, after which they go on skiing or skating parties till about 10 P.M. It sounds a lovely life if you can ski, but my heart aches for the plight of those who cannot, like a dear friend of ours, who, when over fifty, married a square young Viking, American made, whose skis were as permanently attached to her feet as Hermes' wings. His love was such that he followed her down the Cresta Run and sprawled in her wake across the New Hampshire slopes, where he one day had a bad fall. Bill received the news morosely. "Damn it all," he said. "She'll kill him, one way or another."

In Oslo much of the architecture is modern; the city is magnificently situated, but rather dull, although some of the shops were fun—not, however, the one selling gas masks. In 1938 the town had sensed its danger, and masks were modeled by wax manikins in shop windows as though they were new spring bonnets.

From Oslo we went to the enchanting old city of Göteborg and dined one night in a restaurant set in a beautiful garden, and a band in red coats played Viennese waltzes, and the next day we sailed on the *Diana* for a trip through the Göta Canal. The entire journey is life through the other end of a telescope, reduced to miniature. Everything is tiny, except the meals, which are enormous. The cabins are minute, and the bunks so narrow that little hammocks are slung beside them to hold the overflow. You slip through countless locks and past orchards and rolling farmland, and sometimes, rounding a bend, you come upon a squat stone castle, its walls rising from the water. You can sit on deck, and if you lean over ever so little, the branches of the trees will brush your face as you pass. From time to time the boat stops, and you wander leisurely over the country-side to visit one of the castles or an old church, where, since the twelfth century, no Sunday service has ever been missed.

It is an idyllic trip, and exactly my idea of the way water should be taken, with large doses of land. At last the channel broadened, and we came at sunset into the harbor of Stockholm, and docked not far from the famous town hall, with its beautiful square tower. Stockholm is a superb city, built on a network of canals and rivers, so that it inevitably makes one think of Venice, though it has none of the decayed rococo splendor of the southern city, and none of the smells. Some have told me they find this antisepsis dull, but I don't. To my way of thinking, the northern cleanliness is poetic; the clear air, the water, the forests, and the towering mountains touch my imagination. This is the North, the countries evoked for me by surging sym-phonies, the lands which have haunted me ever since, when a small child, I first read about Kay in the *Snow Queen* of Hans Christian Andersen.

But I must admit that as a locale, though preferably for pictures or plays rather than my own person, the tropics appeal to me too. The minute it's frightfully hot and the characters sit around sipping gimlets to the distant throbbing of the tom-toms, I am entranced. I don't care how shoddy the plot as long as nerves begin to snap and the heroine gets feverish. It is my old preoccupation with the weather. As soon as it is the motivating factor of life or of the plot, the magic begins to work for me, and it is a force even more significant in the countries where the climate is extreme.

In Scandinavia life is molded by the elements, and I am in mine. Stockholm that summer was lovely: warm and sunny, but fresh. We spent hours wandering in the market place, which was alive with color—the fruit and flower stands festive under the striped awnings—gazing with admiration at the lean and lovely Orpheus of Mr. Carl Milles which towers above the square, and in the evenings dining on the terrace of the Grand Hotel overlooking the Canal.

There was also a Texas oil man in Stockholm, Arne Molso. The way he pronounced it, it had a jaunty, lilting sound; he was tall and flat, and very good-looking, and took us everywhere. He showed us the modernistic apartments, so designed that everyone had windows facing south and window boxes brimmed with flowers; and there was an especially distinguished one where lots of unmarried mothers lived, with a charming nursery on the roof where the children were taken care of during the day while their mothers were at work. When he asked me why I smiled, I said I thought the Swedish men were cutting off their own noses; if women could live not only with security but with comfort and charm without their men providing it, they might find the ladies more and more reluctant to assume the burdens of matrimony. But he said quickly that it worked just as well for married couples; they too were allowed to send their children to the nurseries, which was important, because such a large percentage of married women work. Though he remarked that he and his family did not patronize them, he spoke admiringly of the co-operative stores. My own downfall was the Nordiska Kompaniet, the magnificent department store where they sold Orrefors glass and exquisite porcelains. I wandered there for hours, and only the pangs of hunger and the thought of smörgåsbord wrenched me away. We went one day to Skansen, the park where there is a famous zoo, and the bears stand up and hold out their arms to be fed. And we visited the majestic castle, Gripsholm Slott, where there is one of the oldest theaters in Europe, with the original scenery still in perfect working condition. We ground a crank, and the elaborate machine which used to bear the God descended from heaven; we turned something that looked like a rolling pin, and blue canvas waves churned furiously. I turned quite pale, remembering the North Sea. And the upstage side of the wings still bore their little wire shields which once protected the flying skirts of the ballet dancers from the candle flames.

That day we had persuaded Arne Molso, who considered it a silly New York notion, to spend a few hours at his desk, and we took the trip on our own. Our driver rather hesitantly recommended a restaurant across the road from the castle, saying it was only a simple country inn, and the American lady and gentleman must not expect too much. We went in willing to settle for a slight snack, the Swedish version of scrambled eggs, perhaps, and two hours later the driver had to come and carry us out. We had gorged ourselves on one of the

most sumptuous repasts of a lifetime and had just
strength to murmur, *"Tack för mål,"* which Arne Molso
had taught us was the polite Swedish custom of thank-
ing one's host for a meal.

I would say that on the whole Europeans eat more
than we do, but we bear the old adage in mind, for I
have noticed that not only in Rome but in Madrid,
Stockholm, or Paris, the traveling American adapts himself nobly to the native custom and is right in there
pitching with the local champs, with every indication
of pleasurable reaction, only now and then murmuring
wistfully, "Oh boy, what I'd give for a steak!"

When we were in Stockholm we nearly flew to Fin-
land with our letter of introduction to Sibelius buttoned
tight over our thumping hearts, but our schedule would
have allowed us only a few hours there, and I rebelled
at behaving like those tourists who rush through galleries in pairs, one of them snatching fleeting glances
at the pictures while the other reads Baedeker. In a way
I am now sorry we didn't go; I should have liked to have
seen Helsinki even with the eye of an express train.
Instead we went on to Copenhagen, which is a jewel
box; a small but extraordinarily cosmopolitan city,
packed with shops and diplomats, museums, theaters,
restaurants, and bars. As we descended from our taxi
at the Hotel d'Angleterre, who should be quietly sipping
his morning coffee on the terrace but that old Nordic,
Dwight Fiske, temporarily released from the vicissitudes
of Ida, the Wayward Sturgeon.

In Copenhagen the entire population bicycles, and in
the late afternoon at the rush hour it was amusing to
see the swarms pumping vigorously down the streets,
coming to an abrupt halt when the lights turned red,

like people in a mechanical ballet. We wandered through the Tivoli, one of the most famous city playgrounds of Europe, which is part garden and part amusement park, but it showered intermittently, and we had to run for cover. Our last night we ate at Wivel's, and that dinner was the first of the two most unforgettable meals I have ever swallowed in twenty-four hours, for the next night we dined at Larue's in Paris. Wivel's smörgåsbord was the kind of thing they must serve in Heaven on Easter morning, with God in full-dress uniform, and the golden trumpets blaring. The next morning we left by plane for Paris after an early breakfast of smoked salmon and beer, which, regardless of what you may be thinking, dear reader, was, under the circumstances, an excellent idea.

The trip was magnificent, in an American plane piloted by Dutchmen, which made everything seem very solid and safe, although there was one bit of European *laissez faire* which I found beguiling. To everyone's surprise we came down at Brussels, a stop which was not scheduled, but the pilot smilingly explained that though we had made a landing at Rotterdam, the airport had run out of gas, so they'd sent us over to Brussels to borrow a cup. That is what lends charm and excitement to air travel in Europe; there is a slight element of uncertainty, and you never know in what exotic land you may be grounded. Instead of calling out Kansas City, Cleveland, and Des Moines, the dispatchers send you winging to Moscow, Paris, and Prague.

I was glad, though, when we took off from Rotterdam, as I had been humiliated before the entire airport. I had gone into the ladies' room, but as I had no guilder—my last Danish crown had gone to Mr. Georg Jensen of Copenhagen for a silver coffee pot, and Bill and I between us had only enough French francs to get us through the customs—I could put nothing in the saucer, and I thought to sneak out before the watchful eye of the fat Dutch attendant pinioned me. I was living in a fool's paradise. Just as I was slipping through the door, she caught sight of me and followed in hot pursuit, bellowing words I couldn't understand but whose meaning was all too clear both to me and every traveler in Rotterdam. I was a dirty foreigner trying to gyp a hard-working woman out of an honest living; and the more rapidly I walked, trying to pretend the tirade wasn't directed at me, the more pointed it became. The whole restaurant burst out laughing, and I finally ran out the door, blushing furiously in ignominious defeat.

There was one ominous moment as we were flying over the North Sea. A German sitting behind us tapped us on the shoulder. Our eyes followed his pointing finger, and there far below, through a gap in the clouds, we saw a tiny island. "Helgoland," he muttered with a nasty leer. I half expected him to lick his chops; his expression as much as said, "We got them there once, we'll get them again." I shivered and turned to contemplating the still free skies. It was lovely when we were over France, the soft, rolling country, and soon the forest of Compiègne and then Paris.

For once we went through the French customs like a breeze, our porter and ourselves chanting firmly in unison, "Rien à déclarer." It was just as well, as our funds were running low and the excess baggage charge from Copenhagen to Paris had been a stunner. Bill and I kept congratulating each other that we had our fare home paid in advance.

We went to the Crillon. I myself would have been
content with more modest lodgings, but I am happy to
say Bill travels in the grand manner. "God knows," he
said piously and more prophetically than we realized,
"when we shall pass this way again." It was mid-July,
and Paris was quiet, but it didn't matter to us. We dined
at Larue's on *canard à la presse,* we roamed the lovely
streets, we strolled through the Luxembourg gardens. I
went shopping to no great avail; it was the off season,
and the collections were all in the making. And I would
meet Bill in the Ritz Bar in the late afternoon. We saw
the Bromfields there, Mary and Louis, and they asked
us to Sunday luncheon at Senlis. It was a beautiful
day; the little river slipped by the old gray walls of the
house; Louis proudly showed off his Lima beans and
corn; and after we had eaten Mary's delicious luncheon,
we stretched out on the lawn. Mainbocher, the dressmaker, was there, the pride of Chicago, plump and
smooth under his French béret; the Italian Schiaparelli,
lean and wiry, with her round, sullen daughter, Gogo;
George Hawkins, the Bromfields' close friend and Louis'
secretary; four or five others; and ourselves. It was a
peaceful, pleasant day, caught in my memory like a fly
in amber.

We were in Paris for the Fourteenth of July and
watched the shining planes of France roar overhead as
the French army swung in review down the Champs
Elysées and thought what a great fighting race they
were and how invincible.

After a week in Paris we flew to London for a few
days before sailing for home. London was very gay,
and we dressed every night and went to the theater
and to supper at the Savoy; and Bill began to look like

a character out of *Esquire;* and we bought our last
presents; and were wined and dined by Harry Foster,
the English William Morris and his pretty wife, Florence; and we lunched at the Ivy with Tilly Losch, the
enchanting Viennese dancer, who is now Lady Car-
narvon and mistress of one of the greatest castles in
England. Tilly is pretty as a kitten, with a shrewd eye
for this world's goods. Just before her wedding another fair young creature who had once contemplated
marrying the noble lord herself, but who had since
become allied with the motion-picture hierarchy, perhaps brooding on what might have been, cautioned
her earnestly.

"It would be a pity, darling, if you were making a
mistake," said she. "Dukes and earls and things are
his only friends, and they can get very dull."

"Perhaps you are right, my darling," murmured the
kitten, her blue eyes dewy. "But they are surely no
duller than the top executives of Hollywood studios."

Also that day at the Ivy were Gina and Romney
Brent, those good people; they are now working in the
theater over here, and I am glad, because they are
witty and gay and gentle, hating sham and pomposity,
with ribald tongues and kind hearts, with pride and
inner dignity, outspoken in what they stand for, and
standing for the right. They picket night clubs where
the Vichy French congregate, they laugh their foolish
heads off, and they donate their blood to the Allied
wounded.

Those sunny July days in London we all laughed
a great deal and enjoyed ourselves hugely. We sailed
home on the *Ile de France,* and I think we will never
see that world again.

CHAPTER TWELVE

Free as Air

THE ADVERTISING AGENCY, AS IT STANDS today, is a peculiar manifestation of American business life of the twentieth century—glossy, brash, and insecure. I believe the pioneer offices have been functioning something like fifty years, but the boys began reaping the biggest hay with the advent of radio advertising in 1928.

Although the profits to be gained are enormous, the harvest hands are insecure, as they are at the mercy of the client's shifting mood, and the competition is cutthroat. Advertising men have raised the humble profession of traveling salesman to a high art. As the great manufacturers of household products live far from the East Forties in New York City, the habitat of most agencies, the slick young advertising men are constantly on the move, flying from Minneapolis to the Carolinas, from Chicago to Cincinnati, to persuade the purveyors of flour, cigarettes, beef, and soap that they are better able than the wretched outfit now handling the account to present the sponsor's product in an irresistible manner to an avid public.

If the sponsor's wife's Cousin Hetty has dined with them the night before and happened to remark that she didn't like the radio program, the competitive agency's seed of doubt falls on fertile ground. In order to sell his goods at a profit, the sponsor's appeal must necessarily be to the masses, whose intelligence in the aggregate he considers subnormal, and knowing Hetty, he feels she is a sound reaction barometer.

Once again the puckish quality of big business which makes it such an interesting study to the layman is manifest. The human element, which the imposing offices, stiff striped shirt fronts, and shiny dictaphones would seem to preclude, but which like an underground river is ever present, bubbles forth again. Because of it we are treated to the entertaining spectacle of one well-known advertising agency paying high fees for the strikingly indifferent services of a publicity organization, because said organization has an in with the better madams and the more amenable young ladies of the town, and regardless of one's lofty station, nature must be served. Besides, if one is able to render some such little service as this to an out-of-town client, well, after all, that's not the kind of thing a man forgets, and who knows but what it won't clinch the deal?

Though not so ubiquitous as in Hollywood, family ties are strong in the advertising business too, and more than one agency has been founded because a fair damsel whose poppa perhaps sells the nation its canned goods has looked with favor upon a winsome Yale man, has annexed him in holy matrimony, and has snuggled up to the old boy after dinner, murmuring wouldn't it be nice if he should set Joe up in business advertising the family edibles?

Agencies frequently quiver with internecine strife, and these battles are discussed with relish and chop-licking over the lunch tables of Louis and Armand's and Toots Schor's, restaurants catering largely to an advertising clientele. The lunchers are 90 per cent men, which demolishes the old theory that only women gossip. The boys love a good get-together, and I have heard the rival merits of favorite tailors discussed quite as heatedly as those of the ranking dressmakers, and the foibles of their colleagues are whooped over with joyful malice. Did you know that at Blank's Agency, Ralph and his girl spy write each other secret reports in a kind of code with no salutation and no signature, so that if anybody in the office picks them up they won't know what they're about? And did you know that over at Wynken, Blynken, and Nod's they keep that bum director on two shows because the fellow who's in charge of their radio department had a little trouble with a bank a few years back in his home town, and the bum director knows the details but he won't talk so long as he's well heeled? And it's notorious that a certain copy-writer gets a raise every six months because he is so adept at saluting the posterior of his immediate superior. It's very enlightening, and I am always happy when invited to lunch with the trade.

Though advertising can be a discouraging and un-grateful business—you may have cherished an account as a mother her ailing child, only to have it snatched away by an unscrupulous rival—it's a great wit-sharp-ener, and ingenuity is highly prized. I was myself much awed to realize that I worked for William Esty, the man

who, while handling the Lifebuoy account, hit upon
the idea that body odor was due to nervousness and not
necessarily lack of bathing. It was a tactful and subtly
flattering explanation, implying, as it did, that one was
sensitive and high-strung, and certainly as nice a way
as any of saying to somebody, "You smell."

Mr. Esty has a philosophy which, while chilly, is
probably sound, and that is, don't mix with the talent.
I worked for him for nearly two years and saw him once
for five minutes. He came into the office of Don Bernard,
who was directing *Luncheon at the Waldorf,* and suggested to me that while doing the broadcasts from
Boston, where I was going for the tryout of *Keep off the
Grass,* I get Hooton of Harvard for a guest. Having
worked at the agency for only a few weeks, I did not
know that it was a visitation from on high, and so I took
the boss in my stride, but everyone else was pale and impressed, and had I known, I probably would have been
too.

I didn't shake, but I didn't know what he was talking
about either. The fame of Mr. Hooton, the anthropolo-
gist, had not reached me, and when Mr. Esty left the
room, I admitted my ignorance to the assembled staff.

"Oh, you know him," said Rosemary Colihan airily.
"He was in *Life.*" I seemed dimly to recall some photographs of a gentleman in a white coat, surrounded by
lots of little skulls.

"Apes, dear," said Don Bernard.

"He loves monkeys," said Sylvia Dowling, who wrote
the commercials. "He thinks everybody's reverting to
them. He'll be crazy about you." And she flounced off to
lunch. With this meager and scarcely reassuring information I approached the eminent scientist.

Mr. Hooton came to the Ritz in Boston for the interview. He was tall, shaggy, a little stooped, and he held forth on mankind with penetrating insight and malice. He was delighted when he found my husband in agreement with his theories on progressive education, as they are both violent classicists. Bill complained that his son, who had spent several years at one of the best-known "progressive" schools in New York, at the age of eleven could only print.

"Ha," snorted Hooton, "there you have it. After thousands of years, man finally invented rapid cursive writing. It was one of the great advancements in learning of the human race. But what happens? Your modern schools scoff at that and deliberately set the children back to the old laborious way of forming letters. Boys come to me for examinations, and even if they know the subject (which is rare), fail time and again because they can't do the written exams in the allotted periods."

Bill chuckled gleefully when Hooton said he had recently delivered a lecture at Princeton on "Progressive Education, or the Decline of Literacy."

While we were in Boston the Hootons came to see *Keep off the Grass* and seemed to be entertained. I was relieved, as the revue was fairly bawdy in spots, and I didn't know how queasy the academic stomach might be. Mr. Hooton, on his side, was uncertain about actresses, and the day I lunched with him at Cambridge he confided gravely that he wouldn't have gone on the air for an ordinary actress, but that I was not ordinary. I thought it sweet of him to say that, as I don't suppose he meets many; academicians lead sheltered lives.

After luncheon he took me through his laboratory,

but the exhibit which interested me most was from the scientific point of view, I suspect, the most charlatan— a human head, in all its perfection, shrunk by Peruvian Indians to the size of a small doll's head. I believe they make a hole, remove the bones, and fill it with sand. What goes on after that, I don't know, nor do I intend to tamper with esoteric Indian rites. Mr. Hooton also showed me a big map of Ireland, stuck full of pins like a war map, but the pins showed where expeditions from Harvard had found ancient curious human skulls which were sent home for measurement and study. I am addicted to skulls, and it gave me a melancholy pleasure to see them, lying in neat rows on the great trays. They were wonderful in color, with the deep patina of old ivory. It was strange to hold a human head in one's hands and to think, "I too."

Another guest on our program was a very prominent gentleman, the head of one of New York's largest department stores, who behaved so badly that the rehearsal developed into a kind of verbal free for all, with insults winging like fly balls through the Empire Room. As he had been distinctly stuffy when I had talked to him, in writing the interview we had tried to insert a few witticisms to make him seem more interesting than he was, but he resented this departure from his stodginess and said laughter detracted from his dignity. He became so disagreeable that when he said we were trying to make a fool of him, I could only murmur that the Creator had beat us to it. His talk was largely about how young people should look for jobs.

"And he's the kid to tell them," snorted the lad from the Morris office, who was keeping an eye on rehearsal. "How would you like your boy to work for that fascist?"

"Listen to the son of a bitch," said the trumpet player with reluctant admiration, impressed that anyone should behave with such gall. But the fight was hardly fair— there were about twenty of us against one of him, and so, deciding perhaps to reserve his strength for more worthy opponents, he finally quieted down and is still, I do not doubt, being bumptious and aggressive to others in his rich paneled office atop his store.

The more I write the more I find literary integrity a problem. Should you recount exactly what happened, or should you be interesting? When our program went on the air at night as *Penthouse Party,* it was more of a vaudeville show, and reality was tossed overboard. But on *Luncheon* we were presenting bona-fide personalities, tops in their fields, and the trick was to write the interviews so that they told the truth, but were, whenever possible, entertaining. How to please the Pee-pul? Do they want to keep their illusions about celebrities, or is it not perhaps comforting to know that the illustrious are also flesh and blood, subject to life's crises? The cooks of the famous walk out on them too, and their children get runny noses; the rich can be as dull or insolent as the most obscure village boor, and the bright young novice does not always marry the boss's daughter; but this is not the kind of thing people yearn to hear, and so, although we told the truth in the interviews, it was not always whole and nothing but.

I would say that the most charming person I met while doing the program was Dr. Randolph Ray, the famous rector of New York's Little Church Around the Corner. At that time, his church had married 100,000 couples, and he told us that the groom is generally the more nervous, as he sees the doors of matrimony yawning before him and thinks, with a cold little shock, "I never thought it would lead to this when Archie said he had a sister."

He said that his church got its name back in 1870, when, under the Puritan influence, actors were taboo socially. George Holland, an eighty-year-old comedian, died, and his friend, Joe Jefferson, went to the Church of the Atonement to arrange for his burial, but Dr. Sabine refused to officiate, because Holland had been an actor.

"There's a little church around the corner," he said patronizingly, "which might take the funeral." And Joe Jefferson replied, "Then God bless the little church around the corner."

It is curious to see how class distinction is so deeply ingrained that it persists beyond the grave. I was particularly struck by this when on a lecture tour. In Detroit even the dead are rich. They lie in miles of spacious cemetery, under carefully tended lawns, differing scarcely at all from their Grosse Pointe estates; and at Arlington it is reassuring to find that rank is maintained in the afterlife, with the officers sleeping through eternity on one side of the driveway and the men at a respectful distance on the other.

Another guest on the program was Victor Hammer, one of the brothers who run the Hammer Galleries, where they are still selling off the magnificent collection of Russian crown jewels. He brought with him to the broadcast the elaborate and exquisite mirror which Napoleon gave to Madame Walewski, and when you press a button at the bottom of the handle, a small golden rose at the top of the mirror opens, and a little bird pops out and sings. He held it close to the microphone, and

it was strange to think that the liquid notes heard by a
lady beloved of an emperor a hundred and thirty years
ago were sounding soft and clear across a land, which,
if she thought of it at all, must have seemed to her an
eternal wilderness. There was a lump in my throat, because delicate and tinkling melody always touches me,
and I am more moved by a music box than by Wagner.

It is generally that way—the trivial things which are
gay and sad seem to me the most appealing; they have a
kind of poignant grace, and an ephemeral quality which
catches the heart. I am not ashamed of this, because in
their fragile scale such delights as a delicate tune, a
witty tale, an elegant piece of furniture are the flowering of discriminating and sensitive imaginations. But
I must also admit to a susceptibility to bathos, which is
less creditable: the little match girl on Christmas Eve,
a dog searching for its master, Old Glory fluttering in
the breeze—all the standard tear-jerkers reduce me to
pulp, and I go gulping, sobbing, and kicking myself at
the same time. And whenever they play the "Battle
Hymn of the Republic" or "Auld Lang Syne" there is a
cloudburst. It so happens that those are two stirring airs,
but tears are not necessarily a gauge of quality, although we are inclined to think they are and to consider that if we have wept over a play or a book it must
be very fine indeed. Sometimes, however, our enthusi-
asms are sound, and one of my pet music-makers is
Larry Adler, who evokes magic tones from a harmonica,
so that you think the bass fiddle and the oboe are
united in sonorous concord, and Mr. Adler now plays
solo with Philharmonics, and he and Paul Draper give
concerts in Carnegie Hall, and he is considered a serious
musician and his musical knowledge is great, but he has

an urchin face, and I don't care how grand he looks in his white tie and tails, Mr. A. is a classy dresser. I remember him in a room of the Ritz Hotel in Boston, when Eileen, his enchanting wife, and I sat on the bed, and Larry, in his undershirt, with a towel wrapped around his freshly shampooed head, his flexible fingers caressing the harmonica, played Bach like a soul inspired.

Another intimate concert I shall always remember was the night Bill and I and Heywood Broun and two or three other people sat in Tony's kitchen about two o'clock one morning. They said there was a man outside who wanted to see Heywood, and he left the table but came back in a few minutes and said, "It's Paul Robeson. I asked him to come in, but he said he didn't like to unless I asked you if you minded." We said of course we didn't and to have him join us; so the great Negro baritone came and sat with us, and in a little while he started to sing very softly some of the oldest spirituals of his race. The kitchen was quiet and empty, except for ourselves and a waiter dozing on his chair, as in a voice like the muted tolling of a bell Robeson sang "Go Down, Moses." It echoed the nostalgia of his people and it was the loneliest sound I ever heard, like the far-off whistle of a train on the night prairies.

At one time I was most anxious to have Dorothy Maynor, the famous Negro soprano, sing on my program, but I was refused permission to ask her, on the grounds that she sang like a cultivated white singer. If she sang spirituals or boogie woogie, or otherwise showed that she knew her place, that was all right, but this raising oneself above the ruck is not to be encouraged. Many and strange are the ways of censorship in the land of the free.

Swinging from the art world, we brought to the microphone that prodigious old party, the cornerstone of café society, Lady Mendl. She had recently arrived from Europe, the swankest refugee, complete with Rolls-Royce, maid, secretary, Sir Charles Mendl, Johnny McMullin, and two miniature dogs, and had established herself and retinue at the St. Regis, where she promptly redecorated her suite. The hotel was delighted, because when she moves from one suite into another, which happens frequently, they are able to rent them immediately at high prices, on account of the Elsie de Wolfe touch. Within the green walls against masses of white flowers she entertains profusely at cocktail parties the same shifting international set who wandered from Versailles to the Lido to St. Moritz before the junkets of the German armies interfered with civilian travel. From Berlin to Paris, to London, to Lisbon, to New York they have fled, desperately evading danger and discomfort, feverishly seeking a refuge where the cannon and the marching feet will not rumble in their ears. But even to New York the echoes reach; one wonders where they will go next.

The cracked, raucous voice of the hostess may be heard echoing down the corridors as she receives her friends, exquisitely dressed and looking like a chic old bug, her eyes snapping, a pert velvet bow in her hair. Her fame is well merited, because she is immensely entertaining, and at eighty her vigor is unimpaired. I think she admits to over seventy, but Johnny McMullin, the old friend who lives with the Mendls, says he and

Sir Charles have reason to believe she is a ripe eighty. About ten years ago Elsie lost her passport, Johnny relates, and he is convinced a little sleight-of-hand work went on when the new one was issued. Perhaps she should indulge in the old trick attributed to Sarah Bernhardt, who, as she grew really old, piled on the years so that her friends would say how young she looked.

During her business life Lady Mendl's achievement was great. When she worked as a decorator, her prices caused oil kings to blench, but the Elsie de Wolfe cachet was a guarantee of more than expense; it also meant incomparable elegance. I happened to remark how well Condé Nast's apartment still looked and she said, "You know, I was very touched. I dined there the other night; there were only six of us, but Mr. Nast had lighted all the candles for me, hundreds of them. Nothing had been changed since the day I finished the house for him nearly twenty years ago, and I think his rooms are still lovely." I replied that that was because the beautiful things had been loved and cared for—they had the enduring quality of the lady who placed them there—and she said, "Thank you, my dear. That is my only boast, that I did good work. The other day I met a woman in Southampton, and she said to me, 'You don't remember me, but thirty years ago you decorated my house, and it is still in excellent condition.' People used to say I was expensive, but I gave value received!"

Probably Elsie de Wolfe's greatest influence was in the use of chintz. "Americans thought chintz was like calico," she says scornfully, "only to be used in country cottages, but I brought it out of the kitchen into the drawing room, the way they did in the great houses in England." When the ignorant Americans got the bill, they hastily started designing ballrooms as the only places grand enough for this costly fabric. In reminiscing about the old days Lady Mendl referred wistfully to a favorite client. "She was the heiress to the Atlantic City wheel-chair fortune. I think of her tenderly; she always paid cash, dear—carried hunks of it around in her handbag." And then there was the woman who insisted on buying the chairs from Miss de Wolfe's own dining room because she liked to think of the famous people who had sat on them.

Once she got a taste of ether, Lady Mendl was crazy about radio and wanted Bill to get her a program of her own. Bill admired her because she was so mettlesome during the broadcast, putting in the expression, thumping the table and jingling her bracelets, and when the portable microphone hindered her from reading her script, she pushed it firmly away with a fine disregard for the listeners-in. We enjoyed it, but the engineer went slightly mad, and Bill tried to dissuade her from the idea of a program of her own, fearing she was perhaps too perishable for twenty-six-week options, but I'm not so sure myself. She is a hardy perennial.

Another lady of stamina and achievement and one who hides her brains behind a bland baby face is Elizabeth Arden, the flutterbug. Miss Arden is one of the richest women in America. She has built an industry independent of masculine aid and has held it against the encroachments of banks and syndicates who wished to help lap up the gravy. Yet to meet her is to wonder whether she knows about coming in out of the rain. She does, but she burbles on so happily about her creams and lotions and the new mask—"I didn't *know* we could do such *wonderful* things"—and her dear horsies in Kentucky that you smile indulgently and think funny little thing; and while you are thinking it, she is whipping up another million dollars.

We had her on the program, and at rehearsal she chortled and burbled and fussed like a yellow chick and read her script so uncertainly that we became alarmed for her performance, till it occurred to me that probably a pair of specs would turn the trick. She was reluctant at first, fearing, I suppose, to dispel the glamour, but she finally hauled out the old horn-rims, and our troubles were over.

One of the most able and human women I ever interviewed was Henrietta Additon, the superintendent of Westfield State Farm, the women's prison at Bedford Hills, New York. She is a kindly and humorous person with a zest for life, remarkable in one whose days must be largely devoted to much that is gloomy and tragic. She told me something of the great strides being made in women's prisons, the efforts to rehabilitate the girls, to give them interests so that they may find some happiness even in jail, but much that she said we couldn't use on the air, for fear of arousing the displeasure of the Philistines and politicians if they heard that prison wasn't unadulterated hell. She told me that pregnant women are frequently brought into detention houses, but at Westfield Farm they go outside for the birth of their babies, so that no child shall carry through its life the stigma of having been born in jail. The babies are kept in a nursery just outside the prison walls, and the mothers are allowed to see them frequently, until they are a year old, when they are sent away.

She was interested in my interest in her job, because she said she had asked her friend Fannie Hurst

about me, and Miss Hurst had said I was very nice but
frankly she couldn't imagine my caring about penology.
There she was wrong, I care a good deal but it reminded
me a little of the time a reporter asked Sibelius what he
thought of Stokowski, and the master answered that he
thought him a fine man, very interesting, very interested
in many things, but he added, "Not, I think, in music."

When I asked Miss Additon if some such social work
had always been her ambition, she answered, "Heavens,
no. When I was a kid I wanted to be a professional
baseball pitcher. I really had a good curve."

My acquaintance with baseball players is slight, but
I know the best, for Mr. Joe di Maggio and I are on
limited but cordial terms, and I can say, "Hello, Joe,"
any time I meet him in Toots Schor's, and he knows
who I am. The fact that he is friendly shows a generous
nature, because my ignorance of baseball is so abysmal
that he must have found conversation with me uphill
work. When he came to the house for the interview he
was accompanied by four or five large men who all
sat around in complete silence, except for the abrupt
guffaws they emitted at every question I asked him. My
husband was also present, enjoying himself, rather
cruelly I felt, and my stepson, Bill, aged fifteen, who
had come on the run when he heard the great Di Mag
was to be at the house. Young Bill didn't laugh at my
boners. He just shook his head in sad bewilderment and
said, "Gee, Ilka," in a hopeless tone. Mr. di Maggio was
charming, and neither laughed nor looked pained, but
tried ever so patiently to explain the esoteric mysteries
of hitting safely in consecutive games and striking out.
I asked him if his position in the game was that of
batter, and he said very nicely that that wasn't the way

they worked it in baseball, and when I said that baseball
seemed quite horticultural, what with the bush leagues
and the ivy leagues, he agreed. I questioned him about
those uniforms too—ball players look so unaesthetic
running around in their gray union suits—but he explained that that was for practicality, because what with
all that exercise and heat, they sweat, and otherwise
they might catch cold. And it was certainly interesting
when he told me that the first time he was at bat he
hit a triple to the right field fence. I could tell right
away that was an achievement from the expression of
reverence on young Bill's face, and all the large men
said in unison, "Yeah, he hit a triple."

We touched on other topics as well, because Joe owns
a restaurant, The Grotto, on Fisherman's Wharf in San
Francisco, where he and his five brothers grew up. Their
father was an Italian fisherman, and all his sons have
been attached to ball clubs at one time or another in
their lives. Joe says the restaurant was his brother Tom's
idea. "It seemed to him a good one," he continued,
"since I was the fellow with the capital. You know how
those things are. Tom estimated ten thousand, I agreed
to forty, and in the end it cost sixty." I gathered, however, that the diamond king was doing all right on his
little flier in the culinary department, and that he is
his own largest consumer of chiappino. He says it's a sea-
food dish with red gravy, and you have to wear a
catcher's mask to eat it.

Another gourmet of renown, Mr. Maury Paul, has
also been our guest. Mr. Paul would be that Cholly
Knickerbocker who dishes out to his gaping public the
doings of the *haut monde,* the chronicler of the births,
deaths, marriages, and recurrent divorces of the inmates

of the *Social Register*. The Paul style is richly be-
sprinkled with quotation marks around words which
seem quite run-of-the-mill to other writers: home, party,
gag, social refugees, hubby, youth, deb, no news, and
such names as Jack, Sonny, Bea, and Ed. But I like it;
I think it shows a spirit not blasé; one still alert to the
commonplace. I have kidded Maury about this habit,
and he says cheerfully that there are so many words he's
uncertain of that he does it for protection; if anyone
calls him to task, he can always say he was only kidding.

I think the story of his early beginnings shows enter-
prise. Apparently when he announced to the editors of
the Philadelphia press—Philadelphia is his native city—
his ambition to be a social reporter, they were blind to
the riches he offered, but, nothing daunted, he per-
severed. His methods were ingenious, if a teensy bit on
the nefarious side. The Philadelphia *Evening Times*
was owned by Frank Munsey. "My dear, it couldn't
have been a more obscure sheet," says Mr. Paul candidly.
"They already had a kind of society editor, but he was
also the office factotum, handling impartially society,
theatrical notices, the obits"—I here interrupted to remark that the two were often closely akin—"dog shows,
church notices, and the rag, tag, and bobtail of news
items. The upshot of it was that the harried wretch
had no time to check his sources, so that he slapped
into his columns any information sent in, regardless of
accuracy, with, one may suppose, a mute and hurried
prayer that there'd be no law suits."

At this point in his story I began to suspect my good
friend of practice the least bit sharp.

"Maury," I said sternly, "did you do what I think
you did?"

"Well, dear," he replied, "it's a hard world; a fellow has to use his wits. I bought about ten boxes of swell assorted stationery and mailed that poor *Times* a raft of incorrect social items."

This dastardly scheme worked. Yelps went up from social Philadelphia when they read the announcements that Mrs. Thistleton Cadwallader had entertained at a luncheon for twelve at her house in Spruce Street Thursday last when the whole world knew that Mrs. C. lived in Walnut Street, wouldn't be seen dead at the luncheon table, but had given a dinner for twenty on St. Swithin's Eve.

When he had collected sufficient ammunition, Maury bearded the editor. "Look at this," he cried triumphantly, waving a sheaf of his own false clippings. "You can't afford to go on printing these boners, and I'm the fellow who can track down the truth. How about taking me on as Editor of Society?"

"And," said I, "I suppose the man said, 'Come in, my boy. You're the answer to our prayers.'"

Maury grinned, "Well, it was a reasonably accurate facsimile."

It appears that when his Philadelphia editor could bear no more, Frank Munsey removed the budding Ward McAllister to his New York *Press*. "That was in 1914, my pigeon, and I barely knew an Astor from a Vanderbilt," says Mr. Paul, "but nothing fazed me." His big night came when he covered his first Metropolitan Opera opening. He didn't know who the box-holders were, but the old ingenuity didn't desert him; he just went around and took the names down from the brass door plates. There was only one slight hitch: he didn't know that even after people died, in those days their names remained on their opera boxes, and so he briskly reported that the opening had been attended by several gentlemen whose only possible interest in music could have been twanging harps. The following morning Mrs. Stuyvesant Fish called Mr. Frank Munsey to remark tartly that he must have a ghoul as a social editor: he had looted every grave in Woodlawn Cemetery. Fortunately for Maury, his boss had a sense of humor and was more amused than sore.

He has worked for Hearst for the past twenty-five years, and his column of social gossip is syndicated in more than one hundred and nineteen papers. If it is the servant girl's delight, it is also pored over by the spotlighted creatures whose doings it retails with the same avidity with which actors read their notices. This was brought home to him at his first meeting with Mrs. Cornelius Vanderbilt. "To tell you the truth," he recounts, "I'd been writing pretty freely of Mrs. Vanderbilt's comings and goings for a good many years without ever having met her. One day I was unexpectedly introduced to her at a luncheon of Vincent Astor's. She fixed me with a fishy and hostile eye; I gulped and said, 'Mrs. Vanderbilt, I'm really not the disreputable person you must think me.' For an instant she did not reply, then her eyes began to twinkle. 'But, Mr. Paul,' she said, 'after reading about myself in your column all these years, I had come to the conclusion I was the disreputable one.'" This, it seems, cemented a bond which still endures.

Of all the people I have interviewed on the air, and there have been dozens of them, I regret to say that the dullest are the actors. To be sure, they speak up and they have a sense of timing, but their lifelong training undermines them; they have nothing amusing to say on their own, and you have to provide the material. Give them the script, tell them to read it, and they do all right. Try to get them to tell you entertaining and colorful stories about themselves, to express some philosophy or viewpoint, and you're up against a stone wall. The notable exceptions to this are Cornelia Otis Skinner, Howard Lindsay, and Tallulah Bankhead. The first two are, after all, writers as well as actors, and so their brains are more spry, and Miss Bankhead is a colorful belle with a mind of her own and an eloquent tongue.

When Tallulah was on the program we had a fine display of the censorial mind at work. When *Penthouse Party* switched to a different network for the summer of 1941, everybody said to me, "You'll love it over there. They're heaps more lenient and human. You'll be able to get away with lots of things this setup frowns on. It's kind of cozy." It is, eh? I find that censors are censors, regardless of the network they serve, and muzzling of free speech is enforced with a practiced hand.

In the Bankhead interview I had Tallulah saying in reply to some remark of mine about her success on the London stage, "Well, Ilka, I love England. You know I lived there for many years." It was shortly before we entered the war, and this apparently innocuous statement was not allowed, on the grounds that it was British propaganda. The Intellects changed it to read, "I love the English theater." Tallulah, at the time, had a lion cub named Winston Churchill, which name was likewise anathema to the censors, but that one we slipped in anyhow. When I asked her what she called her pet, she replied, "A courageous lion? Why, what else could he be named but Winston Churchill?" and the audience burst into applause. I waged a pitched and bloody battle over the "I love England" business, pointing out with what I hoped was scathing sarcasm that our relations with England were, on the whole, friendly, and that would they review the newspapers of the past few months they would find some interesting items anent lend-lease bills and destroyers. My jibes fell on concrete. Had the Camel people themselves objected to the script, that would have been a different story, because, regardless of my feelings, they could have said with justification that they were paying the piper, and it may be supposed that manufacturers of cigarettes are indifferent to their customers' political leanings so long as they smoke their brand. As the agency had no objection, it seemed to me the network was overofficious, nor was I impressed by their obvious fence-straddling so as not to offend Axis sympathizers. I thought it a risk they might well afford, as the trend was obvious. It was like the busybody who quibbled over the wisdom of making a picture called *A Yank in the R.A.F.* on the grounds that public sentiment had not crystallized. He was silenced by the retort that it had crystallized enough to make a production called *A Yank in the Luftwaffe* inadvisable.

My battle was in vain, however; the offending line was removed. "But why don't you say it anyhow?" people ask. The reason is because it's useless; the master control will take you off the air. During the ASCAP row (this was a little difference of opinion between the American Society of Authors, Composers, and Publishers and the national networks on the matter of royalties), while I was describing a New Year's Eve party, I said that at midnight someone played "Auld Lang

Syne" on the piano, adding as a mild little joke, "Because it's not ASCAP." The broadcasting company,
hypersensitive and goaded to the quick by the number
of ASCAP jokes on the air, which always got tremen-
dous laughs from the audience and highly entertained
irresponsible comedians, clamped down on the use of
the word. This seemed to me a new high in silliness, and
as it had neither political nor moral significance, I informed them I would read the line as it stood. I did,
it got a big laugh, but we were off the air for five
seconds. The listeners, hearing their radios go dead,
must have thought they needed new tubes.

The networks' alarm that the talent might in even the
most innocuous terms express a personal opinion about
the war (before we were in it) was pitiable. In one
broadcast, describing the Luce dinner for China, I
ended by saying, "It is to be hoped it yielded a rich
harvest for a courageous and gallant people. Another
people certainly deserving of our help are the Dutch
(this was shortly after the invasion of that country),
and Yvette will sing for us the charming little song
about two Dutch children." The tune was "My Sister
and I," and the reference to Holland was by way of
a song cue. This was changed to read, "It is reported it
[the dinner] yielded a rich harvest for the Chinese,
and now as a gesture to another land across the sea,
Yvette will sing, etc." One may protest, and rightly, that
these changes in no way impair the literary integrity of
the speaker's deathless prose, but they rankle at the time
and are an interesting sidelight on the breathtaking
feats of tightrope walking performed by the major networks.

Of course the agencies themselves have another whole

set of taboos, which the talent soon learns they must accept or else. It is death to mention the word "lucky" on the Camel program. One may not say, "What a lucky break," or, "You lucky boy," which sometimes leads to such circumlocutions as, "What a fortuitous circumstance," and, "You favored child of fortune." The word "strike" is also anathema, and it is the copywriter's headache when he must write a whole commercial on bowling without once mentioning the obscene syllable. When I interviewed Joe di Maggio it was a neat trick not to let it slip when discussing baseball.

I understand that packers are just as bitter. On the Armour program no one is swift; they are quick, brisk, or agile. And on the Swift offering, knights in armor are taboo. It is a lamentable truth that a remunerative and once free element, the air, is permeated by fear. The talent fears dismissal by the advertising agencies; the agencies fear their clients' whims and the withdrawal of accounts; in a showdown on material or policy the clients must bow to the networks, who in turn live in dread of having their license revoked by the Federal Communications Commission. I suppose that the Federal Communications Commission exists in uneasy anticipation of squawks from the public should it not care for messages born on the ether bands, although considering the quality of much of the material which the listeners endure with sheeplike submission, their revolt will probably be long in coming; over a period of time their finer sensibilities will have been dulled by the balderdash meted out to them. Why those so devoted to censorship have never set up a board of aesthetic standards is mystifying, but it may be assumed that the censorial mind is scarcely of a caliber to recognize such a standard when it sees one. It is only when it has been well stung by its own gullibility that the public's temper is quick to flare, as was evinced by the overwhelming and farcical reaction to the Orson Welles Martian broadcast, which still holds the record as radio's most gargantuan pain in the neck. When we see the grotesque and humiliating spectacle of adult human beings fleeing in panic and swallowing poison in preference to combating the imaginary invasion of the mythical gents from Mars, it is time either to despair of human common sense or drastically to revise our educational system.

Signor Marconi must squirm in his grave when he hears some of the uses to which his great invention has been put. It is ironic that men suffered and studied, sacrificed and labored to perfect a medium to unite all men, to disseminate knowledge, only to have 90 per cent of the messages conveyed through it geared to the comprehension of a twelve-year-old mentality, the standard I.Q. of the mass mind. Radio, which might be an incomparable channel for enlightenment, has done more than its share to debase our intellectual standards.

CHAPTER THIRTEEN

Luncheon at the Waldorf

FOR SOME TIME BILL HAD HAD THE IDEA OF
a daytime radio show which would star me and be a departure from the soap operas with which the ether is
surfeited. Neither of us felt that I would be convincing
as a village maid who sees good in everything and who is
able to lift the mortgage, remaining virtuous the while.
That is a neat trick, said my William, and requires more
the Martha Scott type. He finally got together with
Richard Marvin, of the William Esty agency, who
handles the Camel account, and between them they
evolved the idea of *Luncheon at the Waldorf*.

It was considered revolutionary, because although
presented in the daytime, it was aimed to appeal to the
upper middle class and the slightly educated instead of
the lowest mental and income brackets, which is supposedly the audience of the soap opera, so called because the endless serials are for the most part sponsored
by soap manufacturers, Rinso, Ivory Flakes, Camay, etc.

There is a curious assumption, on the part of radio magnates, that the national mentality is at lowest ebb during the daytime, so that the fare they parcel out then is even more innocuous, if possible, than the evening menus. This attitude is as unflattering as it is false, and I have found, at least among those who listen to my broadcasts, that audiences are pathetically grateful because I have presupposed they have a mind. As my own is nothing which is likely to overwhelm them, we have always gotten along very well, and I am proud that my program is considered, in a small way, an intellectual stimulus—two-syllable words and a more sophisticated point of view. It turns out that the listeners can take it. If I boast a little, it is because we were modest pioneers, the Esty agency apparently feeling that the R. J. Reynolds Tobacco Company could afford to be, as the adventure would cost but a pittance. A pittance in radio parlance, that is to say, for despite that simile glibly tossed about, the air is far from free; from the purchaser's point of view it is in the same category as jewels, furs, or yachts. But in the case of *Luncheon at the Waldorf,* for a mere few thousand bucks a week the sponsors could tap the literate moneyed and, they fervently hoped, smoking women of the country. For many years Camels had been sold on their rugged appeal, but the policy had recently been switched to lure the gentler bred—the ladies whom the Reynolds Tobacco Company was paying to smoke its cigarettes while sipping coffe and piloting their planes on the back covers of the slick-paper magazine. These ladies smilingly confide to the admiring subscribers that Camels are delicious and soothing to the nerves, and the implication is that if you smoke them, you too may marry a wealthy scion, jump purebred hunters, and cop prizes with your setters or your peonies. The ladies are the McCoy, but whether or not they smoke Camels, once the photographer is out of sight, is their own dark secret.

When Bill came home and told me the contract for the broadcasts had been signed, I was delighted at the thought of the lovely dross I would pocket and which I do not hesitate to mention, as, God knows, my salary is no secret from the Collector of Internal Revenue, and I was pleased at the idea of the publicity, as I thought it would be good for me in the theater. I did not expect to enjoy the work, being of the school who thinks, "Dear Heaven, daytime radio!" In this I was wrong, as it turned out to be a lot of fun.

Bill told me that Esty thought the idea of the *Luncheon* was good, but he feared that I might not be able to deliver the guests. "But I know you can," said Bill stanchly. "There'll be no difficulty about that." And he proceeded to paint bright pictures of distinguished people streaming to my door. Having followed Dorothy Dix for many years, I know it is woman's place to encourage her helpmate, not to tear down his confidence, but a chill rippled up my spine. I thought, suppose nobody will let me interview them, and I started awake at night in a cold sweat from dreaming I stood alone at the microphone, surrounded by a milling throng of Wigman dancers wagging enormous masked heads and cackling shrilly, "She can't get anyone, she can't get anyone." I might have slept on undisturbed, as the guests were almost without exception not only extremely agreeable about appearing, but generally snapped at the chance. After the program became *Penthouse Party* and went on at night, the setup was different, with professional enter-

tainers exclusively, who are blasé about radio and are
paid rich sums. But in the *Waldorf* days it was amusing
to watch the dawn of speculation in the eyes of those
who had an ax to grind when it was brought home to
them that thousands of people would hear them, that
their names and words would carry into people's intimate lives, however briefly.

As it had been decided in conclave that there should
be one spot on the program devoted to the parties I had
been to—"your glamorous life, dear"—my first purchase
was a diary, a chunky black book like a small Bible,
which said "Daily Reminder" on the cover. I have never
been able to sustain a diary for any length of time, but
as my memory is a guttering candle, lighting the unim-
portant with fitful flares and leaving the good copy in
deepest gloom, I needed the Daily Reminder's steady
glow to illuminate my activities.

I sometimes worry about my preoccupation with the
trivial, but it is the intimate, personal, and simple things
of life which seem to me to have warmth and color and
which really evoke a personality. The sonorous orations
and weighty documents leave me cold. What books did
the great man read? What quirks of personality annoyed
him? Was he a jealous lover? These are the things
I wish to know. On a trip to Washington I was enchanted to learn that one morning Mr. Stimson, the
Secretary of War, and Mr. Hull, the Secretary of State,
had had a violent argument, from which Mr. Stimson
was still smarting as he sat in the late afternoon in the
grounds of the Wardman Park Hotel, where Mr. Hull
lives. Mr. Hull, having emerged victorious from the
matutinal skirmish, was engaged in an unruffled game
of croquet, upon which, it appears, he dotes. The two-

year-old son of a Department of War assistant was playing in a near-by sand pile, gazing with interest upon the
prowess of the Secretary of State. The Secretary of War
saw his chance for sweet revenge. "Peter," said he, "how
would you like to go and kick Mr. Hull's ball away from
that wicket while he isn't looking?" Peter started off
with happy crows, and it was only his mother's grabbing
him by the seat of his jiffy pants which averted an Inci-
dent whose repercussions one quails to contemplate.

I regret to say I derive more satisfaction from these
stories than from a penetrating analysis of international
politics. It is like the wondrous book, *The Scandal and
Credulities of John Aubrey*, a treasure-trove of gossip
of the late sixteenth and early seventeenth century, in
which that busybody relates that, sitting around the
Mermaid Tavern, Ben Jonson was heard to observe
testily that although Will Shakespeare bragged that he
never blotted out a line in his life, he, Jonson, could wish
he would blot out a thousand. And Aubrey goes on to
tell us that as a boy Shakespeare worked in his father's
butcher shop, but that when he "killed a calfe, he
would doe it in a high style, and make a speech"; also
his accounts of some of the smart set's hotter love affairs
are graphic and hugely entertaining.

Although I have seldom found out about their love affairs, I have been amused by the foibles, prejudices, and
pastimes of some of the celebrities whom I have interviewed on the air.

Lotte Lehmann was our first guest, and she was a
pet, large and placid and looking just like my idea of an
opera star. Her gentle smile and soft eyes have nothing
of professional razzle-dazzle, and she talks simply and
charmingly with her pretty Viennese accent. At the

time I met her she had recently taken up painting and was keen about it. In telling me of Nikol Schattenstein's reaction to her first endeavors, she assured me gravely that he had been "flabbergoosed." This delighted me, and I wanted her to say it on the air, but when we came to the broadcast, someone had unfortunately enlightened her as to the Hollywood usage of goose as a verb, and she felt uneasy and wouldn't repeat it. She ended her interview with a brief plea for contributions to save the opera. Indeed, all through the winter of 1940 everybody you met was hell bent on rescuing classical music; the Metropolitan was in danger of perishing from lack of funds, and there were benefits galore. One of the gayest was given in the tiny theater atop the Chanin Building; it was a kind of burlesque concert, with the final number conducted by the maestro himself, Toscanini.

Lawrence Tibbett, whom I had never thought of as a comedian, having seen him in movies, sang an hilarious version of "Drink to Me Only with Thine Eyes." His musical audience was convulsed, because it seems it's very hard for a good musician to sing deliberately off so many keys. Personally, I was not impressed—singing off key is no trick at all for me. The climax of his performance, however, was very fine, as he had accompanied the song with a breathtakingly skillful bit of pantomime. His pants kept causing him embarrassing difficulty, and he kept trying inconspicuously to hike them up. He clutched surreptitiously at the retreating garments, a fixed, desperate smile on his face, his voice swooping and breaking from key to key, but with the final note they dropped in a swift cascade to his ankles. He stood revealed in tails and shorts to thunderous applause.

The finale to the concert was a rendering of "Perpetual Motion" by an orchestra of precocious kiddies. Little Jascha Heifetz in middy blouse and knickers played the first fiddle, tiny Alfred Wallenstein sawed away at the cello, and wee Vladimir Horowitz pounded the ivories. The rest of the ensemble was composed of obscure talents such as William Primrose and Nathan Milstein. Sour notes rent the air, and Toscanini mopped his brow with a huge red handkerchief and shook his fists to heaven in mock fury. Then they played Paganini's exercise in technique as it should be played, but for one who is not a glutton for the food of love, it was a little monotonous. Supper was served in a large room across the hall from the theater, but when we complimented Toscanini on his pupils and the masterly way he had handled them, and especially on the sly use of the commodious handkerchief, he was in despair. "I have a big red one from Wagner, from Wagner," he cried. "Every day I put it out ready for tonight, and tonight I forget to bring it." This struck me as being so typical of myself that I was charmed. It is doubtless, thought I, that you too are a genius, little one. There having been no further evidence of our kinship, I have since discarded the idea.

For sometime I had been commenting on the Fox Technicolor fashion shorts, and so I thought it would be a good plan to interview Vyvyan Donner. The shorts had gone well, because luckily I had hit on the idea of kidding them, and apparently it was the first time a commentator's remarks had echoed the audience's sentiments. Men began to enjoy them too, as the models were luscious, and they also got a few laughs. Vyvyan Donner, who had been producing them for a long time, is plump and fluttering, and the nearest thing to a pigeon

you can get in the human race. She is no Mrs. Harrison
Williams for chic, but she is an extremely able producer,
and we had good times working together, and she has a
romantic and sentimental soul. She would generally
chortle at my quips, but she would utter little protest-
ing cries when she thought I was being too tough on her
young ladies who modeled the clothes. They were certainly fair of face, but even the elementary histrionics
which they were called upon to deliver in a fashion short
often proved too much for them, and I would sometimes
hurl a few vocal darts, which brought laughter from
the audience but pierced the soft breast of my sentimental pigeon, and she would cluck and plead and beg
me to soften my attack the next time, and I would try,
but the saccharine sweetness of the vapid smiles would
bring out the beast in me, and I would forget that I had
taken the pledge and let fly.

My first real coup on the program, because I had to
screw up my courage for the attack, was Dorothy Thompson. I was eager to interview her, because she was obviously an excellent name and a strong personality, but
there was also another reason. I had long admired the
lady and had felt for her that friendly interest which
ripens into a kind of affection when one shares many
common experiences, although for the most part she was
unaware of our mutual participation. The first time I
met her was at the Toscanini party, when she and her
escort shared a supper table with Bill and me. She knew
a great deal about everything and was very articulate.
Even Bill, who generally knows more than anybody
present, had to play second fiddle. When they were in
college together, a friend of my husband's once observed
that Bill didn't know as much as God, but that he knew

as much as God knew at his age, and it is indisputable
that he has an acquisitive mind and a retentive memory,
but so has Miss Thompson, and she has a firmer jaw
than Bill.

Toscanini came up to our table and greeted her with
a warm kiss, and she observed complacently that he always did that, because she was the one person who
didn't fuss over him. I wish I could learn to maintain
this nice balance in the presence of the great. When I
am genuinely impressed by people I behave like a fool.
Either I am awed to dumbness or else, in an access of
shyness, I babble and gurgle in a way that congeals my
own blood. When I met Aldous Huxley in Hollywood
at a Sunday luncheon party of George Cukor's, I distinguished myself by my gaucherie. I think Mr. Huxley
one of the most adroit writers of our day, though I admit
to complete bafflement through the greater part of *After
Many a Summer Dies the Swan,* and I drooled over
him, "Oh, Mr. Huxley, I think you're the most wonderful writer there is; I think you're absolutely marvelous; I
just love your books, Mr. Huxley." The look of one who
has bit into a bad shrimp flitted across his face, and I
was mercifully silenced. I think everyone enjoys admiration, but my trowel technique was repugnant to the
aesthetic Mr. Huxley, who might have lapped it up
from a fine silver spoon. To me he didn't talk again, but
I overheard him telling Elsa Maxwell, his left-hand
neighbor, when he could get a word in edgewise, that
Metro had decided to shelve the life of Madame Curie,
because after working on it for some months, he one
day told them the story, and they had said in alarm,
"Jesus, who's going to go for a dame who goes for
chemistry." This cheered me up a bit, but I still felt I

had behaved stupidly, so when I got the chance I listened to Miss Thompson that I might get a few pointers on the care and handling of celebrities. In fact, our whole group became so engrossed that the party melted away around us, and we were roused and sent on our way only by the malevolent clatter of the waiters piling tables.

After that, though we seemed to frequent the same places, we moved in separate spheres. I have glimpsed her at Twenty One, surrounded by her intellectual friends; I have spied her whisking up and down the aisles at Philharmonic concerts. She is apparently devoted to music, which bond my husband shares, and I don't mind it either. I could wish for more comfortable chairs, but one can't have everything.

The night Clare Boothe's play, *Margin for Error*, opened, Dorothy Thompson came with Henry Luce. He and I exchanged a few words, but Thompson passed quickly into the theater. It was close though; I felt that had I had a little salt I would have made the grade. Our most unlikely meeting was on the platform of the Hanover station in the early morning. We had gone up to see Dartmouth play Cornell, and were dumped out of the train at an ungodly hour, and who should be dumped after us but my will-of-the-wisp. It was an icy morning, and she was looking very snug in gray astrakhan. I smiled and said, "Hello," and so did Bill, and as she looked receptive but bewildered, we hastily added who we were. I believe in that. I think people who leave you dangling are triple pigs. My own suffering from mental-pause in these situations is acute.

She said, "Oh yes," gave a vague smile, and hurried away. The next night after the game we were on the same train going home. I suggested to Bill we ask her in for a drink, but at that moment, the door of her compartment was banged to, and my courage ebbed.

Ordinarily I would have pursued the lady no further —either accepting fate or else hoping that in the normal course of social life I should again have the pleasure of meeting her. What precipitated my quest was the program. Gee whiz, I asked myself, do you suppose she'd do it? What the hell? I replied, ask her. All she can say is no. At last, after a search for her address, leading over hill, over dale, over the *Herald Tribune,* and over Central Park West, I presented my request, by letter. Her answer came prompt, courteous, and in the affirmative. There were further negotiations through the phalanx of secretaries, and a meeting was arranged.

I went to Miss Thompson's apartment in the late afternoon. I don't know what she was having for dinner, but it smelled delicious, and I sniffed happily as I sat in the large, pleasantly conventional living room overlooking the park.

She came in wearing a simple dark blue frock and looking very pretty. Miss Thompson's brains have been considerably publicized, but I don't think people realize how attractive she is. Her hair is lovely, short and silvery and curly, and she has a clear fresh complexion.

Considering how much work she does, how organized her life is, and the number of people she knows, my judgment must obviously be wrong, but I had that day the distinct impression of a woman at a loose end. It may have been only a mood, but she seemed vague and distracted. She was nice and co-operative, and I got plenty of material for the interview, but I felt her heart lay elsewhere. In European chancelleries, maybe.

She was grand on the air, funny and sincere and self-possessed, but I had been a little worried, because at luncheon she had appeared very upset. A friend of hers, an Austrian, it seems, had died. I understood at first that Hitler had been directly responsible, and was beginning to boil myself, but it later developed that the woman had died of an illness in Switzerland, so Der Fuehrer's culpability was, in that particular case, oblique.

I can understand that there are those who take Miss Thompson with a grain of salt, but at the time she agreed to the interview she certainly had nothing to gain, yet she went out of her way to do a friendly and helpful thing, to give a younger woman a boost, and I am very grateful to her. Because I had had her, it was easier to get other big names, and besides, I respect a lady who can dish out the vitriol with the same high hand as her eminent colleagues, the Messrs. Pegler and Johnson, and who, when days are darkest, is never guilty of any of that "Cheer up, it all happens for the best" nonsense. Her gloom is gargantuan, but her fighting spirit is as unquenchable as Donald Duck's, and glows through the chaos like a steadfast flame.

CHAPTER FOURTEEN

"Celebrity Proves Quite Modest"

I HOPE MY CAREER TOUCHED ITS NADIR with a Metro-Goldwyn-Mayer atrocity in which I participated in the summer of 1939. I say, "I hope," as it would indeed be bitter to think of sinking to depths lower than the picture called *Stronger than Desire*. This shambles starred Virginia Bruce and Walter Pidgeon, and I wandered through it like a banshee. We all thought it a fright and were at no pains to conceal our opinion, and I enhanced my prophet's reputation when I predicted it would be box-office poison, although the prophecy was unworthy of my powers, as a blind Eskimo could have foretold its fate. The supervisors were the only ones not in on the secret. They went around saying, "You shouldn't talk that way. This is not a bad little picture at all." It wasn't bad, it was putrid, and I learned with pleasure that it grossed the all-time low at the Capitol Theatre in New York.

I should be unfair, however, if I neglected to record

that the making of it afforded me one exquisite thrill. The cameraman ordained that I bleach my hair for photographic purposes, and the results enchanted me. Having been a sultry brunette from birth, I was overwhelmed by the novelty of my titian tresses, and in the middle of the night I would hop out of bed to admire myself in the mirror. The sight of me was an ever fresh and delicious shock, but one which I could not long afford. While I was working on the picture, the studio paid for the paint job, but when I retired from their service, the maintenance fees were staggering, plus which my family howled with pain and disapproval. When I returned to New York from the Coast, Bill eyed me grimly, but held his peace, saying only, "Let's wait till Edna gets home." Mother was in Europe, and the day she landed, we went to the dock to meet her. She spied my flaming head practically at Quarantine, and sailed up the bay, shouting loudly, "I don't like it, you look awful. It isn't my baby," and making strong negative gestures, wagging her head violently, and turning thumbs down. "You look like one of those awful Hollywood Totty Coughdrops," she said, among other uncomplimentary things, so outweighed, I dyed it back. I do not understand photography. Why should Hedy Lamarr's dark locks look like a soft, shining cloud about her face and mine like a shapeless black wad reminiscent of the overpowering millinery of the Edwardian era? I realize that to be in your early twenties and a raving beauty has some bearing on the problem, but even the back of the Lamarr head looks well on the screen, whereas mine just looks as if the film had been underexposed, and it gives me an inferiority complex. I elbowed glory, however, because Miss Lamarr's false eyelashes and mine lay side by side in the drawer of the make-up room, and at seven-thirty in the morning, minus lips, eyes, and powder, the kinship between the glamorized studio beauties and the transient Eastern talent is not so distant. You've got to really settle down in Hollywood to acquire the permanent high-gloss finish. If you work in pictures only spasmodically, you achieve but a thin veneer, which cracks as soon as the draught from the Holland Tunnel hits it, and there you are, walking down Fifth Avenue, with that ladylike, dull look, the exotic, expensive, candidly artificial mask wiped quite away. Even the widely touted natural beauties, the Hepburns and the Bergmans, have the Hollywood aura; I guess it's the publicity and their bone structure.

But though my career during the filming of *Stronger than Desire* was distinctly in the doldrums, my social life was not. As they were sure I would be there for only a limited time, my friends spread themselves, and I was invited to many parties, at one of which I distinguished myself by pulling what was probably the most exuberant boner of the season.

My friend, Buff Cobb, was living in Santa Barbara with one of her husbands. Buff is a dear creature, but she marries every hour on the hour, and it is difficult, when you see her only occasionally, to remember just which lap she's on, and this is not intended as a pun. She had invited Edwin Justus Mayer and me to Sunday luncheon, and so we drove up from Hollywood for the day. As I recall, there were eight of us at the table, and as we sat over the coffee cups the conversation drifted to literature. Something was said about profiles and character sketches, and I remarked that

I had once read a book on famous mistresses of history. It was years since I had read it, and I can't imagine why I brought it up, but I did. I criticized it fulsomely, lambasting it with a will, describing with considerable skill its bathos, lack of insight and imagination, and its cloying sentimentality, and was adding by way of envoi that it was the worst book I had ever read when I became aware of an icy chill dispelling the California warmth. There was a moment's silence, and then the ax fell. "I wrote it," said my host. After that there was quite a long silence. Then I heard a rather dry, rasping sound; it was my own voice. "Have you a gun?" it said. Then everybody but the host and Mr. Mayer began to guffaw in what I considered an unnecessarily loud and vulgar way. Mr. Mayer behaved like a king of men, not trying to disclaim acquaintanceship or pretend that he had driven up to Santa Barbara alone and was amazed to find that I had secreted myself in the rumble seat, though he said afterward he felt like doing both those things. The host understandably went into the house to pour himself a drink, and Eddie went with him.

When we left, which was soon, Eddie said, "I think I fixed it up a little. Of course I had to make you out a moron, but it was worth it. I said to him, 'Wasn't your book a collection of essays?' And he said 'Yes,' and I said, 'Well, then, that wasn't the book Ilka meant at all. She got it confused with some bum novel. Why, the girl's never read an essay in her life.'"

"Did he believe it?" I asked dubiously.

"Well, dear," said Eddie, "I don't think he did really, but a ray of hope came into his eye. I'm a writer myself, and I know the feeling. We clutch at straws." That is what I call true friendship, and Mr. Mayer can have half my kingdom any day in the week.

That trip to Hollywood was my last sortie of any magnitude for some time. The following two years I was working in radio and went no further than Long Island and Connecticut except for a four-day jaunt to New Orleans for Mardi Gras. I suppose the other fifty-one weeks of the year the city is given over to sleepy Southern charm, but during Carnival Week the effete visiting Northerner is run ragged. In most towns if you arrive at your hotel from the airport, at 4 A.M., life is pretty quiet, but not in the little Paris of the South in the gladsome time of Carnival—there it's the shank of the evening. Taxis are jockeying for position, luggage hurtles to the sidewalk, and the lobby is crowded. To be sure, a few carousers had collapsed and were sleeping on sofas in an atmosphere reminiscent of the Hotel Astor when the American Legion Convention met in New York, but they were the weaklings; the elevators kept disgorging the sturdier element, all of whom were riding high, and we were a little startled to see emerge a magnificently upholstered specimen, dressed like Marie Antoinette. She carried before her a sheaf of red roses, giving her somewhat the appearance of Birnam Wood on the march, and we were told she was left over from Mystic, the great costume ball of the evening. Fortunately, our rooms at the Roosevelt overlooked Canal Street, so we had reserved mezzanine seats from which to view the festivities, and Sunday noon we sat at breakfast and watched the Krewe of Mid-City parade. Each float was supposed to represent one of the best movies of the last few years; Bill and I are generally quite bright at guessing

games, but some of them were little stumpers which
would have stopped the Quiz Kids. However, they
were all lavish and gorgeous creations, with the maskers
in riotous costumes tossing gimcracks and geegaws to
the crowd. They parade all night too, and that is even
more spectacular, with boys running beside the floats,
bearing aloft great flares, and the costumes and jewels
blazing in the torchlight.

We were taken about by the Lawrence Williams,
a delightful pair of people who live in a lovely old
house and have three little girls with smooth hair and
pinafores, exactly like Alice in Wonderland.

Mardi Gras itself starts as early as the children's
Christmas, and by seven or eight o'clock Canal Street
was thronged with nearly half the citizens in dominoes,
purple and blue and red and poison green, shouting,
strolling, snaking through the crowds, as they waited
for the Parade of Rex to begin. The king himself was
resplendent in a discreet little outfit of solid diamonds,
and the floats represented tales from *The Arabian
Nights:* Sinbad the Sailor entwined with fat papier-
mâché mermaids, and Aladdin, and Ali Baba and the
Forty Thieves popping from huge oil jars.

William and I put on our costumes rented from
Mildred's Costume Shoppe; mine was a Chinese tent,
a little draughty, but spacious, with trousers like tun-
nels, and Bill, playing no favorites, was sensational as
a red and white Russian. With him running inter-
ference, we plunged into the caldron, which by that
time looked like Times Square on New Year's Eve,
and plowed our way across Canal Street, down Royal in
the French Quarter, till we came to the Bounders
Club where the Williams had invited us for luncheon.

Those two old French apéritifs, Ecossais and Bourbon, were drunk from twelve to three, but the number of guests still upright when the meal was served was surprising.

Carnival Week is climaxed by the Ball of Comus, so in our best bibs and tuckers we went that evening to the Auditorium. My stepsister, Lillian, had the good taste to marry into the Navy, and fortunately, her husband, Captain Thomson, is commandant of the New Orleans territory, so that, what with her social grace and his diplomatic position, we were assured of call-outs, which entitled us to sit on the ballroom floor instead of the balcony. Lillian had patiently tried to explain to me the intricate working of the call-outs, but though the finer points escaped me, I grasped the main idea: they are the invitations to the waltz, and if you don't get any, you are a wallflower. The thought is alarming, for you are not allowed to hold on to your own man. If he is not a masker—that is, not one of the costumed boys who has ridden the floats—he is relegated to the balcony, which he loves, for there are many refreshing, surreptitious nips passed around up there, and there are none on the dance floor. Not that the maskers need them; by the time they hit Comus they are floating without mechanical aid, but a little spiked punch would be nice for the ladies. Comus is bound round with tradition, and I was surprised to see how many snow-capped peaks were firmly entrenched in the front rows on the dance floor. Their husbands and sons are more or less on a spot and have to call them out, or the little women will Know the Reason Why.

The ball is opened by the arrival of the Queen and

her maids. Nobody is ever satisfied by the choice of the Queen, except her mother, as there are dozens of warring factions, each with its own candidate, and I understand local politics play a considerable part. The maids are hand-picked debutantes who are already out, but the more of these affairs they participate in, the farther out they get.

After the King and Queen have mounted the steps of the throne, the ball is opened, and the maskers crowd toward the ladies, whose names are called by the members of the Floor Committee. When your name is called, you join your partner for one dance, and it is not considered cricket to recognize him behind his mask. They were safe with me; I was a stranger in their midst and would have recognized none of my partners had he stood revealed stark naked. After the dance your partner returns you to your seat, but just before he relinquishes you he reaches into a little bag he carries and hands you a small present prettily wrapped up. I think this is a charming custom, and one I would like to see spread among Northern gentlemen.

Bill had thought that we should go to Midnight Mass in the old Cathedral to mark the beginning of Lent, but the idea didn't wear; instead we went back to our hotel and had a quiet supper by ourselves, and flew to New York the next morning. Mardi Gras is quite an experience, but I haven't the stomach for continuous drinking, and on the whole I am allergic to any organized fiesta on a gargantuan scale; it depresses me. I feel that Christmas has become sadly distorted by the ballyhoo of the merchants, and it is less for the glory of God than of Saks, Nieman-Marcus, and

Bullock's-Wilshire. Not that the shops are to be blamed for reaping their profits where they find them, but there always seems something a little shoddy in commercializing a generous instinct. Filial devotion is ridden to a fare-you-well by enterprising merchants throughout the country, who, if they didn't think up Mother's Day and belatedly, in true American fashion, Father's, were quick to seize their advantage. The advertising men have so effectively sold its parents to the nation that the stores clean up a tidy profit, and the touching occasion is a Western Union field day.

The New Orleans jaunt was the longest flight I have ever made, but since that time I have become the darling of the airlines and the greatest short-distance flier on record, for since that time I have been on a lecture tour.

The idea was borne in upon Harold Peat, an enterprising impresario, from hearing my broadcasts. He reasoned that if all those people listened to a disembodied voice, they might come to see the source in person if she were handy. He was also spurred on by the fact that there were apparently some requests for me, and that I had already delivered one lecture to The Women's Institute of St. Paul, an aggregation of twelve thousand ladies who gather in a homey building resembling Madison Square Garden to hear the twelve-thousand-and-first lady talk at them. They plow through the snow and ice of a Northwest winter for this dubious privilege, and the welcome they accord one is as warm as the weather is cold.

The night before I spoke in St. Paul I previewed myself in Duluth, to a mere handful of two thousand. Mai-Mai Sze, Gloria Hollister, and I were on the

same program, bolstering each other's morale. Gloria
had fine slides of fish and Mr. William Beebe frater-
nizing under the sea, and Mai-Mai Sze had China to
fall back upon, but I was strictly on my own. When
the idea of a lecture had been broached to me, I took
it lightly. To begin with, I was sure the day would never
come, as in wily fashion the St. Paul committee had
taken the precaution of asking me some months in
advance, and in the second place I thought that if it
did turn up, I would murmur a few diplomatic words,
five or ten minutes at the outside, and withdraw to
gracious applause. What I didn't know about the lecture business! I learned that a one-hour talk is the
minimum, and it's preferable if you can run on for an
hour and a half. This I wouldn't do, and told them so.
"Winston Churchill," said I, and I think my point
was well taken, "is probably the greatest living prac-
titioner of English prose, but an hour and a half of
even Mr. Churchill would prove tedious, and who am
I to play the spellbinder?" This sound and modest viewpoint was ignored. "The people pay to hear you," said
the impresario. "They drive into the cities from the
suburbs and farms, and they wish to feel they have
had a full morning or evening's program, as the case
may be. You whip up a speech which will take at
least an hour to deliver."

This gave me pause—perhaps coma would be a better
word—while I waited for an idea to bubble to the surface. I didn't want to talk about the theater, because
I have always held that conversation about it interests
the general public far less than its protagonists fatuously
believe, and besides, there are the Messrs. John Mason
Brown and Maurice Evans, both shining lights of the

theater world in their respective departments, who lecture to packed houses on matters histrionic. So I reasoned that any theater-hungry audiences would hear enough about that. An hour's talk on fashion, which I might be expected to know something of, seemed to me dull, and besides, Schiaparelli had scooped the field the season before, complete with models. What to talk about? I discussed it with Mother, who was also a little troubled, for as she said right away, "You are really quite ignorant, darling." But in the end, we decided that I might talk about the philosophy of being a woman. Whatever my shortcomings as a radio personality, actress, or author, I was indisputably a woman, and the fears, hopes, and foibles common to women were common to me. This, then, was the topic of my lecture. I was extremely lucky in that it was well received, and it certainly gave me scope. I touched on fashion, humor, etiquette, children, food, men, and love—lots of love. The love parts were generally very popular, although in Detroit a friend of mine sitting in the audience told me that behind her were two middle-aged women, unmistakably spinsters. As they started out at the end of the lecture, one of them said to the other, "Hmph, who does she think she's talking to? A bunch of young girls?" and the other one said wistfully, "Well, I don't know, it's kind of nice to *hear* about love."

The lecture tour was an adventure to me, because I know New York and Hollywood, but I am provincial about the in-between parts. It always seems to be Kansas, for even if one has toured with plays, and my touring has been limited, theatrical people are clannish and generally stick together, and in strange towns one rarely meets the audience. Not so in lecturing; one's

audience is flatteringly firm in its determination to meet
one, and as almost all lectures are sponsored by women's
clubs or organizations, in many cities and over a period
of time the ladies who head these groups come to have
for the transient speaker a kind of composite personality,
their faces and characteristics shifting and overlapping
in a super-movie montage. They meet you at the train
in nervous knots of four or five; when you come by
plane you find your own way in from the airport, and
it is much less strain for all concerned. They have
Bosoms with little tags dripping from them, as from
a shelf, with the word *Hostess* printed on them. They
wear pince-nez, and round patches of unblended rouge
on their cheeks, and expensive, rather fancy clothes.
The majority are firm and capable, and so formidable
in appearance that you are pleasantly surprised to find,
on herding them to your hotel, that they are not averse
to a drink or two. A few of them are bird-brains, which
makes the sterner minds very ashamed, as the bird-
brains get things badly tangled and think you mean
to lecture at night when your contract specifically states
afternoon, and you are booked out of town on the 4
P.M. plane and are, what's more, hell bent on catching
it. They are cordial and call you Dear, when they first
meet you, and kiss you good-by at the station two hours
later. They are always kind and insistent on driving
you there themselves, when you would prefer a cab
as a surer method of locomotion, because no matter
how small the town, the location of the station and
airport comes as a surprise to the feminine inhabitants,
who drive slowly, motivated by a sense of smell rather
than a bump of location, and you are on a griddle,
fearing you will miss your connection. A lecture tour

is just like playing one-night stands. You get so engrossed in timetables that the reason for which you are doing all this traveling, the performance itself, becomes negligible.

Club ladies swing erratically from chumminess to chilling formality, referring to their husbands either as Poppa or Mr. Jones. When they introduce you they say, "Shake hands with Mr. So-and-so," or they go grand and present people to each other, but they get a little confused and present the ladies to the gentlemen and the old people to the young. They are sketchily informed about you, as frequently you are a pig in a poke foisted on them by the lecture bureau, and from years of experience they don't expect much. My own case was a little different, in so far as most of my audience knew me from my radio programs, *Luncheon at the Waldorf* and *Penthouse Party*. They enjoy being spoken to at eleven o'clock in the morning, and after that there is an enormous luncheon, and when you try to beg off, pleading fatigue, their brows darken and they say with an ominous tightening of thin lips that it is in their contract they are to have you for lunch. At this alarming announcement you struggle like a panicky lamb, but the iron hand makes itself felt, and you file in obediently to the sacrifice.

Aside from their determination to eat you, they are extraordinarily kind and will go to no end of pains to make you comfortable; indeed, it's all you can do to squeeze in a bath between their ministrations; and as audiences, with but few exceptions they are unbeatable: warm and receptive, quick and hearty in their laughter, and they turn out en masse—endearing traits in any citizens, regardless of locale—shows they live right. I think one reason for their alert response to one's effort is because the lecture business is so far reaching that it can bring to the smallest towns of the United States some of the most distinguished figures, not only of this country, but of Europe and Asia as well, for the Oriental, as it turns out, is as ubiquitous a speaker as your Englishman, and though New Yorkers are inclined to look down their metropolitan noses, the fact remains that the unassuming sticks are more widely interested and more genuinely informed on matters cultural than the self-assured gentry of my own home town, whom I love but who are very provincial folk indeed. They read *Variety* and Mr. Winchell and in perilous taxicabs ride happily to work on the fifty-second floor, snug in their delusion that America is bounded on the west by the Hudson River.

The audiences who came to hear me speak were gratifyingly large, and I even had a good house in Urbana, the University of Illinois—not packed, but better than two-thirds full. Still my pride was a little piqued. I had had them swinging from the chandeliers, and I didn't like to see a slump in trade. A member of the faculty explained it to me. "You did all right, Miss Chase," said the head of the short-story department as I sat with him and a colleague after the talk. "You must realize that in a university listening to a lecture is no treat. As a rule, no matter how distinguished the speaker the student body stays away in droves. Two-thirds full is by way of a record." This assurance perked me up no end, as did the highball the understanding man poured me.

I was also gratified by my notices, the headlines of the college paper reading, "Celebrity [that was me]

Proves Quite Modest." I was profusely interviewed in every town in which I spoke, by both the professional and amateur press. When the high-school reporters drew me as an assignment it was obviously not their happiest day; they sometimes suffered from painfully tied tongues, and I found it was easier for all of us if I interviewed myself. I would babble along, and they would gulp and scribble down the pearls I so graciously tossed. There always seemed to me something touching about the young professional reporters who interviewed me, because they were most knowledgeable about books and plays and tremendously interested in the theater, but they had a kind of shy, embarrassed feeling, because they hadn't seen the current Broadway productions. The clubladies definitely did not share this sentiment and took a melancholy pride in telling me what a bad theater town theirs was.

As my route zigzagged through the Middle West, no matter where I went I was always landing at the Detroit Airport, a gruesome spot which I came to know by heart. When one thinks of the wealth of that area, the dirt and discomfort of the airport is a crying scandal. I do not know whether it is indifference or politics, but I hope the Chamber of Commerce hangs its head in shame when it broods upon it.

Although a timid flier—"Why should the plane stay up here," I ask myself; "Who is man to toy with the laws of gravity? What about that apple?"—I nevertheless came to enjoy the flights tremendously. The breathtaking moment of suspense when the plane takes off— "Doubtless overloaded," I think to myself. "Will never make the grade"—the relieved feeling when it does, and we rise and level off, and then the magic sensation of freedom when the earth lies far below and we fly through the blue airy regions with the clouds rolling beneath us, an undulating expanse of white, fields of cotton, fields of snow, yet shimmering with color like a pearl. The way the sun strikes through the haze hanging over the cities in the daytime, and the way the lights twinkle like a million diamonds in the dark is a faery sight to see.

When you come down you are right back in the workaday world, at the Mizpah Auditorium in Syracuse, although that building has a slight element of fantasy too, combining as it does church, lecture hall, nursery, drugstore, and restaurant. Syracuse was the last stop on my lecture tour, and since then my goal has been the hermit's existence, which I have not achieved. I used to think it was an affectation when authors went to Coney Island in the winter, or the Maine woods, that they might write undisturbed. I now see the wisdom of their choice. What with the radio, the telephone, the theater, the war, and one's friends, turning out what my secretary refers to as the Deathless Prose gets more and more complicated, and the reader will be no happier than I when my life is a closed book.

CHAPTER FIFTEEN

Sheer Prejudice

I SUPPOSE ONE MAY BE SAID TO HAVE achieved adulthood if not maturity, the terms not being necessarily synonymous, upon reaching his early twenties, and certainly if one has experienced love, marriage, parenthood, business, bitterness, and joy— in short, the collected works—he should feel firmly ensconced in the grown-up world; but at the risk of appearing fay, I must confess that such is not my case. God knows I have been clattering about in the more advanced brackets long enough to have become habituated, and if I follow the precedent of my ancestors, who never had the grace to totter from the mundane scene until well into their nineties, I shall eventually become the oldest living inhabitant. But though aware of this, a periodic wonderment still sweeps over me that I, Ilka Chase, am grown up, and I giggle to myself while performing certain adult rites.

To borrow a phrase from show business, one reason for my delayed take may be that for most of my life

I have associated with people a good many years older than myself. I was baby Ilka in any gathering for a long while, but this has ceased to be true, and it is a distinct shock on looking around the room to see the nasty, unlined little faces of my juniors with that unpleasant dewy look about them.

High on the list of my adult rites stands Dealing With Wall Street. I once said to my secretary, "Get my broker on the phone," and at the sound of the phrase burst out laughing. At that I was lucky; most people burst out crying, and the secretary probably thought I laughed in bitter irony—a still unfulfilled ambition of my childhood. My current laughter, however, is merry and mocking when I think of my three shares of Standard Oil of New Jersey and the headache I cause the good man who handles them for me, but even so, brokers seem to me frightfully advanced—not mentally, of course, but as component parts of the grown-up world.

Psychologically, this is probably not hard to trace. I was deplorable in arithmetic, and still don't know what I'm talking about when I largely discuss shares and percentages, but it affords me much pompous delight. Such gentlemen as Mr. Stanton Griffis, of Hemphill Noyes, Mr. Lewis Wurzburg, treasurer of the Condé Nast publications, and Mr. Gilbert Miller, of the theater and, by marriage, of the brokerage house of Jules Bache, have at one time or another striven to enlighten me on the mysteries of finance. They draw little pictures looking just like the fever charts of streptococcus patients, and write letters neatly paragraphed and full of phrases like "in re the above securities" and "liens on first mortgages" and "the maturity value of preferred investments." They are patient, and I am grateful, but it seems easier to put my ten dollars in the Dry Dock Savings Institution or wait for a war to break out, which it always handily does, and buy a couple of Defense Stamps. Though I do not understand money, I love it as one does a complex and alluring Lothario, and the whole economic structure seems to me ingenious, if faulty, and I wonder how they thought it up. My winsome feminine incompetency in finance, however, is limited. For a long time I have been able to balance my own checkbook, and now Bunny Koehler does it for me, so that I don't see that men are so unique. It's a far cry from my boarding-school days, when the fellow who was a kind of porter and courier of the school was going over my checkbook with me and said, "But you can't do that, Miss Ilka, there's no more money in your account." I was the original girl who thought that when there were checks in the book there was money in the bank. I have since become aware of the fleet manner in which the cash outruns the symbols, so that it is refreshing to me when I am working and can pay my bills promptly, because in the entertainment field there are often long lapses between contracts, when the savings dwindle and the correspondence begins. Dearest Saks Fifth Avenue—— Darling Bergdorf—— I do not seek to welsh on my just debts, and if you will just be patient, etc., etc. Your loving customer, Ilka Chase. That is definitely a time when the other team seems much more grown up than I.

Then there is Staying up Late. It is ironic indeed, after planning all through childhood daily to greet the sun in wild carouse, to find on reaching maturity that one's idea of bliss is supper on a tray in bed at seven.

It is a topsy-turvy world. Where is that poise one thought to attain as a matter of course? Where are those perfect grownups one met as a child? One didn't like them perhaps, but it didn't occur to one that in their various unpleasant ways they weren't perfect. They never cried; no one scolded them; they could tell time; they found newspapers absorbing reading; they were finished beings; they were perfect. One was ill-prepared for the fear, the restlessness, the loneliness, and, most surprising of all, the embarrassment which adults are prey to. One hurdle to better comprehension, I think, is that children and adults are treated as two distinct species instead of as parts of the same whole. That is one advantage of the close-knit family life of Europe; it has its drawbacks, but different generations mingle together with less restraint and greater understanding and pleasure.

On the other hand, there are some things that now baffle me completely which as a child I took for granted, and it certainly simplified my life. Scientific inventions, for instance. Take electricity—why, when you flip the switch, does the light go on? There's no use trying to harangue me on the subject of Benjamin Franklin and that kite. I too have seen the lightning but still can't read the message. The telephone I find incomprehensible, but I don't feel so apologetic about that, as it apparently baffles the operators too. And as for radio! Engineers have wilted under their efforts to clarify for me the mystery of the curving ether bands, but how can the human voice circle the world in a split second? I don't know, and I suspect that they too come to the door to which there is no key, just as the most knowledgeable obstetricians have penetrated the mystery of

gestation and birth and are ignorant only of the greatest
mystery of all—what is the human spirit? That is another surprising discovery one makes on entering the
adult world—the ignorance and insecurity which pre-
vail there.

I am still embarrassed by many of the same things
which distressed me as a child. I hate going into a
roomful of strangers; I hate telephoning to people whom
I don't know well. I dislike being left to sit alone at a
table in a restaurant while my escort sees a man about a
dog, which last humiliation children are able to avoid by
the simple expedient of dining at home. I can't bear
asking for anything, which makes me the world's worst
money-raiser for Causes and disgusts the committees on
which I am asked to serve. However, as my husband
negotiates most of my business deals for me, I do not
feel a bit shy about discussing with him the salary I
so richly merit; actually his ideas are even sounder than
mine, and he is a lovely man with no shame at all when
it comes to telling employers what they will pay his
clients.

Another childish fallacy which has evaporated since
I have burst into glorious womanhood is that grownups
don't cry. They cry all the time. In the theater, at the
movies, when they lose their jobs, when people die—
they are great ones for crying over death, an event
which children accept for the most part with imper-
turbability—when their own true love walks out on them,
and when they are tired, especially on moving day.
Personally, it is practically impossible for me to watch
children putting on plays or singing Christmas carols.
They look so grave and work with such concentration
that I am dissolved. Nor is it correct to think that only

women cry. I have known men who wept copiously, but whether from love, which they said, or from self-pity, which I suspected, I have never been sure.

I have outgrown being afraid of the dark, except when I am reading a murder mystery, but if I hear ominous sounds in the night I am terrified, too terrified to put my head under the covers. I am galvanized into outraged action and spring from my bed with loud and angry cries of "Who's there?" and I go stampeding through the house, switching on every light, till the place is ablaze. Having seen many movies, I know how such things are done, and so I don't peer timidly into a room but bang the door wide open so that the robber will be squashed behind it.

The feeling that someone is following me in the street makes me most uncomfortable. The place between my shoulder blades itches in anticipation of the cold steel, and if I am driving on a lonely road at night and feel I am being trailed by another car, I accelerate to a brisk eighty, driven by visions of being forced to the side of the road and raped. The trouble with me is my imagination, plus too heavy a diet of the gory sensationalism of Mr. Luce's *Life*.

With the daylight these hobgoblin fancies vanish, and no truer bromide was ever coined than "Things will look different in the morning." To be sure they sometimes look worse—this is especially true since Mr. Hitler has been with us—but on the whole, daylight is a gloom dispeller. For me the worst time of the twenty-four hours comes around four or five o'clock in the morning. Then the dreams are bad, and if I waken, it is to black depression. My failures, my fears, and my phobias come to haunt me. The strange thing is that no matter how often one lives through these heavy small hours, no matter how firmly one says to oneself, "This is because my resistance is low," the suffocating feeling still persists.

There are doubtless easily traceable causes, physical and psychological, for it, but knowing them doesn't change the sensation. That is why psychoanalysis has never seemed to me as all-illuminating as it does to some. Knowing it is cancer from which you suffer does not alleviate the pain. In the same way awareness of the cause of a reaction or an emotion does not necessarily alter it.

I remember once reading a French novel called *La Belle de Jour,* in which a beautiful creature could find sexual satisfaction only in the arms of gross men, because as a child she had been caressed by a workman, a plumber, I believe, come to fix the drains. She felt very badly about this, as she was married to a refined fellow with whom she was in love, but in spite of knowing about the plumber—in fact, because she'd never forgotten him would be my diagnosis—there was nothing for it but to sneak off with traveling salesmen and stevedores on rainy afternoons to a dubious establishment on Montmartre.

And even if my friend Lawrence Langner is right, and the reason I am indifferent to orthodox religion is because I was hit on the head by a drop of cold water in the cathedral as a child, I have always remembered the occasion without its having to be probed out of me, but I still don't go much to church. If I wanted to, such an insignificant body of water would not bar my way. I don't go because I am lazy and like to sleep late on Sunday morning and have never been able to convince myself that doing so was a mortal sin—my God not being a victim of an inferiority complex who has to have people kneeling and praying to Him on a certain day in the week or He gets in a huff and condemns them to hell fire—and the other reason is that I look with jaundiced eye at those dogmas which exploit fear and superstition and impose ignorance on their followers, forbidding them scientific and critical reading when it differs from the tenets of the Church. Also it is not every clergyman whom it is possible to respect as an intelligent, charitable, and disinterested man. This is not remarkable, as there are few human beings who have those qualities; but one hopes for them in leaders.

If churchmen *haven't* got them, they should at least be masters of oratory, and much of the preaching is deplorably bad. Besides, one has only to look at the stars by night, or the sea, or the marching forests, a fleet animal or a snowflake or a shell, to know there is a power and rhythm governing the universe, complex, majestic, and infinite. I have always felt nearer to the source while outdoors, and away from people, than when sitting crowded in a pew, being harangued from the pulpit, but for those who feel uplifted through intimate religious contact with their fellow beings, churches are satisfying and necessary.

As the hierarchy and history of religion have engrossed the great mystics of the ages, and as I am as unmystic as they come, I do not pretend to a dissertation on the church, but I will say that religion compressed into an airtight compartment on Sunday mornings seems to me shockingly superficial, and that for our current needs there is still too strong a survival of medieval academic hairsplitting. How many angels shall stand on the head of a pin is dusty stuff in a bloody, fighting world. It seems to me it would be a fine thing to have a church militant in the sense of one which actively combated the powers of darkness by which we are surrounded today in a very literal sense, for they are the powers which would destroy all learning and culture and self-admittedly reduce mankind to the status of slaves. The Church's failures must be laid at the church door, for the clergy are still concerned with academic dogmas and creeds and the snatching of brands from a burning which on closer inspection turns out to be only watchfires illuminating a different road to the same gate. Too frequently the dyed-in-the-wool churchman is bitterly condemnatory of those who use an unorthodox light to find the way. It is the old story —orthodoxy is my doxy, heterodoxy is yours. When the need is desperate, what does it matter? Flare or candle, lantern or flash, they all light up the dark. But such musty bickerings becloud and sidetrack the urgent need for guidance, and the beacon from the Church flickers but dimly.

Sunday morning isn't enough. To live the good life is not that simple. It takes doing twenty-four hours a day, and far from churchly precincts.

I happen to believe that through clear vision, relaxed nerves, and sustained effort man works out his salvation, but I know that there are millions who believe that a personal God takes an interest in their personal welfare, and it must give them a cozy, protected, and irresponsible feeling. Confession relieves the soul, and it is this fundamental need in human nature to which the psychoanalysts cater; and certainly if one is able to afford it, it is very agreeable indeed to talk about oneself for an hour at a stretch three times a week. I read a book by one of New York's leading men in the field of psychoanalysis in which he recounted a cure he had effected on a man who was in love and wanted to get out. The system worked like a charm, because the young man's dreams all pointed to the conclusion that his lady was a heel, and she finally began to shock him so much and he got to feeling so superior that he shed her like an old garment, though to be sure, he didn't do it in a trice—it took him about as long as it takes most men to shed their old clothes without a psychoanalyst—but anyhow he was finally free of her and quite alone in the world, which seems to me poor exchange for the rapture and agony of love, not to mention the several thousand dollars it cost him to get that way, but that is the psychoanalyst's story, and presumably the patient was satisfied. It is, I suppose, comforting to know that if we are too hard hit and have the price, we can always pay a magician to turn our heart's darling into an ugly toad. Or many a layman will oblige free of charge, as slander and vilification come easy.

For a long time I felt that I had poor judgment or bad taste when I would hear criticisms leveled at the people I liked, and I felt bashful about them, and on occasion I cravenly denied them, but as I grow older I am coming to realize that almost nobody thinks highly of anyone else. The human being doesn't live who won't be picked to pieces by his friends. Look for kindness in a stranger. If even Mr. Abraham Lincoln had and still has his violent detractors, it is obvious that ordinary mortals won't be spared. Gossip is the cheapest commodity in the world, but it always comes as a little shock when someone says, "We were talking about you the other day." I think to myself, "Good heavens, what would they have to talk about?" and answer ringeth, "Plenty." It is interesting to ponder on the universal popularity of gossip when one considers that it is generally inaccurate, frequently vicious, and always a waste of time. It is, I think, so universally indulged in because the average mind is of indifferent caliber, versed in lazy habits, and it is easier to babble idly about personalities than to cultivate our gardens and unearth fresh and original material. If I gossip less than many women I know, it is not from nobility but rather because I am busy and most people are not sufficiently interesting to dwell on for very long. The truth of the matter is I don't see how it's possible to care much for humanity, and though, like Sadie Thompson, I feel sorry for the whole damned world, I do not feel called upon to love it. In return, I do not ask that it yearn over me. In defense of this unpopular viewpoint I will say that I think the great humanitarians are the people who work for the betterment of the human race, appreciating full well its stupidity, apathy, and ingratitude. Most of mankind is below par. Mediocrity is the passing mark, and unfortunately it is not the underprivileged who are always the most remiss. I say unfortunately, because if that were so, our troubles would be well on their way to extinction. Better education, more vitamins, a redistribution of wealth, and everything would be jake, but we are faced with the sorry fact that the educated and the comfortably off are just as banal and prejudiced as their proletarian brothers; frequently more so, as they quite naturally wish to maintain the status quo. If it is only a minute percentage of the population who may be called rich, how infinitely smaller is that percentage who may be considered the elite in the world of spirit and intellect. We have only to look around us in streets, in trains, in theaters—in how many faces do we find nobility or happiness or even alertness? Pitiably few. Even when given every advantage, it is infrequent that human beings seek to enrich their spirit. Human soil seems to be mostly submarginal.

That is why democracy is, or should be, the governmental ideal; the foundation must be broad and low. The creating of opportunity whereby the few may exploit the many is the basis of Fascism and is profoundly reprehensible, because, like them or not, human beings are the inhabitants of the earth, and our only permissible goal must be the democratic one—the greatest good for the greatest number, with the rights of minorities respected, and the people themselves the judges of what they consider their own good. Democracy is not an easy form of government, because it is never final; it is a living, changing organism, with a continuous shifting and adjusting of balance between individual freedom and general order.

In connection with government for and by the people, it is, I think, interesting to remember that our Constitution was framed not by simple sons of the soil and the man in the street but by the most trenchant and aristocratic minds of the era: Thomas Jefferson, Benjamin Franklin, Alexander Hamilton, James Madison, etc., etc. The great events of our country were fathered by men unequaled in moral integrity and intellectual prescience. That is what must recurrently discourage political idealists with democratic convictions. The People in whom they believe and for whom they are

working arrive like the famous clown, Marcelline, eager
to help when the work is done. The individual thinks,
but the aggregate is a lethargic, sheeplike mass, and the
spry, eager, ambitious little collies who have their welfare at heart hound and harry them for their own betterment. The majority is too humble and too grateful for
too little, though I can see the eyebrows raising, and
with justification, if one construes majority to mean
labor. Bosses are royally fleeced by those union leaders
who are dishonest and irresponsible, and are forced to
go, hat in hand, to the gentlemen with the large cigars
and the feet on the desk, frequently to be ignored when
they lodge a just complaint of slackness or poor work-
manship. The gangster methods whereby incompetent,
superfluous men must be kept on a payroll breed hatred
and distrust where there should be mutual understanding and clear thinking.

Of course as labor has been underdog for so long, I
suppose it's natural that now it's in the saddle, it should
often ride roughshod, suspicious of everything, and with
small regard to fairness, responsibility, or even common
sense, but it would be nice if the boys could more generally awaken to the fact that their own leaders may be
venal too, even without striped pants and a cutaway. I
say this who am a member of and pay dues in three
unions: Equity, American Federation of Radio Artists,
and Screen Actors Guild. Nobody can shut his eyes
tight and say, "Daddy, I want the best for me," and
think that he will be safe.

It takes a long time and bitter humiliation before men
will realize that freedom is more vital than security, that
indeed freedom is the only security, and that true freedom is achieved by those willing to shoulder its twin,

responsibility. When a people can accept both, they may hope to attain democracy. The democratic process is a curiously right one, because it is the synthesis of human nature, inspiring and laughable, lumbering and apt, struggling by infinitesimal degrees toward dignity and peace. When by some happy chance an outstanding leader comes to the fore, everybody but the self-seekers profits, and when he doesn't, the governors and the governed muddle along together. When it comes to muddling, the British have no monopoly. We have muddling, and with orchestral accompaniment, right here in our glorious republic. When one witnesses some of the goings on of the representatives of the United States in Congress assembled, the marvel is not that many things are done badly but that anything is done at all. Sometimes, reading the utterances of various members of the legislature, considering the boners, chicanery, and pigheadedness of the gentlemen in charge of our destinies, and then looking upon the might and progress of America, one is forced to the inescapable conclusion that this must indeed be God's country.

CURTAIN